D1009075

# SAN
# FRANCISCO
## ENCOUNTER

**ALISON BING**

San Francisco Encounter

**Published by Lonely Planet Publications Pty Ltd**
ABN 36 005 607 983

| **Australia** | Head Office |
| | Locked Bag 1, Footscray, Vic 3011 |
| | ☎ 03 8379 8000  fax 03 8379 8111 |
| | talk2us@lonelyplanet.com.au |
| **USA** | 150 Linden St, Oakland, CA 94607 |
| | ☎ 510 250 6400 |
| | toll free 800 275 8555 |
| | fax 510 893 8572 |
| | info@lonelyplanet.com |
| **UK** | 2nd fl, 186 City Rd |
| | London EC1V 2NT |
| | ☎ 020 7106 2100  fax 020 7106 2101 |
| | go@lonelyplanet.co.uk |

This title was commissioned in Lonely Planet's Oakland office and produced by: **Commissioning Editor** Suki Gear **Coordinating Editors** Gabrielle Stefanos, Ali Lemer **Coordinating Cartographers** Andy Rojas, Brendan Streager **Coordinating Layout Designer** Wibowo Rusli **Assisting Editor** Kirsten Rawlings **Assisting Cartographer** Barbara Benson **Senior Editor** Helen Christinis **Managing Editor** Sasha Baskett **Managing Cartographer** Alison Lyall **Managing Layout Designer** Laura Jane **Project Manager** Glenn van der Knijff **Cover Designer** Pepi Bluck **Thanks to** Glenn Beanland, Lucy Birchley, Yvonne Bischofberger, Jessica Boland, Ruth Cosgrove, Ryan Evans, Wayne Murphy, Piers Pickard, Raphael Richards, Fabrice Rocher, Mik Ruff, Julie Sheridan, Celia Wood

ISBN 978 1 74104 996 1

Printed through Colorcraft Ltd, Hong Kong.
Printed in China.

**Acknowledgement** Bay Area Rapid Transit © 2008.

# HOW TO USE THIS BOOK
## Color-Coding & Maps

Color-coding is used for symbols on maps and in the text that they relate to (eg all eating venues on the maps and in the text are given a green knife and fork symbol). Each neighborhood also gets its own color, and this is used down the edge of the page and throughout that neighborhood section.

Although the authors and Lonely Planet have taken all reasonable care in preparing this book, we make no warranty about the accuracy or completeness of its content and, to the maximum extent permitted, disclaim all liability arising from its use.

**Send us your feedback** We love to hear from readers – your comments help make our books better. We read every word you send us, and we always guarantee that your feedback goes straight to the appropriate authors. The most useful submissions are rewarded with a free book. To send us your updates and find out about Lonely Planet events, newsletters and travel news visit our award-winning website: **lonelyplanet.com/contact**

Note: We may edit, reproduce and incorporate your comments in Lonely Planet products such as guidebooks, websites and digital products, so let us know if you don't want your comments reproduced or your name acknowledged. For a copy of our privacy policy visit **lonelyplanet.com/privacy**.

**MIX**
**Paper from responsible sources**
FSC™ C021741
www.fsc.org

## ALISON BING

Author, arts commentator and adventurous eater Alison Bing was adopted by San Francisco 16 years ago. By now she's done everything you're supposed to do here and a few things you're definitely not, including gorging on burritos before Berlioz symphonies and falling in love on the 7 Haight bus. Alison holds a graduate degree in international diplomacy, which she makes every effort to undermine with opinionated commentary for magazines, newspapers, public radio and books.

## ALISON'S THANKS

Big, smothering California bear hugs to editorial luminaries Suki Gear, Brice Gosnell and Gabbi Stefanos, the cartos at Lonely Planet, and to the Sanchez Writers' Grotto for steady inspiration. Thanks always to Marco Flavio Marinucci, who turned a Muni bus ride into the San Francisco adventure of a lifetime, and to June and Tony Bing, whose passions for food, art and freethinking are apparently heritable traits.

Many thanks to San Francisco icons Raj Patel, Daniel Handler and Idexa Stern, and cheers to fellow picky eaters Warren and Lindsay Braunig, Becca Bing, DeeAnn Budney, Sahai Burrowes, Yosh Han, Luke Hass, Mini Kahlon, Dave Knox, John Lorance, Kirsten Menger-Anderson, Lisa Park, Sean Scullion and Ann Trausch.

## THE PHOTOGRAPHERS

Special thanks to the staff members who contributed images of their hometown to this edition. Specific credits are listed below.

**Our readers** Many thanks to the travelers who wrote to us with helpful hints, useful advice and interesting anecdotes: Diana Huidobro, Wes Snow.

**Cover photograph** Vesuvio and the Transamerica Pyramid, North Beach, Sabrina Dalbesio. **Internal photographs** p93, p121 by Alison Bing; p179 by Meredith Heuer; p17, p199 Avi Martin; p6 (top left), p20, p26, p64, p100, p128, p178 Aimee Goggins; p22 Heather Dickson; p4 Kevin Berne; p47 Mary Polizzotti; p29 Suki Gear; p186, p103 Tim Griffith. All other photographs by Lonely Planet Images, and by Anthony Pidgeon p69, p139, p162; Christian Aslund p21; Diana Mayfield p24, p32 (bottom); Emily Riddell p74, p82, p87, p154; Hannah Levy p79; Holger Leue p19, p23; Jim Wark p36; John Elk III p27, p58; Kevin Levesque p13; Lawrence Worcester p6 (bottom); Lee Foster p60; Nicholas Pavloff p8; Ray Laskowitz p52; Richard Cummins p31, p172, p183, 190; Roberto Gerometta p18, p25; Thomas Winz p11.

All images are copyright of the photographers unless otherwise indicated. Many of the images in this guide are available for licensing from **Lonely Planet Images:** www.lonelyplanetimages.com

MICHELLE

Pompadour or pompadon't? SF's comedy-cabaret hit Beach Blanket Babylon (p54)

# CONTENTS

# THIS IS SAN FRANCISCO

Whenever you get completely carried away, you're halfway to San Francisco already. Here love is perpetually in the air along with dinner plans and stray glitter, because this rambunctious city can't wait for a fresh excuse to flirt, dine out or throw a parade.

Let's face it: SF gets away with a lot because of its good looks. Just when its beauty seems familiar, you turn a corner to find a glorious alleyway mural, Victorian roofline or sea-breeze-sculpted pine that entirely changes your outlook. The Pacific forms a dazzling natural boundary to the west, but there are no other observable limits here. One San Franciscan wearing nothing but combat boots is possibly wacko – and probably chilly – but two could be a date, three is a theme party and four makes a parade. And if you get goose bumps in the fog, march your rear guard across town: when it's drizzling downtown, it's probably sunny in the Mission.

Yet somehow the city with its head in the clouds hasn't lost its grip on the continent or reality, despite earthquakes, fires and prognostications of certain doom by the righteously indignant. With free thinkers and wild parrots nested on its 43 hills, San Francisco refuses to be brought down to earth, and instead forces cable cars and spirits to rise to the occasion. Through unrelenting outlandishness, this city of fewer than a million people has become a global capital of cuisine, technology, gay liberation, skateboarding, eco-consciousness, comics, street art, documentaries and poetry.

Spontaneity is the only law obeyed without question in San Francisco. No one can commit to a date next week, but everyone suddenly shows up when there's a war that needs protesting or someone's handing out free cupcakes at same-sex weddings in City Hall. San Francisco's stratospheric booms and breakneck busts aren't for the weak of heart, but as anyone who's clung onto the side of a cable car will tell you, this town gives one hell of a ride. Anyone up for a parade?

**Top left** Wild parrots rule the roost in San Francisco **Top right** Gay revelry abounds at the annual Pride Parade (p27) **Bottom** Sunday services sing at the Glide Memorial United Methodist Church (p87)

# >HIGHLIGHTS

The majestic Golden Gate Bridge (p16) stands guard by the bay

# >1 GOLDEN GATE PARK

## WALK ON SF'S WILD SIDE IN GOLDEN GATE PARK

As you've probably heard, San Francisco has a wild streak about a mile wide. Everything San Franciscans hold dear is found in the 1-by-4.5-mile wilds of Golden Gate Park: free spirits, free music, Frisbee, protests, fine art, bonsai and a balding penguin.

This green scene started with a forward-thinking citizens' petition in 1865 to turn 1017 acres of SF sand dunes into a park, which scared off even New York's Central Park designer Frederick Law Olmstead. Idealistic 24-year-old William Hammond Hall championed the effort, and spent the next two decades tenaciously fighting casino developers, theme-park boosters and slippery politicians to create the world's largest developed park – one-upping Olmstead. By 1886, sunny days brought one-fifth of the city's population to their park, ignoring the city's newspaper dire warning that its scenic benches could lead to 'excess hugging.'

Hugging remains a constant danger in the romantic park, from sunset views near quixotic oceanside windmills to Hippie Hill, where a daily drum circle does its rhythmically challenged best to restart the Summer of Love. The park has been updated since the 19th century – the wacky 'Eskimo village' is gone, and the Conservatory of Flowers (p175) was recently retrofitted to keep the carnivorous plants from catching cold – though if anything, the park has become even less tame. Pritzker Prize–winning architect Renzo Piano's 2008 landmark green building, the California Academy of Sciences (p175), houses Pierre the Penguin and 38,000 other weird and wonderful animals under a 'living roof' of California wildflowers. Across the music concourse where lindy-hoppers swing on Sundays is another showstopper: the MH de Young Museum (p178), a landmark collection of arts and crafts in Herzog & de Meuron's sleek copper-clad bunker, now oxidizing green to match the park.

Wild as it is, the park has its contemplative moments. The National AIDS Memorial Grove offers consoling shade, while the stand of old-growth redwoods at Strybing Arboretum is ideal for meditation before a fierce match at the Lawn Bowling Club (p185). Wiccan offerings are made on the marble remains of a Spanish monastery behind

the baseball diamond, and overstimulated visitors can enjoy a moment of Zen at the Japanese Tea Garden (p175; pictured above).
    See p174 for more information.

# >2 ALCATRAZ

## MAKE YOUR OWN GREAT ALCATRAZ ESCAPE

Even before your ferry arrives on the Rock, you'll start plotting your getaway. The obvious gambit is laundry duty, and sneaking out in a load of sheets. But then what? If you're caught you'll get sent to D-Block solitary, a tiny cube where days are marked by a light shaft traveling across the wall – or you might be interrogated using techniques only alluded to in the otherwise thorough Alcatraz audio tour, with first-hand accounts by prison guards and prisoners of the Rock.

For maximum creep factor, book the popular night tour to watch the sun set over the Rock and tour the darkened cell house. Pause in the library to check out the books the average prisoner read at a rate of 75 to 100 per year – though none of the books could have references to crime, violence or sex. Tense 20-minute meals were served under armed guard in the mess hall, where no spoon was left unaccounted for and a sign ordered prisoners: 'Take all that you wish – eat all that you take.' If you dare, step inside a cell and take off your headphones for a moment, and listen to the sound of carefree city life traveling 1.25 miles across the water. This is the torment that made perilous prison breaks and flying leaps into riptides worth the risk, from the 19th-century founding of the prison to hold Civil War deserters and Native American dissidents until Bobby Kennedy officially ordered its closure in 1963.

Outside the cell block, you'll notice faint graffiti on the water tower that reads, 'This is Indian Land.' This declaration was made by Native American activists, whose request to turn the closed prison island into a Native American study center was repeatedly turned down in the 1960s. Finally, on the eve of Thanksgiving, 1969, 79 Native American activists broke a Coast Guard blockade and took over Alcatraz in protest of the violation of treaties and appropriation of lands from 106 Native groups. Over the next 19 months, some 5600 Native Americans visited the occupied island, sparking Native American activism nationwide. Before the FBI seized the island in 1971, public support pressured President Richard Nixon to restore Native territory and strengthen self-rule for Native nations. The protest is commemorated in 'Red Power' graffiti found throughout Alcatraz

and at the dockside processing center, where an award-winning documentary featuring protesters' first-hand accounts is screened in a small side room.

See p58 for more information.

# >3 CHINATOWN ALLEYWAYS

## FIND THE CITY'S HIDDEN TREASURES IN CHINATOWN

'May you live in interesting times' goes the legendary Chinese curse, and the 41 alleys packed into 22 square blocks of Chinatown have lived through 150 very interesting years. In these narrow streets, San Francisco grew up too fast, surviving booms, bootleggers, bigotry and trials by fire to reach a wise old age.

The alleyways aren't exactly paved with gold as advertised in the 1850s Chinese railroad-labor recruitment posters, but they are rich with history. In the evenings you'll hear the shuffling of mahjong tiles in Spofford Alley (p80), where Sun Yat-sen plotted the overthrow of China's last dynasty. Society swells once sauntered down Nob Hill to smoke opium and gamble on Ross Alley (p79), while sailors stumbled up from the port to Commercial St brothels for 25-cent recreation. Today fortunes are still made on Ross Alley at the Golden Gate Fortune Cookie Company (p81), while Commercial's main enticements are happy hour at EZ5 (p83) and the city's best dim sum at City View (p81).

Since the 1849 gold rush, Waverly Place (p80) has been lined with ground-floor barber shops, restaurants and laundries topped with temples festooned with flags and lanterns. Starting in the 1870s, restrictions on marriage and family immigration turned Chinatown into a community of bachelors and 'paper sons' claimed as relations in a workaround for exclusion laws. Most services in Chinatown were provided not by the city but by tongs, neighborhood associations whose headquarters you can still see along Waverly Place and Spofford Alley.

After the 1906 fire gutted Chinatown, developers planned to oust Chinese residents. But while the altars were still smoldering ruins, worship services were held in Waverly Place, and Chinatown entrepreneurs led by Look Tin Ely reinvented Grant Ave as a distinctive Chinatown deco shopping and dining destination. Spofford and Ross Alleys were not so easily tamed: with corrupt police looking the other way during Prohibition, gun battles raged over the bootlegging trade concealed in a network of alleyway cellars. Again the neighborhood rallied, and forced a truce among gangsters.

Finally in 1943, the Chinese Exclusion Act that had prevented new immigration since 1882 was repealed, and Chinatown welcomed

new arrivals and fresh ideas. Chinatown became a favorite bohemian haunt, dishing dumplings to local artists like street photographer Benjamin Chinn and slinging hooch to Allen Ginsberg, Jack Kerouac and the rest of the Beat scene installed in the booths at Li Po Cocktails (p83). Today the colorful history of Chinatown's alleys are captured in murals in Spofford and Ross Alleys, and retold with pride by Chinatown teens in nonprofit Chinatown Alleyways walking tours (p205).

See p76 for more information.

# >4 GOLDEN GATE BRIDGE

## SEE THE GOLDEN GATE BRIDGE AT ITS BEST

Leftists pretty much run SF, but fierce right-wing and left-wing debates rage over the best bridge viewpoint. On the bridge's left are Seacliff mansion owners with multimillion-dollar vested interests in believing their view is best, plus nudists on Baker Beach (p165) convinced that the only way to appreciate the bridge in all its glory is to see it in theirs. To the right are Crissy Field (p165) fitness freaks with Ironman jogging strollers who brake for beauty, and cinema buffs who believe Hitchcock got it right: seen from below at Fort Point, the bridge induces a thrilling case of *Vertigo* (p210).

To see both sides of the Golden Gate debate, you can hike or bike it yourself: pedestrians can walk across the bridge on the east side, while bicyclists zoom along on the ocean side. But no matter how you look at or obsessively photograph it, this 1937 engineering marvel never fails to make a scene. Sunny days make you hope for afternoon fog, spilling over the towers like dry ice at a Kiss concert.

Hard to believe that this bridge was originally the idea of a certified nutcase, and was almost built of concrete painted like a bumblebee. Back in the 19th century, a bankrupted San Franciscan eccentric declared himself Emperor Norton, ruler of San Francisco and protector of Mexico, and decreed that a bridge should be built 2 miles across the mouth of the bay. Since the emperor also banned the term 'Frisco,' with violations subject to a $25 fine payable directly to himself, laughter was the initial response to his imperial bridge proposal. But when ferries became impractical to accommodate growing automobile traffic to and from the North Bay in the 20th century, the US War Department took up the emperor's cause. The navy's notion was to plunk hulking concrete pylons into the bay, slap a highway on top, and paint the whole thing with caution-yellow stripes for maximum visibility at sea.

Thankfully, architects Gertrude and Irving Murrow and engineer Joseph B Strauss intervened on the side of taste, and instead suggested an elegant art deco suspension bridge painted a signature shade called International Orange to harmonize with the natural environment. When their plan got the nod in 1933, the Murrows and Strauss worked quickly before the navy could protest. Daredevil laborers dove into the treacherous riptides of the bay to sink the foundations,

and four years later balanced triumphantly atop the 746ft suspension towers of the completed Golden Gate Bridge. But the bridge doesn't just wake up glowing golden every day – 25 fearless painters freshen up those looks with 1000 gallons of International Orange every week.

HIGHLIGHTS

# >5 THE FERRY BUILDING

## GO GOURMET BY THE BAY IN THE FERRY BUILDING

Deciding where to eat can be a major dilemma in a city with one restaurant for every 28 people, but there's one place everyone can agree on: the Ferry Building. Saturday picnickers raid the Ferry Plaza Farmers Market (p59) and blithely gorge themselves under the statue of a famished Gandhi, while lazy Sundays are ideal for watching chefs whip up beignets at the communal chef's table at Boulette's Larder (p62). Weekday lunches become mood-altering events with sparkling bay views, sustainable Baja fish tacos, and organic jicama, grapefruit and avocado salads at Mijita (p63). With advance reservations, that local Dungeness crab you saw hauled in down the block can be yours atop Vietnamese cellophane noodles at Slanted Door (p63). Savor that flavor by the bay, and let life and lunch exceed your expectations.

See p59 for more information.

# >6 TELEGRAPH HILL

## GET GIDDY IN THE CITY ATOP TELEGRAPH HILL

For breathless views of the bay, there's no topping Telegraph Hill. No crampons are needed, though you may want to pack poetry from nearby City Lights (p47) and a sandwich from Molinari (p50) for pit stops on the uphill climb. Rock quarrying by a ruthless 19th-century entrepreneur left one side of the hill too steep for roads, so mountaineering locals anchored stairway walks onto the rock face instead. Filbert and Greenwich Steps offer vertiginous views of the bay, winding through gardens blooming improbably along the cliff and cottages perched along wooden boardwalks.

You'll know you're near the crest of Telegraph Hill when you hear squawked hellos from the wild parrots that have claimed the treetops. Topping this surreal scene is the enormous white fire-hose nozzle of Coit Tower (p41), which eccentric millionaire Lillie Hancock Coit had built in 1934 to honor San Francisco's firefighters. The lobby is lined with Diego Rivera–inspired WPA (Works Progress Administration) murals of sweet-faced workers, once denounced as dangerously communist. But for truly woozy vistas, take the elevator to the viewing platform for a 360-degree panorama, 210ft above San Francisco.

## >7 MISSION MURALS
### DISCOVER YOUR SECRET MISSION

Passion and protest became permanent parts of the San Francisco
landscape starting in the 1930s, when Diego Rivera and fellow WPA
muralists risked their financial backing with monumental tributes
to workers in the San Francisco Art Institute (p44) and Coit Tower
(p41). But like Rivera's brief San Francisco reconciliation with ex-wife
Frida Kahlo, San Francisco's love affair with murals was star-crossed.
Public art projects were shelved with the onset of WWII and the rise
of McCarthyism, and artists came under federal scrutiny for glorifying
the everyman.

By the 1970s, San Francisco muralists couldn't wait anymore for
financial backing or city planning approval. Mujeres Muralistas (Women
Muralists) and PLACA (meaning 'mark-making') took their concerns
over US Central America policies directly to the streets of the Mission,
where sympathetic neighbors along Balmy Alley offered up garage
doors and fences for full-color protest murals. Today arts nonprofit Precita Eyes (p118) restores these murals, commissions new ones by San
Francisco artists and leads tours that cover 75 Mission murals within an
eight-block radius of Balmy Alley. Murals turned Clarion Alley (p115)
and the Women's Building (p119) into artistic landmarks, and some 250
street artworks bring meaning to the mean streets of the Mission.

# >8 CASTRO THEATRE

## COSTAR IN SF'S BEST MOVIE SCENE AT THE CASTRO

At other cinemas, movies begin with a hush – but at the Castro (p134), you know the show is starting when the crowd stomps and sings along to the mighty Wurlitzer organ pumping out the title song from Clark Gable's classic *San Francisco*: 'San Francisco/Open your Golden Gate/You let no stranger wait outside your door…' After such a dramatic overture, you'd think that any film would be anticlimactic. Not at all, thanks to the Castro's thrilling bills of unearthed silver-screen gems, retrospectives with in-person appearances by the likes of John Waters, Tim Burton and Tony Curtis, and the riveting San Francisco International LGBT Film Festival (p27) in June.

But no matter what's on the iconic Mex-deco marquee outside, you can count on irreverent audience participation inside this perfectly preserved movie palace. The wisecracks at every Rock Hudson–Doris Day kiss are worth the price of admission, and debates in the popcorn line during Fellini tributes condense film-school educations into five minutes. Outspoken, outrageous and occasionally as brilliant as they think they are, Castro filmgoers are San Francisco at its finest.

# >9 JAPANTOWN

## RELAX IN JAPANTOWN AND SAY HELLO KITTY

Perky kitties eagerly await your arrival in Japantown (p156). Atop every noodle-house counter and karaoke bar perches a *maneki neko*, the porcelain cat with a serious expression and one paw raised in permanent welcome. Japantown is a lot like its *maneki neko* mascot: endearing, enduring and industriously charming.

The neighborhood works hard to put you completely at ease, from shiatsu massages at Kabuki Hot Springs (p163) to the new jazz club Yoshi's (p163), featuring such world-class talents as the traditionalist Ellis Marsalis trio and crossover jazz piano sensation Hiromi. Japantown Center is out to prove that 'adorable mall' is not an oxymoron, from its anime photo-sticker booths to vast selections of surreal Japanese fashion magazines and panda-shaped office supplies at Kinokuniya (p160). Under new direction from Robert Redford, Kabuki Sundance Cinema (p163) is introducing moviegoers to eco-entertainment with non-GMO popcorn, cushy recycled-fiber seats and a reclaimed-wood bar.

The deliberate cheer and forward thinking is all the more impressive given Japantown's past. After 19th-century exclusion laws limited marriage and employment for Japanese San Franciscans, Executive Order 9066 sent 7000 Japantown residents to internment camps during WWII. The Japanese American Citizens' League promptly challenged this violation of civil rights, establishing legal precedents for the 1960s civil rights movement and resulting in a 1988 presidential apology. *Kawaii* (cute) as it is, Japantown is also unbreakable.

# >10 ALAMO SQUARE'S PAINTED LADIES

## SEE VICTORIANS GONE WILD AROUND ALAMO SQUARE

Can you blame turn-of-the century San Franciscans for wanting to bust out a little? They had fires, economic crashes, a bubonic plague outbreak and the 1906 earthquake to deal with – not to mention corsets and mustache wax. Yet as buttoned-up as ladies and gents of Victorian society appeared in public, their home decor reveals a Barbary Coast wild streak.

Today's real estate speculators consider Victorian tastes garish enough to bring down property values, so most of the Victorian 'Painted Ladies' in swanky Pacific Heights have been repainted saleable shades of white and taupe. But in the nonconformist Haight and the Castro, there are still many Victorians that stay true to their original outrageousness. Several houses around Alamo Square park (p145) feature lavish Victorian trimmings: high-contrast color palettes, stained-glass windows, fish-scale shingles, gilded stucco garlands and peaked roofs with carved wood 'gingerbread' trim. The famed Postcard Row on the east side of the park is cookie-cutter Victorian – for more outlandish Victorian photo ops, wander along the north side of the park and the blocks of McAllister and Golden Gate between Scott and Steiner.

See also p145.

## >11 THE HAIGHT

### RELIVE THE SUMMER OF LOVE

It was January of 1967, or maybe June, or possibly October of '68…
as the Haight saying goes, if you can remember the Summer of Love,
man, you weren't there. According to hazy collective memory, everything was free: music, love, food, truth, crash pads and then-legal
LSD. At some point the drugs got heavy, and so did the scene.

Many summers later, the legend lives. For decades, the Haight
Ashbury Food Program (p148) has served up free healthy meals and job
training, and you can return the love by volunteering. There's free live
music on the streets and at Amoeba Records (p149), and flowers are
still left on the doorsteps of the Grateful Dead house (p145). Co-ops run
the Red Vic Movie House (p155) and Bound Together Anarchist Book
Collective (p149), and Green Party candidates are the incumbents.

Even nostalgic hippies have to admit there have been improve-
ments since the '60s: Haight Ashbury Free Clinics have helped kick
tricky habits, there's free wireless at Coffee to the People (p153), and
Hell's Angels and hippies pass the organic ketchup at the communal
table at Magnolia (p152) without anyone getting hurt. Golden Gate
Park's Hippie Hill drum circle still hasn't found rhythm after 30 years,
but no one seems to mind. Peace and love, people, peace and love.

# >SAN FRANCISCO CALENDAR

No matter when you hit SF, a jacket and some glitter will come in handy. There's dancing in the streets at summer street fairs, free concerts come fall, and parades even in winter. Run, strut or get spanked for a good cause, then chill out with back-to-back movie premieres. Get inside tips on film, theater and dance at www.sfgate.com/eguide; music and art at http://sf.flavorpill.net and www.sfbg.com; food and drink celebrations at www.thrillist.com; literary events at www.somalit.com/newsletter.html; and organized mayhem at http://laughingsquid.com/squidlist. Join SF shenanigans already in progress at http://sfbay.craigslist.org/act.

Going zither and yon at Chinatown's Lunar New Year Parade (p26)

# FEBRUARY

## Independent Film Festival

☎ 820-3907; www.sfindie.com
Cinephiles get more than 100 indie films and
animations over two weeks. Mid-February.

## Lunar New Year Parade

www.chineseparade.com
Party with a 200ft dragon, tiny-tot martial
artists and lucky red envelopes. Mid-February.

# MARCH

## St Patrick's Day Parade

www.sfstpatricksdayparade.com
Bringing luck and libations to San Francisco
since 1851. Mid-month.

Steppin' out at the St Patrick's Day Parade

## Asian American Film Festival

☎ 863-0814; www.asianamerican
media.org
Two hundred filmmakers debut features and
documentaries at Kabuki Sundance Cinema
(p163). Third week.

## Anarchist Book Fair

http://sfbookfair.wordpress.com
Rise up and read freely at Golden Gate Park's
Fair Building. Third weekend.

# APRIL

## Cherry Blossom Festival

www.nccbf.org
Japantown blooms and booms with taiko
drums. Mid-April.

## San Francisco International Film Festival

☎ 925-866-9559; www.sffs.org
Looking stellar at 50-plus years, with two
weeks of star-studded premieres. Last two
weeks.

# MAY

## Bay to Breakers

www.baytobreakers.com
Jog costumed, naked or inebriated from
Embarcadero to Ocean Beach. Third
Sunday.

## Carnaval

www.carnavalsf.com

Get head-dressed to impress and samba through the Mission. Last weekend.

# JUNE

### North Beach Street Fair

www.sfnorthbeach.org/festival

Swing music, Italian sausages and sidewalk drawings worthy of Leonardo. Mid-June.

### Haight Street Fair

www.haightashburystreetfair.org

They've got the free music, you bring the free love. Mid-June.

## San Francisco International LGBT Film Festival

☎ 703-8650; www.frameline.org

Here, queer and ready for a premiere. Last half of June.

### Pink Saturday

www.sfpride.org

Fifty thousand GLBT women parade from Dolores to Castro St. Last Saturday.

### Pride Parade

www.sfpride.org

The ultimate GLBT celebration: more than 500,000 people, tons of boas and ounces of bikinis. Last Sunday.

Japantown celebrates spring at the annual Cherry Blossom Festival

# JULY

## San Francisco Mime Troupe

www.sfmt.org
Free musical comedy meets biting political satire in Dolores Park. First weekend.

## AIDS Walk

www.aidswalk.net/sanfran
Until AIDS takes a hike, you can: this 10K fundraiser benefits 43 AIDS organizations. Third Sunday.

# AUGUST

## San Francisco Jewish Film Festival

☎ 621-0556; www.sfjff.org
The world's premier Jewish film festival will leave you kvelling. Early August.

# SEPTEMBER

## San Francisco Shakespeare Fest

www.sfshakes.org
Free Shakespeare and sunshine in the Presidio. Weekends.

## Opera in the Park

www.sfopera.com
Divas sing gratis in Sharon Meadow. First Sunday of the opera season.

## Arab Film Fest

☎ 564-1100; www.aff.org
Mideastern moxie at the Roxie Cinema. Second week.

## Folsom Street Fair

www.folsomstreetfair.com
Work those leather chaps and enjoy public spankings for charity. Last weekend.

## SPECIAL EVENTS ON A REGULAR BASIS

### Weekly

**Farmers market** Get easy access to the good stuff almost year-round at the farmers market behind the Ferry Building (p59) on Saturdays and Heart of the City Farmers Market (p94) on Wednesdays and Sundays.
**Sundays in Golden Gate Park** (p174) That's when it's closed to traffic and you're free to roam on foot, skates, bikes, skateboards, unicycles…

### Monthly

**Critical Mass** Last Friday of the month at Justin Herman Plaza at 5:30pm, bicyclists take over the streets during rush hour in San Francisco's trailblazing bike parade, held in protest to make the streets safer for bikes.
**First Thursday gallery openings** Galleries unveil new shows and stay open until 7:30pm or 8pm, and all of arty San Francisco traipses through SoMa galleries and 49 Geary (p68) and 77 Geary (p68) to see what's up on the walls.

### Fringe Festival

www.sffringe.org

More outrageous theatrical antics in SF than usual. Late September to October.

# OCTOBER

### Castro Street Fair

www.castrostreetfair.org

Drag royalty perform and rainbow flags fly. First weekend.

### Hardly Strictly Bluegrass Festival

www.strictlybluegrass.com

Free bluegrass and rock with a twang in Golden Gate Park. First weekend.

### LoveFest

www.sflovefest.org

All you need is love and 100-plus DJs downtown. First weekend.

### LitQuake

www.litquake.org

Stranger-than-fiction literary events. Second weekend.

### Alternative Press Expo

www.comic-con.org/ape

Meet the demented masterminds behind cult-hit comics . Last weekend.

### SF Jazz Festival

☎ 788-7353; www.sfjazz.org

Standards reinvented: greats play with newcomers. End of October.

Four wheels bad, two wheels good: Sundays are car-free in Golden Gate Park

# NOVEMBER

## Diá de los Muertos
**www.dayofthedeadsf.org**
Party to raise the dead with a parade and
altars in the Mission. November 2.

## Green Festival
**www.greenfestivals.org**
The latest in hydro-powered cars, eco-
smarts and green cuisine. Second week.

## Tranny Fest
**www.trannyfest.com**
Cross-dress and transgress with the best.
All month.

# DECEMBER

## Celebration of Craftswomen
**www.celebrationofcraftswomen.org**
Get crafty gifts at this Women's Building
(p119) fundraiser. First weekend.

## Dance Along Nutcracker
☎ **255-1355; www.sflgfb.org/show.html**
You too can tutu with the Lesbian/Gay Freedom Band's *Nutcracker Suite*. First weekend.

## Kung Pao Kosher Comedy
**www.koshercomedy.com**
An SF holiday tradition: Jewish comedy on
Christmas at a Chinese restaurant.

# >ITINERARIES

Follow your nose to Pier 39 (p56)

# ITINERARIES

So you've only got a short stay in San Francisco? Enjoy multiple peak SF experiences on day one, reinvent yourself as a San Franciscan on day two, and stick around to discover the benefits of fog, freebies and cruise control – and see if you still need that return ticket.

## DAY ONE

Hit SF's high points in one day, starting with truffled eggs in the working kitchen at Boulette's Larder (p62). Gold-rush through historic Jackson Square and up Filbert Steps (p41), but take a breather for dizzying views over the bay. Wild parrots cheer your arrival at Coit Tower (p41), where you'll glimpse uplifting murals and parrot's-eye views of the Golden Gate Bridge (p17). Roll down to boho North Beach to refuel at Caffe Trieste (p52), where Francis Ford Coppola wrote *The Godfather* under the Sicilian mural, and find the sublime in the upstairs poetry

### FORWARD PLANNING

**Three weeks before you go** Plot your getaway to and from Alcatraz (p58), book back-alley adventures with Chinatown Alleyway Tours (p205) and plan mural tours with Precita Eyes (p118). Start walking: you'll need stamina to handle SF's hills and Mission bar crawls. Register for workshops to bring out your inner lamp designer at Craft Gym (p98), documentary filmmaker at Bay Area Video Coalition (p129) or wino at Cav Wine Bar (p97).

**One week before you go** At www.sfbg.com, find out who's playing at SF's hot music venues: the Fillmore (p162), Café du Nord (p142), Slim's (p113), the Great American Music Hall (p99) and the Warfield (p101). Relax: it's not too late to get tickets for American Conservatory Theater (p98) matinees or book a table at Slanted Door (p63), Gary Danko (p62) or Michael Mina (p73).

**One day before you go** See what San Franciscans are buzzing about at www.sfgate.com and www.sfist.com, and find out at www.indybay.org/sf if there's an upcoming protest worth packing a picket sign for. Check the calendar for the Booksmith (p154), San Francisco Public Library Main Branch (p88) and City Lights (p47) to see if you can get your favorite book signed by the author. You can still make dinner reservations at Jai Yun (p82) – and start cramming if you're going to attempt pub trivia night at Edinburgh Castle Pub (p99) or Mad Dog in the Fog (p153).

**Top** Sidewalk fruit sellers, Chinatown (p76) **Bottom** San Francisco Museum of Modern Art (p107)

ITINERARIES

section of bookstore City Lights (p47). Stumble over the sidewalk poetry of Jack Kerouac Alley (p45) to pagoda-roofed Grant Ave and up to Waverly Place (p80), where prayer flags have fluttered from temple balconies for almost 150 years. Take lunch to another level with scrumptious shrimp and leek dumplings at nearby City View (p81), then reach new artistic heights at the San Francisco Museum of Modern Art (p107). Head to Union Square to score last-minute half-price tickets to the American Conservatory Theater (p98), topped with a highly satisfying sustainable dinner at Fish & Farm (p94).

## DAY TWO

Discover your inner San Franciscan, starting with eye-opening coffee and political slogans at Coffee to the People (p153). Next, drag yourself into Piedmont (p150) for a feather boa, get a retro rocker makeover at Wasteland (p151) or score a streetwise hoodie from SFO Snowboarding & FTC Skateboarding (p150). Then head into the wilds of Golden Gate Park to do as the locals do: lecture flesh-eating plants on vegetarianism at the Conservatory of Flowers (p175), raise your eco-consciousness along the rainforest ramp at the California Academy of Sciences (p175) or find inspiration for your next art project at the MH de Young Museum (p178). Enjoy chili-laced lunch with an exclamation at Spices (p182), followed by cooling green-tea ice-cream crepes at Genki (p181). Browse your way past Clement St bookstores to the Legion of Honor (p178), where a path leads to Lands End (p175). Absorb sunset over the Pacific, then beat the fog down Geary to your organic Cal-Moroccan feast at Aziza (p181) and *soju* cocktails at Rohan Lounge (p184).

## FREE DAY!

Free love is only the beginning in SF, where free concerts happen year-round at Amoeba Records (p149) and Golden Gate Park, from opera (p28) to bluegrass (p29). First Tuesdays of the months are free at most SF museums, and on first Thursdays at 49 Geary (p68) and 77 Geary (p68) there's free wine and cheese to wash down your art. Take your pick of free performances by the San Francisco Mime Troupe in Dolores Park in July (p28) or at the San Francisco Shakespeare Fest in the Presidio in September (p28). Reserve ahead for a spot on the free tour and beer tasting at Anchor Brewing (p111), and catch SF Giants games for free along the waterfront promenade behind AT&T Park (p112).

## CRUISING THE COAST: SANTA CRUZ TO SONOMA COUNTY

For a quick, spectacular change of scenery, take Hwy 101/880/17 to surf capital Santa Cruz, 70 miles south of SF, then follow coastal Hwy 1 all the way back up to Sonoma wine country. Pull over to take a wooden roller-coaster ride at the **Santa Cruz Beach Boardwalk** (www .beachboardwalk.com), watch surfing stunts along West Cliff Dr, and hike to beaches packed with sunbathing sea lions and elephant seals 15 miles north at **Año Nuevo State Reserve** (www.parks.ca.gov). Swing by Pescadero's **Duarte's Tavern** (www.duartestavern.com) for the catch of the day and Grandma Duarte's olallieberry pie, then head 66 winding miles along Hwy 1 for a peaceful pause among the great redwoods of **Muir Woods National Monument** (www.nps.gov/muwo) and tea in organic gardens at **Tassajara Zen Center** (www .sfzc.org/tassajara). Follow Hwy 1 north through 23 miles of pastures and parkland to Point Reyes Station, a Wild West outpost with unbelievable cheese at **Cowgirl Creamery** (www .cowgirlcreamery.com). Stick with Hwy 1 through 23 miles of oyster flats and rolling pastures to **Rocker Oysterfeller's Kitchen & Saloon** (www.rockeroysterfellers.com) for a tasting menu of oysters, pork shoulder soused on bourbon, and all-local wines.

## FOGGY DAY

Make like a San Franciscan and wander around with your head in the clouds, starting with the Cartoon Art Museum (p103). Hop the historic F line streetcar past misty Market St flatirons, and pop by the Luggage Store Gallery (p88), San Francisco Public Library Main Branch (p88) and City Hall (p86) to see big ideas emerge from the fog. Lunch is self-served at the café in the Asian Art Museum (p86), and upstairs you'll see clouds drift through classic Song dynasty scroll paintings. If there's a bright spot anywhere in SF, it's in the Mission, with riotous murals lining Clarion Alley (p115), Balmy Alley (p118) and the Women's Building (p119). On stormy days, stop by 826 Valencia (p115) to load up on pirate supplies and fiction, or dance up a storm of your own with a West African dance class at the ODC Theater (p130). Drift into Jardinière (p94) for a mood-altering meal before a cloud-clearing night at the opera (p100) or symphony (p98).

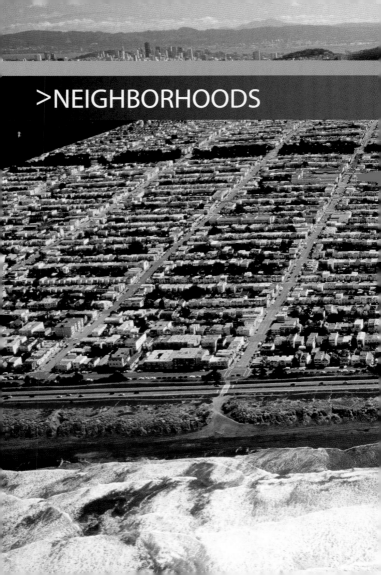

>NEIGHBORHOODS

Swimmers, beware: a rip-roaring surf pounds Ocean Beach (p180)

# NEIGHBORHOODS

Even meteorologists are mystified by San Francisco's microclimates, where a bus ride can take you from rain to sunshine in 20 minutes. But there's another shift that happens, too, as downtown awnings give way to gabled Victorian roofs, and a pungent whiff of chili hitting a hot wok fades into the smoky-savory scent of *carne asada* on the grill.

Locals respond to these shifts in the weather and culture from one block to the next as matters of course: add a sweater here or leather chaps there and you're good to go in San Francisco.

Here's what to look for in San Francisco's microclimates of community:

**North Beach & the Hills** Poetry and parrots, top-of-the-world views, Italian gossip and opera on the jukebox.

**Embarcadero & the Piers** Gourmet treats, sea-lion antics, 19th-century video games and getaways to and from Alcatraz.

**Downtown & the Financial District** The notorious Barbary Coast has gone legit with banks and boutiques, but reveals its wild side in provocative art galleries.

**Chinatown** Pagoda roofs, mahjong, revolution and fortunes made and lost in historic alleyways.

**Hayes Valley, Civic Center & the Tenderloin** Grand buildings and great performances amid dive bars and cable cars, foodie finds and local designs.

**SoMa** Where high technology meets higher art, and everyone gets down and dirty on the dance floor.

**Mission** A book in one hand and a burrito in the other, and murals all around.

**Castro** Out and proud with samba whistles, rainbow flags and policy platforms.

**Haight** Flashbacks and fashion-forwardness, free thinking, free music and spendy skateboards.

**Japantown, the Fillmore & Pacific Heights** Sushi in the fountains, John Coltrane over the altar and rock at the Fillmore.

**Marina & the Presidio** Boutiques, organic dining, peace and public nudity at a former army base.

**Golden Gate Park & the Avenues** SF's mile-wide wild streak, surrounded by gourmet hangouts for hungry surfers.

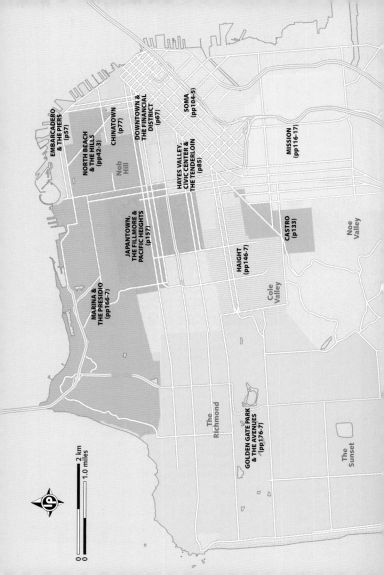

EMBARCADERO
& THE PIERS
(p57)

NORTH BEACH
& THE HILLS
(pp42-3)

CHINATOWN
(p77)

Nob
Hill

DOWNTOWN &
THE FINANCIAL
DISTRICT
(p67)

SOMA
(pp104-5)

MISSION
(pp116-17)

HAYES VALLEY,
CIVIC CENTER &
THE TENDERLOIN
(p85)

JAPANTOWN,
THE FILLMORE &
PACIFIC HEIGHTS
(p157)

CASTRO
(p133)

Noe
Valley

MARINA &
THE PRESIDIO
(pp166-7)

HAIGHT
(pp146-7)

Cole
Valley

The
Richmond

GOLDEN GATE PARK
& THE AVENUES
(pp176-7)

The
Sunset

2 km
1.0 miles

0

0

# >NORTH BEACH & THE HILLS

Strange landscape formations occur wherever tectonic plates touch in California – but in these hills, where SF eccentricity rubs up against natural splendor, the scenery is even stranger. Stairways are the only way to scale the heights of Russian and Telegraph Hills, yet residents have dragged old car parts uphill to repurpose as sculpture and wild parrots have settled into the treetops. Nob Hill started out as a forbidding crag where hermits lived with chickens in shotgun shacks, and though cable cars have made it more accessible, this is still the location of choice for reclusive millionaires with dozens of pets.

Downhill in North Beach, a bohemian wellspring bubbles up from the poetry section of City Lights bookstore, and alleyways named after poets fill with opera arias from cafés where Italian is still spoken. On a good night at neighborhood jazz clubs and bars, the air seems atomically charged with primal forces and nascent revolutions.

# NORTH BEACH & THE HILLS

Please see over for map

#  SEE

## ◉ BEAT MUSEUM

☎ 800-537-6822; www.thebeatmuseum
.org; 540 Broadway; admission $5;
🕐 10am-7pm Tue-Sun; 🚌 15, 30, 41, 45

The closest you can get to the complete Beat experience without breaking a law. The one-room ephemera collection ranges from such literary relics as the banned edition of Allen Ginsberg's *Howl* to tawdry tidbits like a Jack Kerouac liquor store check. Starving artists can skip the museum and peruse limited-edition poetry titles in the adjoining shop (entry is free).

## ◉ COIT TOWER & FILBERT STEPS

☎ 362-0808; Telegraph Hill Blvd;
elevator adult/senior & child $3/2;
🕐 10am-6pm; 🚌 39

Firehouse groupie Lillie Hancock Coit left a fortune to build this peculiar 210ft concrete tower as a monument to SF firefighters. When it was completed in 1934, the worker-glorifying, Diego Rivera–style WPA (Works Progress Administration) lobby murals were denounced as communist, as were the 25 artists who worked on them, but these views were eventually

See the best minds of their generation at the Beat Museum

NEIGHBORHOODS

NORTH BEACH & THE HILLS

trumped by the colorful murals and panoramic tower views. The climb here along the Filbert Steps is its own adventure, scaling the rocky face of Telegraph Hill past sculpture gardens in bloom, with sweeping vistas of the Bay Bridge and wild parrots squawking encouragement along the final stretch.

### COLUMBUS TOWER
**916 Kearny St; 🚌 15, 41**
Bad luck, good reggae and cannoli worthy of a Corleone are the back-story of copper-topped Columbus Tower. Shady political boss Abe Ruef had only just finished the building in 1905 when it was hit by the 1906 earthquake, and restored it right before his 1907

bribery conviction. The Kingston Trio bought the building in the 1960s, and recorded reggae and the Grateful Dead in the base-ment. Since 1970 the building has belonged to filmmaker Francis Ford Coppola, who leases the top floors to fellow filmmakers Sean Penn and Wayne Wang, and offers mean desserts and his own-label Napa wine at the ground-level Niebaum Coppola Café.

### DIEGO RIVERA GALLERY
☎ 771-7020; www.sfai.edu; 800 Chest-nut St; admission free; ⏰ 11am-6pm Tue-Sat; 🚌 30; 🚋 Powell-Mason
Hidden inside the San Francisco Art Institute, through the entrance courtyard and under the archway

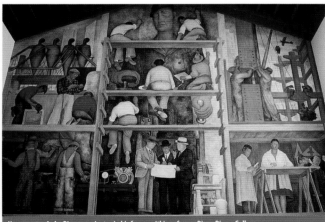
Heavy meta, dude: Rivera ruminates in his fresco-within-a-fresco, Diego Rivera Gallery

on the left, is a San Francisco treasure: *The Making of a Fresco Showing the Building of a City*. This wall-size mural painted by Rivera in 1931 is a trompe l'oeil fresco-within-a-fresco, showing the back of the artist himself as he pauses to admire the work in constant progress that is San Francisco. For another standout SF panorama, head to the school's rear courtyard for surprisingly tasty café food overlooking the bay.

### GRACE CATHEDRAL

☎ 749-6300; www.gracecathedral.org; 1100 California St; ⏱ 7am-6pm Sun-Fri, 8am-6pm Sat; 🚌 1, 27; 🚋 **California**
Third time's a charm: this progressive Episcopal church has been rebuilt thrice since the gold rush and it still keeps reinventing itself. Additions include an AIDS Memorial Chapel with a bronze altarpiece by the late artist and AIDS activist Keith Haring; stained-glass windows dedicated to Human Endeavor, including one of Albert Einstein floating in a swirl of nuclear particles; and a mystical stone labyrinth, meant to guide restless souls through the spiritual stages of releasing, receiving and returning.

### INA COOLBRITH PARK

**Off Vallejo St;** 🚋 **Powell-Hyde**
California's first poet laureate was Ina Coolbrith, who mentored Jack London, Isadora Duncan, George Sterling and Charlotte Perkins Gilman – all while keeping secret from her bohemian crowd the fact that her uncle was Mormon prophet Joseph Smith. Scenic Russian Hill staircases lead to hilltop gardens named in her honor, with vistas worthy of her trademark romantic rhapsodies and multiple exclamation points.

### JACK KEROUAC ALLEY

**Btwn Grant & Columbus Aves;** 🚌 **15, 30, 41**
'The air was soft, the stars so fine, and the promise of every cobbled alley so great…' The *On the Road* author's ode to San Francisco is now inscribed in the pavement of the signature shortcut between Chinatown and the Beat hub of City Lights (p47). Spiffy with murals yet fragrant as ever, this is the very alleyway where Kerouac was tossed after one epic binge at Vesuvio (p54).

### SAINTS PETER & PAUL CHURCH AND WASHINGTON SQUARE PARK

☎ 421-0809; www.stspeterpaul.san -francisco.ca.us; 666 Filbert St; 🚌 **15, 30, 39, 41, 45;** 🚋 **Powell-Mason**
Wedding-cake cravings are to be expected upon sight of this frosting-white, triple-decker 1924 cathedral where Joe DiMaggio and Marilyn Monroe famously posed for wedding photos (since they were both divorced, they were denied a church wedding here).

The church overlooks Washington Square, where nonagenarian *non-nas* (Italian grandmothers) feed wild parrots and practice tai chi by the 1897 statue of Ben Franklin, donated by an eccentric dentist who made his fortune fitting miners with gold teeth.

### ☞ STERLING PARK
Cnr Greenwich & Hyde Sts; 🚌 19, 41, 45, 47, 49; 🚋 Powell-Hyde

'Homeward into the sunset/Still unwearied we go,/Till the northern hills are misty/With the amber of afterglow.' Poet George Sterling's 'City by the Sea' is gushingly romantic, but when you watch the sun set over the Golden Gate Bridge from this hilltop park, you'll concede his point. SF's 'King of Bohemia' loved poetry, women, men, nature, opium and San Francisco (not necessarily in that order). The park was named in his honor two years after his apparent suicide by opium in 1926, and offers recently resurfaced public tennis and basketball courts, zigzagging paths and stirring, Sterling views.

# 🛍 SHOP
### ☐ 101 MUSIC
*Music & Instruments*
☎ 392-6369; 1414 Grant Ave; 🕙 11am-8pm Sun-Mon & Wed-Thu, 11am-9pm Fri & Sat; 🚌 15, 30, 41, 45

DJs maintain a Cosa Nostra–like code of silence about this place, and you'll have to bend over the $5 bins to let determined vinyl collectors pass you in single-file aisles. Dig through the bins to score original Dead Kennedys, William S Burroughs singing, and live North Beach jazz c 1959. Try not to bang your head on the vintage guitars overhead, and don't be surprised to bump into Tom Waits by the checkout counter.

### ☐ ARIA *Antiques*
☎ 433-0219; 1522 Grant Ave; 🕙 11am-7pm Mon-Sat, noon-5pm Sun; 🚌 15, 30, 41, 45

The antiques here aren't the glitziest, but the most poetic: anatomy diagrams of the human heart, iron keys to wine-cellar doors somewhere in Italy, 19th-century letters in French still in their glassine wax-sealed envelopes. These relics seem perfectly placed atop well-worn benches and inside salvaged medicine cabinets, yet just forlorn enough that you'll feel obliged to give them a good home.

### ☐ BABYLON FALLING *Books*
☎ 345-1017; www.babylonfalling.com; 1017 Bush St; 🕙 noon-9pm Tue-Fri, noon-7pm Sat & Sun; 🚌 19, 38; 🚋 Powell-Hyde

What skeptic can resist a bookstore that boasts '3,000 titles, NO FILLER'? Babylon Falling isn't exaggerating: herein lies all the lit you could ever need to lead a revolution and inspire your next graphic novel, plus locally designed T-shirts and art shows highlighting the talents of San Francisco's many streetwise social commentators.

### 📷 CITY LIGHTS Books
☎ 362-8193; www.citylights.com; 261 Columbus Ave; 🕑 10am-midnight; 🚌 15, 30, 41, 45
Ever since manager Shigeyoshi Murao and founder and Beat poet Lawrence Ferlinghetti successfully defended their right to 'willfully and lewdly print' Allen Ginsberg's magnificent *Howl and Other Poems*

in 1957, this landmark bookstore has been a magnet for poets, politicos and omnivorous readers. Celebrate your freedom to read willfully and lewdly upstairs in Poetry, load up on zines on the mezzanine, or entertain radical ideas downstairs in sections on Muckraking and Stolen Continents.

### 📷 DELILAH CROWN Clothing
☎ 765-9060; www.delilahcrown.com; 524 Green St; 🕑 11am-6:30pm Tue-Sat, noon-5pm Sun; 🚌 15, 30, 41, 45
Casual flair with crafty details – pin-tucking, silkscreened mushroom prints, tiny red vintage

Trip the lit fantastic at San Francisco's shrine for Beat-loving bibliophiles

buttons – for women and precociously hip babies. The sales table by the dressing room often features graphic-patterned Orla Kiely tops, but the most irresistible deals are sweet dandelion-printed dresses by SF designer Kristina De Pizzol for Delilah's own label.

### 🏠 ECO CITIZEN
*Sustainable Clothing*

☎ 614-0100; www.ecocitizenonline
.com; 1488 Vallejo St; 🕐 11am-7pm
Mon-Sat, noon-6pm Sun; 🚌 19, 47, 49;
🚃 Powell-Hyde

Idealism meets street chic in this boutique of eco-conscious must-haves, from recycled cotton lace camis to handbags made of salvaged muscle-car upholstery. Prices are reasonable and sales a steal – for $25 you can keep a poem up your sleeve, with the organic, fair-trade cotton Edgar Allan Poe T-shirt that has a Poe ode inside the left arm. And once you've worn out those fabulous silver molded-rubber flip-flops, Eco Citizen will recycle them.

### 🏠 POLK-A-DOT
*Gifts & Stationery*

☎ 346-0660; 1742 Polk St; 🕐 11:30am-
6:30pm Mon-Sat, noon-6pm Sun; 🚌 1,
19, 47, 49; 🚃 California

Spectra the cat is the only one present who isn't squealing with joy over tiny Japanese drawers filled with treasures under $2.50: antique mahjong tiles, fake mustaches and enough horseshoe charms to keep you lucky for life. Five dollars will get you a vintage Japanese stuffed dog smoking a pipe or a tin kazoo, and if your haul adds up to $40, you get a free grab bag of treats.

### 🏠 STUDIO *Arts & Crafts*

☎ 931-3130; www.studiogallerysf.com;
1718A Polk St; 🕐 11am-8pm Wed-Fri,
11am-6pm Sat & Sun; 🚌 1, 19, 47, 49;
🚃 California

So maybe shopping is a substitute for Prozac after all. Try on a silver necklace in the shape of a serotonin molecule, meditate on street signage reorganized by Mike Farruggia to read 'Simplify then Glorify' and cure insomnia counting Chiami Sekine's quizzical sheep paintings. Better yet, take a look at the price tags on all these locally made arts and crafts – most are under $100.

### 🏠 VELVET DA VINCI
*Jewelry & Crafts*

☎ 441-0109; www.velvetdavinci.com;
2015 Polk St; 🕐 noon-6pm Tue-Sat,
noon-4pm Sun; 🚌 12, 19, 47, 49, 76;
🚃 Powell-Hyde

Breakfast at Tiffany's is a yawn compared with afternoons spent poring over this brilliantly curated selection of handcrafted embellishments, including knockout shows of enamel badges in celebration of the Universal Declaration of Human Rights. Distinctive styles and materials range from Cynthia Troops' felt octopus-tentacle bracelets to silhouette cameos of people talking with their hands, produced with a 3-D scanner by portraitist Arthur Hash.

# 🍴 EAT

### 🍴 1550 HYDE *Californian* $$
☎ 775-1550; www.1550hyde.com; 1550 Hyde St; 🕑 7-10:30pm Tue-Sun; 🚌 12, 19; 🚋 Powell-Hyde
Low lights, mood music by Dave Brubeck, succulent seasonal cuisine and glimpses of passing cable cars through bay windows: 1550 Hyde is putting all the San Francisco moves on you. Go Sunday to Thursday for the $29.95 three-course dinner and $15 wine flights, and be seduced.

### 🍴 ACQUERELLO *Cal-Italian* $$$
☎ 567-5432; www.acquerello.com; 1722 Sacramento St; 🕑 7-11pm Tue-Sat; 🚌 1, 19, 47, 49, 76; 🚋 California
Chef Suzette Gresham converts Italian purists into true believers in Cal-Italian cuisine with generous pastas and ingenious seasonal meat dishes, all served in a renovated former chapel. An anteroom where brides once steadied their nerves is now lined with rare, limited-production Italian vintages, which the sommelier will gladly pair by the glass. Order up heavenly quail salad or lobster panzerotti (stuffed dough pockets in a spicy seafood broth) à la carte, or the seasonal prix fixe of three courses for $60, four for $72 or five for $82.

### 🍴 BRIOCHE BAKERY *Bakery* $
☎ 765-0412; 210 Columbus Ave; 🕑 7am-6pm Mon-Fri, 8am-4pm Sat; 🚌 15, 41
When gold rush miners struck it rich they treated themselves to 'Frenchy food' here on San Francisco's Barbary Coast – and now you too can start your day the decadent way, with flaky cinnamon twists, not-too-sweet *pain au chocolat*, and namesake brioches golden with butter.

### 🍴 CINECITTÁ PIZZERIA *Pizza* $
☎ 291-8830; 663 Union St; 🕑 11am-10pm Sun-Thu, 11am-midnight Fri & Sat; 🚌 15, 30, 41, 45; 🚋 Powell-Mason; Ⓥ ♿
Squeeze in at the counter for your thin-crust pie and Anchor Steam on draft with a side order of sass from Roman owner Romina. Vegetarians swear by the Funghi Selvatici (wild mushroom with grilled zucchini and sundried tomato), but that saliva-prompting aroma escaping the wood-fired oven is probably the Travestere (fresh mozzarella, arugula and prosciutto) or the classic Capricciosa

NEIGHBORHOODS

NORTH BEACH & THE HILLS

(artichoke hearts, olives, fresh mozzarella, prosciutto and egg).

### 🍴 IDEALE *Italian* $$
☎ 391-4129; www.idealerestaurant.com; 1315 Grant Ave; ⏱ 5:30-10:30pm Tue-Sat, 5-10pm Sun; 🚌 15, 30, 41, 45; Ⓥ ♿
Other restaurants pass off spaghetti with meatballs as authentic, but Ideale is the one restaurant where you'll find actual Italians in the kitchen, on the floor and at the table, thoroughly enjoying the experience. Roman chef Maurizio Bruschi grills a mean fish and whips up a gorgeous truffled zucchini, but try any pasta involving house-cured pancetta and ask the Tuscan staff to recommend wine, and everyone goes home happy.

### 🍴 LIGURIA BAKERY *Focaccia* $
☎ 421-3786; 1700 Stockton St; ⏱ 8am-2pm Mon-Fri, 7am-2pm Sat, 7am-noon Sun; 🚌 15, 30, 41, 45; Ⓥ ♿
Bleary-eyed art students and Italian grandmothers are in line by 8am for the cinnamon-raisin focaccia, leaving 9am dawdlers a choice of tomato or classic rosemary and 11am stragglers out of luck. Take what you can get, and don't kid yourself that you're going to save it for lunch.

### 🍴 MOLINARI *Italian Deli* $
☎ 421-2337; 373 Columbus Ave; ⏱ 8am-5:30pm Mon-Fri, 7:30am-5:30pm Sat; 🚌 15, 30, 41, 45

Grab a number and wait your turn ogling Italian wines and cheeses. By the time you're called for your sandwich order ($5 to $7), the aroma of house-cured salami dangling from the rafters, buffalo mozzarella glistening in milky baths, and translucent sheets being sliced from a Parma prosciutto will have made your choice for you.

### 🍴 NAIA GELATO *Ice Cream* $
☎ 677-9280; www.gelaterianaia.com; 520 Columbus Ave; ⏱ 11am-11pm Sun-Thu, 11am-midnight Fri & Sat; 🚌 15, 30, 41, 45
Chinatown and North Beach cross-pollinate with creamy concoctions that improve on the ordinary, elevating the usual green tea or pistachio ice-cream options to a decadent choice of Kyoto maccha tea or locally roasted California pistachio gelato. Local, seasonal flavors and constant experimentation introduce entirely new sorbet and gelato obsessions with flavors ranging from white peach to black sesame.

### 🍴 SWAN OYSTER DEPOT *Seafood* $$
☎ 673-1101; 1517 Polk St; ⏱ 8am-5:30pm Mon-Sat; 🚌 1, 19, 47, 49; 🚋 California
Superior flavor without the superior attitude of most seafood

## SAN FRANCISCO BY THE BOOK

Share the love for books at SF's best literary landmarks.
> Hall of fame: City Lights (p47), LitQuake (p29), San Francisco Public Library (p88), 826 Valencia (p115)
> Poetry: City Lights (p47), Sterling Park (p46), Ina Coolbrith Park (p45)
> Graphic novels: Isotope (p90), Alternative Press Expo (p29), San Francisco Public Library (p88), Babylon Falling (p46)
> Beat literature: City Lights (p47), Vesuvio (p54), Jack Kerouac Alley (p45), Beat Museum (p41), bathroom at Caffe Trieste (p52)
> Noir & Mystery: John's Grill (p75), Hemlock Tavern (p97), LitQuake (p29), Castro Theatre (p134)
> Memoirs & First-person: 826 Valencia (p115), Make-Out Room (p129), Edinburgh Castle Pub (p99)
> Zines: Anarchist Book Fair (p26), Needles & Pens (p122), Bound Together Anarchist Book Collective (p149), Adobe Books (p119)

restaurants. The downside is an inevitable wait for the few counter seats, but the upside of the high turnover is unbelievably fresh seafood. On sunny days, place an order to go, browse Polk St boutiques, then breeze past the line to pick up your crab salad with Louie dressing and the obligatory top-grade oysters with *mignonette* (wine with shallot) sauce. Then bus or hike up to Sterling Park for superlative seafood with ocean views.

### ZA *Pizza* $

☎ 771-3100; 1919 Hyde St; ⏰ noon-10pm Mon-Wed & Sun, noon-11pm Thu-Sat; 🚋 41, 45; 🚡 Powell-Hyde
Sit down and savor that slice, already: you don't get a gourmet, cornmeal-dusted, thin-crust slice

like this every day. Pizza-lovers brave the uphill climb for slices piled with fresh ingredients, a pint of Anchor Steam and a cozy bar setting with highly flirtatious pizza-slingers – all for under 10 bucks.

## 🍸 DRINK

### 🍸 BIGFOOT LODGE *Dive Bar*

☎ 440-2355; www.bigfootlodge.com; 1750 Polk St; ⏰ 3pm-2am; 🚋 1, 19, 47, 49, 76; 🚡 California
No, it's not the signature cocktail of ginger brandy and Wild Turkey talking: there really is an 8ft-tall stuffed Sasquatch over your shoulder. By the end of the 3pm to 7pm happy hour, everyone's telling tall tales over Toasted Marshmallows (vanilla vodka, Bailey's and a flaming marshmallow). All that's

missing is the campfire, right? Stick around and stand back at midnight, when the bartenders set the bar on fire.

### ▼ CAFFÉ ROMA *Café*

☎ 296-7942; www.cafferoma.com; 526 Columbus Ave; 🕙 6am-7pm Mon-Thu, 6am-8pm Fri & Sun, 6am-11pm Sat; 🚌 15, 30, 41, 45

Follow the smell of espresso beans roasting to this authentic *caffé*, where your order is served according to the Italian proverb: 'Black as night/strong as sin/sweet as love/hot as hell.' After mass on Sundays, North Beach regulars converge here for *vero* (real) espresso and possibly true gossip from the old country.

### ▼ CAFFE TRIESTE *Café*

☎ 392-6739; www.caffetrieste.com; 601 Vallejo St; 🕙 6:30am-11pm Sun-Thu, 6:30am-midnight Fri & Sat; 🚌 15, 30, 41, 45

Poetry on the bathroom walls, opera on the jukebox, accordion on Sundays and, on occasion, a

Indulge your inner Italian at Caffe Trieste

sighting of poet laureate Lawrence Ferlinghetti: this is North Beach at its best, as it's been since the 1950s. Linger over a legendary espresso, join aging anarchists debating how best to bring down the government and have your opinion solicited about the expressive potential of hair by young performance artists.

## ⛉ SPECS MUSEUM CAFÉ
*Dive Bar*
☎ 421-4112; 12 William Saroyan Pl; ☽ 5pm-2am; 🚌 15, 30, 41, 45
If you've ever wondered what do you do with a drunken sailor, here's your answer. The walls are plastered with Specs' collection of mementos from the Merchant Marine, and you will be too if you try to keep pace with the salty old-timers holding court in back. With this much nautical memorabilia, your order is obvious: pint of Anchor Steam, coming right up.

## ⛉ TONGA ROOM *Tiki Bar*
☎ 772-5278; www.fairmont.com; Fairmont Hotel, 950 Mason St; ☽ 6-11:45pm Sun-Thu, 6pm-12:45am Fri & Sat; 🚌 1, 27; 🚋 California
Tonight's San Francisco weather: foggy, about 50 degrees, with a 100% chance of tropical rainstorms every 20 minutes on the lower level of the Fairmont Hotel. Don't worry, it only falls around the cover band playing on the

island in the middle of the indoor pool, so you're safe in your grass hut. If you want a more powerful hurricane, get one in a plastic coconut from the bar – but do not attempt to hoist sails after the heavily fried $9.50 happy-hour buffet.

## ⛉ TOP OF THE MARK
*Cocktail Lounge*
☎ 616-6916; www.topofthemark.com; 999 California St; cover $5-10; ☽ 5pm-midnight Sun-Thu, 4pm-1am Fri & Sat; 🚌 1, 27; 🚋 California
Sashay across the dance floor and spend an evening on top of the world (or at least the Mark Hopkins Hotel) with a 360-degree view over SF. Cocktails will set you back $16, but watch the sunset with live jazz accompaniment and then try to complain.

## ⛉ TOSCA *Cocktail Lounge*
☎ 391-1244; 242 Columbus Ave; ☽ 5pm-2am; 🚌 15, 30, 41, 45
Sean Penn, Bobby De Niro and Francis Ford Coppola may be tucked away in the private back room, but they'll probably be basing their next character study on the regulars in the red vinyl booth next to yours. If these tobacco-stained, opera-postered walls could talk, they'd sing arias of great loves and even greater Irish coffees whipped up right here.

NEIGHBORHOODS

NORTH BEACH & THE HILLS

### ▼ VESUVIO *Microbrewery*
☎ 362-3370; www.vesuvio.com;
255 Columbus Ave; ⏲ 6am-2am;
🚌 15, 30, 41, 45

Guy walks into a bar, roars, and leaves. Without missing a beat, the bartender says to the next customer, 'Welcome to Vesuvio, honey – what can I get you?' It takes a lot more than a barbaric yawp to get Vesuvio's regulars to glance up from their microbrewed beers. Kerouac blew off Henry Miller to go on a bender here, and after knocking back a couple with neighborhood characters, you'll understand why.

##  PLAY
### ▣ BEACH BLANKET BABYLON
*Musical Revue*
☎ 421-4222; www.beachblanketbab
ylon.com; 678 Green St; tickets $25-78;
⏲ shows 8pm Wed-Thu, 7pm & 10pm Fri
& Sat, 2pm & 5pm Sun; 🚌 15, 30, 39, 41,
45; 🚃 Powell-Mason

Killer drag, cutting pop-culture satire and oddly touching musical odes to San Francisco in the city's longest-running comedy cabaret. The onstage personalities are as big as the absurdly giant hats, accented with over-the-top costumes designed by Chris March of *Project Runway* fame. Spectators must be 21-plus for the occasionally racy humor, except at cleverly sanitized matinees.

### ▣ BIMBO'S 365 CLUB
*Live Music*
☎ 474-0365; www.bimbos365club
.com; 1025 Columbus Ave; tickets
$15-40; ⏲ shows 7pm & 8pm; 🚌 30;
🚃 Powell-Mason

Anything goes behind these plush lounge velvet curtains since 1951, back when Rita Hayworth worked the chorus line here. More recent bills featured manic Cambodian-Californian dance band Dengue Fever, the occasional singer-songwriter like Iron & Wine, and several full swing bands catering to North Beach's lindy-hopping/rockabilly set.

### ▣ CHEESE SCHOOL
*Gourmet Classes*
☎ 346-7530; www.cheeseschoolsf.com;
2155 Powell St; classes/drop-in nights
$60/25; ⏲ 6:30-8:30pm; 🚌 30;
🚃 Powell-Mason

That glorified plastic called 'American cheese' may fool preschoolers, but it's an insult to California artisan cheesemakers. Learn to discern your West Coast goats from Loire Valley *bucherons,* and kick-start an illustrious career as a serious cheese enthusiast. Begin with drop-in nights featuring tastings of eight to 10 cheeses paired with three to five wines, then graduate to a masters in fondue or a doctorate in American artisan cheesemaking.

## ⭐ COBB'S COMEDY CLUB
*Comedy*

☎ 928-4320; www.cobbscomedyclub.com; 915 Columbus Ave; admission $10-35 plus a 2-drink minimum; 🕐 shows 8pm & 11pm; 🚌 30; 🚃 Powell-Mason

Bumper-to-bumper shared tables make for an intimate (and vulnerable) audience for stand-up acts. Come to see new talents before they sell out for sitcoms, and see if comedic talents Janeane Garofalo, Damon Wayans and Jamie Kennedy can regain their edge after dubious movie and TV roles.

# >EMBARCADERO & THE PIERS

Twelve miles across, 60 miles long, and at points only 6ft deep at low tide, the silvery bay makes a grander entrance to San Francisco than any red carpet. But the bayside Embarcadero where families stroll today was once a dodgy dock area during the gold rush. Saloon owners like Shanghai Kelly and notorious madam Miss Piggot would ply new arrivals with booze and women, conk them on the head and deliver them to sea captains in need of crews.

After the 1906 earthquake and fire leveled most of the Barbary Coast's houses of ill repute, a retaining wall was built to prevent piers from drifting and policed to prevent locals from grifting. Gracing the newly respectable port was an elegant Ferry Building, and San Francisco's shipping business boomed until WWII ended, and the Embarcadero again slipped into decline. But after the 1989 Loma Prieta earthquake brought down an Embarcadero overpass, the Ferry Building was reinvented as a dining destination. Some Wild West manners remain on Pier 39, where sea lions snore and belch like Kelly and Piggot's marks.

## EMBARCADERO & THE PIERS

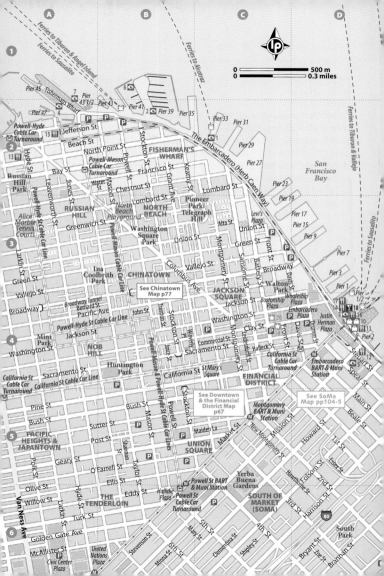

NEIGHBORHOODS

EMBARCADERO & THE PIERS

#  SEE

## ALCATRAZ

☎ 981-7625; www.nps.gov/alcatraz, www.alcatrazcruises.com; Pier 33; adult/senior/child day $26/24.50/16, night $33/30.50/19.50; ☾ day tours depart every 30min 9am-3:55pm & return 9:20am-6:15pm daily, night tours depart 6:10pm & 6:50pm Thu-Mon; ☒ F, 37, 49; ☧

The world's most notorious prison started as a holding pen for Civil War deserters and Native American 'unfriendlies,' including 19 Hopis who refused to send their children to government boarding schools. In 1934 the Federal Bureau of Prisons took over Alcatraz to house high-profile criminals like Chicago crime boss Al 'Scarface' Capone, Harlem poet-mafioso 'Bumpy' Johnson, and Morton Sobell, found guilty of Soviet espionage with Julius and Ethel Rosenberg. 'The Rock' was considered escape-proof, but in 1962 the Anglin brothers and Frank Morris disappeared on a raft. Since ferrying necessities cost more

Escape to Alcatraz, the world's most notorious prison

than putting up prisoners at the Ritz, the state closed the prison in 1963, yet refused a petition for an Alcatraz Native American study center. Native American activists broke a Coast Guard blockade and occupied Alcatraz in protest for 19 months, until President Nixon strengthened self-rule for Native American nations. Ferry fare includes admission, a cell-house audio tour featuring narratives by guards and inmates, and a video oral history of the Native American occupation near the ferry dock. See p13 for more information.

### � AQUARIUM OF THE BAY
☎ 623-5300; www.aquariumofthe bay.com; Pier 39; adult/senior & child $14.95/8; ☀ 10am-6pm Mon-Thu, 10am-7pm Fri-Sun Sep-May, 9am-8pm daily Jun-Aug; ☐ F, 15, 37, 49; ♿
Take a long walk off a short pier right into the bay, and stay perfectly safe and dry as sharks circle, manta rays flutter and schools of fish flit overhead. No, really – this aquarium is built right into the bay, and a conveyor belt transports you through underwater glass tubes for an up-close-and-personal look at local aquaculture.

### � FERRY BUILDING
☎ 693-0996; www.ferrybuildingmar ketplace.com; 1 Ferry Bldg; ☀ 10am-6pm Mon-Fri, 9am-6pm Sat, 11am-5pm

Sun; ☐ F, J, K, L, M, N, 7, 21, 71; ◎ Embarcadero
At this transport hub turned gourmet emporium, no one's in a hurry to get anywhere. Since transbay boat traffic isn't what it was back when the grand hall was built in 1898, the city revived the Ferry Building as a tribute to San Francisco's legendary farmers market. The **Ferry Plaza Farmers Market** (www.ferryplazafarmersmarket .com; ☀ 10am-2pm Tue, 8am-2pm Sat) fans out around the south end of the building on Saturdays like a fabulous garnish, with almost 100 specialty food producers selling their wares. Further reasons to miss that ferry are found indoors: brunches at Boulette's Larder (p62), oyster happy hour at Hog Island Oyster Company (p62), the shaking beef at Slanted Door (p63), sustainable fish tacos at Mijita (p63) and salted caramels swathed in chocolate at Recchiuti Chocolates (p61).

### � MUSÉE MÉCANIQUE
☎ 346-2000; www.museemecanique .org; Pier 45, Shed A; admission free; ☀ 11am-7pm Mon-Fri, 10am-8pm Sat & Sun; ☐ F, 47; ☒ Powell-Mason, Powell-Hyde; ♿
Laughing Sal has freaked out visitors with her coin-operated cackle for 100 years, but don't let this manic mannequin deter you from the best arcade west of

NEIGHBORHOODS

EMBARCADERO & THE PIERS

Coney Island. A few quarters let you start bar brawls in mechanical Wild West saloons, peep at belly-dancers through a vintage Mutoscope, save the world from Space Invaders and get your fortune told by an eerily lifelike wooden swami.

### ⊙ SEA LIONS AT PIER 39

**California Welcome Center at Pier 39; ☎ 981-1280; www.pier39.com; Pier 39 at Beach St & The Embarcadero; ☼ Jan-Jul; 🚌 F, 15, 37, 49; ⚓**

Beach bums took over San Francisco's most coveted waterfront real estate in 1990 and have been making a public display of themselves ever since, canoodling, belching, scratching their naked backsides and gleefully shoving one another off the docks. Naturally these unkempt squatters became San Francisco's favorite mascots, and since California law requires boats to make way for marine mammals, yacht owners have had to relinquish valuable slips to accommodate as many as 1300 sea lions who 'haul out' onto the docks January through July, and whenever else they feel like sunbathing.

### ⊙ USS *PAMPANITO*

**☎ 775-1943; www.maritime.org; Pier 45; adult/senior/child 6-12yr/child under 6yr $9/5/4/free; ☼ 9am-8pm; 🚌 F, 19, 32; 🚋 Powell-Hyde**

Video games can't compare to the real-life drama of this WWII US Navy submarine that completed six wartime patrols, sunk six Japanese ships (including two carrying British and Australian POWs) and battled three others without sinking. Submariners' stories of tense moments in underwater stealth mode will have you holding your breath – caution, claustrophobes – and all those brass knobs and mysterious hydraulic valves make 21st-century technology seem way overrated.

SF's sea lions bask in the sun (and the attention)

NEIGHBORHOODS

EMBARCADERO & THE PIERS

### WPA MURALS AT RINCON ANNEX POST OFFICE

**101 Spear St at Mission St;** 🚃 **F, J, K, L, M, N, 2, 7, 14, 71;** 🚇 **Embarcadero**

Only in San Francisco could a post office be so controversial. This art deco building is lined with WPA murals of Northern California history that Russian-born painter Anton Refregier was commissioned to paint in 1941 and were constantly interrupted by WWII and political squabbles over differing versions of history. The murals were completed in 1948 after 92 changes, only to be denounced as communist by McCarthyists in 1953. They're now a National Landmark.

# SHOP

### FERRY PLAZA WINE MERCHANT *Wines*

☎ **391-9400; www.fpwm.com;** **1 Ferry Bldg;** 🕑 **11am-8pm Mon-Wed, 10am-9pm Thu & Fri, 8am-9pm Sat, 10am-7pm Sun;** 🚃 **F, J, K, L, M, N, 7, 21, 71;** 🚇 **Embarcadero**

Part tasting room, part wine bar, totally tasty (hic). Staff is knowledgeable and the wine list written to make non-snobs feel welcome. For $50 to $75, you can take a class that promises to demystify sparkling wines and unveil pinot noirs – or just take that cash to the wine bar and ask the resident sommelier to surprise you, and enjoy 2oz tastings cloaked in mystery.

### RECCHIUTI CHOCOLATES
*Chocolates*

☎ **834-9494; www.recchiuticonfections .com; 1 Ferry Bldg;** 🕑 **10am-6pm Mon-Tue, 10am-7pm Wed-Fri, 8am-6pm Sat, 10am-5pm Sun;** 🚃 **F, J, K, L, M, N, 2, 7, 21, 71;** 🚇 **Embarcadero**

San Francisco invented the chocolate bar as a convenience food for gold miners, but Recchiuti is reviving a more leisurely, indulgent approach to chocolate with gold-leafed Kona coffee chocolates, dark-chocolate-dipped *fleur de sel* caramels and feel-good truffles with designs by SF arts nonprofit Creativity Explored (p115), which gets 10% of the price.

### SUR LA TABLE *Kitchenware*

☎ **800-243-0852; www.surlatable.com; 1 Ferry Bldg;** 🕑 **10am-6pm Mon-Wed, 10am-7pm Thu-Fri, 8am-7pm Sat, 11am-6pm Sun;** 🚃 **F, J, K, L, M, N, 7, 71;** 🚇 **Embarcadero**

Need $CO_2$ canisters to make tap water fizz, or a terrarium to grow your own salad? Of course you do, and the kindly salespeople at this West Coast culinary emporium will find it for you. The Ferry Building location features free lectures and demos; the 77 Maiden Lane store near Union Square (in the Downtown area) offers evening classes on sushi-making, California cuisine and more, plus SF farmers market tours for $75 to $85.

# 🍴 EAT

## 🍴 BOULETTE'S LARDER
*Californian* $$

☎ 399-1155; www.bouletteslarder.com; 1 Ferry Bldg; 🕙 breakfast Mon-Fri, lunch Mon-Sat, brunch Sun; 🚌 F, J, K, L, M, N, 7, 21, 71; ⊕ Embarcadero

Dinner theater doesn't get better than brunch at Boulette's communal table, strategically placed inside a working kitchen amid a swirl of chefs preparing for dinner service. Inspired by their truffled eggs and beignets? Get spices and mixes to go at the pantry counter.

## 🍴 BOULEVARD *Californian* $$

☎ 543-6084; www.boulevardrestaurant.com; 1 Mission St; 🕙 11:30am-2pm Mon-Fri, 5:30-10pm Sun-Thu, 5:30-10:30pm Fri & Sat; 🚌 F, 1, 5, 7, 9, 14, 38, 41, 71; ⊕ Embarcadero

Pat Kuleto's belle epoque decor could have been a tad too precious in this 1889 building that once housed the Coast Seamen's Union, but chef Nancy Oakes has kept the menu honest with juicy pork chops, enough local soft-shell crab to satisfy a sailor and chocolate ganache cake with housemade bourbon ice cream.

## 🍴 GARY DANKO
*Californian* $$$

☎ 749-2060; www.garydanko.com; 800 North Point St; 🕙 7-11pm; 🚌 10, 30, 47; 🚋 Powell-Hyde

The true test of romance isn't whom you'd take to Gary Danko, but whom you'd be willing to grant a taste of your trio of crème brûlées. You might imagine that sharing three desserts would be easy after two/four other courses for $66/98, give or take a cheese cart and duck course with huckleberries and bacon-braised endive, but Gary Danko is determined to prove you wrong. The covetousness begins over inventive salad courses like oysters with caviar and lettuce cream, and doesn't quit until your casually charming server hands you a tiny chocolate cake as a parting gift.

## 🍴 HOG ISLAND OYSTER COMPANY
*Sustainable Seafood* $$

☎ 391-7117; www.hogislandoysters.com; 1 Ferry Bldg; 🕙 11:30am-8pm Mon-Fri, 11am-6pm Sat & Sun; 🚌 F, J, K, L, M, N, 7, 21, 71; ⊕ Embarcadero

Decadence with a conscience: sustainably farmed, local Tomales Bay oysters served raw or cooked to succulence and a glass of Sonoma bubbly. Go with a $15 to $30 oyster sampler or choose yours au naturel, with caper *beurre blanc*, spiked with bacon and paprika or classic lemon and shallots. Mondays and Thursdays between 5pm and 7pm are happy hours indeed for shellfish fans, when oysters are $1.

### IN-N-OUT BURGER *Burgers* $
☎ 800-786-1000; www.in-n-out.com; 333 Jefferson St; 🕑 10:30am-1am Sun-Thu, 10:30am-1:30am Fri & Sat; 🚍 10, 30, 47; 🚋 Powell-Hyde; 🕭

Gourmet burgers have taken SF by storm, but In-N-Out has had a good thing going for 60 years: prime chuck beef they process themselves, plus fries and shakes made with ingredients you can pronounce, all served by employees paid a living wage. Ask for yours off the menu 'wild style,' cooked in mustard with grilled onions.

### MIJITA *Cal-Mex* $
☎ 399-0814; www.mijitasf.com; 1 Ferry Bldg; 🕑 11am-7pm Mon-Wed, 11am-8pm Thu-Fri, 9am-8pm Sat, 10am-4pm Sun; 🚍 F, J, K, L, M, N, 7, 21, 71; 🚇 Embarcadero

On sunny days you'll have to pounce to find a bayside leather stool, but the wait is worth it to taste award-winning chef Traci des Jardins' twist on her Mexican grandmother's standbys, from jicama, grapefruit and avocado salad to sustainable fish tacos that you'll be craving tomorrow, next week, or possibly next year.

### SLANTED DOOR *Cal-Vietnamese* $$
☎ 861-8032; www.slanteddoor.com; 1 Ferry Bldg; 🕑 11am-2:30pm & 5:30-10pm; 🚍 F, J, K, L, M, N, 7, 21, 71; 🚇 Embarcadero

The toughest table to get without reservations, and with good reason. James Beard Award–winning owner-chef Charles Phan reinvents Vietnamese classics with superb local produce, from fragrant five-spice duck with figs to garlicky Niman Ranch 'shaking beef' atop watercress. The wildly successful venture is still a family establishment, with 20 Phan clan members working the room here and at their sister restaurant in the basement of the Westfield shopping center (p71). If it's fully booked, picnic on takeout from the Out the Door stall.

## 🍸 DRINK

### 🍸 TSAR NICOULAI CAVIAR CAFÉ *Caviar Bar*
☎ 288-8630; www.tsarnicoulai.com; 1 Ferry Bldg; 🕑 11am-7pm Mon-Thu, 11am-8pm Fri, 9am-7pm Sat, 11am-5pm Sun; 🚍 F, J, K, L, M, N, 7, 21, 71; 🚇 Embarcadero

Indulge champagne tastes and caviar dreams with a West Coast twist: grassy, sprightly Sonoma sparkling wine and sustainably farmed California osetra caviar. Pair bubbly by the glass with the Infused Sampler:

NEIGHBORHOODS

EMBARCADERO & THE PIERS

Roe, roe, roe your boat to the Tsar Nicoulai Caviar Café (p63)

caviar with traces of brandy, saffron, wasabi, truffle and ginger. But the most deliciously perverse bar snack ever has to be the ahi and sturgeon sashimi, served in a glass inserted into a fishbowl, with fish flitting around the base.

## ⭐ PLAY

### ⭐ EMBARCADERO CENTER CINEMA *Cinema*
☎ 267-4893; www.landmarktheatres .com; Top fl, 1 Embarcadero Center; adult/senior & child $10.50/8.25; 🚍 F, J, K, L, M, N, 2, 7, 21, 71; Ⓔ Embarcadero
Blockbusters do nothing for the cinephile crowds at Embarcadero –

the lines here are probably for the latest Almodóvar film, critically acclaimed Indian documentary or late-night showings of *Rocky Horror* and *The Big Lebowski*. The snack bar caters to discerning tastes with Caffe Trieste (p52) coffee, Fair Trade chocolate and popcorn with real butter.

### ⭐ PUNCH LINE *Comedy*
☎ 397-4337; www.punchlinecomedy club.com; 444 Battery St; cover $8-20 plus 2-drink minimum; 🕑 shows 9pm Sun-Thu, 9pm & 11pm Fri & Sat; 🚍 F, J, K, L, M, N, 1, 7, 71; Ⓔ Embarcadero
Known for launching promising talents – perhaps you've heard of

Robin Williams, Chris Rock, Ellen DeGeneres and David Cross? – this historic stand-up venue is small enough that you can hear sighs of relief backstage when the comics kill, and teeth grinding when jokes bomb. Toss down your two-drink minimum before the show or during breaks, but be warned: they pack more punch than most one-liners.

# >DOWNTOWN & THE FINANCIAL DISTRICT

Where now stands a forest of sleek skyscrapers was once an unruly gold-rush port nicknamed the Barbary Coast. Sailors abandoned ship to seek their fortune here through the 1870s, filling in the area with as many as 600 rotting boats. San Francisco's finest financial institutions were built on these shaky foundations, gradually replacing muck with money between Montgomery St and the Embarcadero.

Downtown may sparkle today, but it still has its wily ways. Pirates' saloons have morphed into slick lounges where cocktails creep stealthily toward the $15 mark, and dazzling downtown restaurants keep minting top chefs like new money. Contemporary art speculators rush downtown gallery openings, hoping to beat the art fair circuit before it catches onto San Francisco's next Matthew Barney. Conveniently located alongside downtown banks is Jackson Square, where intoxicatingly chic design boutiques and beguiling antique shops somehow make chaise longues and Ming vases seem like sensible souvenirs.

## DOWNTOWN & THE FINANCIAL DISTRICT

# SEE

## ◎ 49 GEARY

**49 Geary St; admission free;** ☼ **most galleries 10:30am-5:30pm Tue-Fri, 11am-5pm Sat;** 🚌 **F, J, K, L, M, N, 5, 7, 38, 71;** ◉ **Montgomery**

The first Thursday of each month is an arty party at 49 Geary, when locals dressed to express-parade through four floors of galleries from 5pm to 7:30pm. To beat the crowds and collectors, go on weekdays instead. Start at the 5th floor for mind-warping painting and sculpture at **Gregory Lind Gallery** (www.gregorylindgallery.com), sublime new media and environmental art at **Haines Gallery** (www.hainesgallery.com) and high-impact photography at **Koch Gallery** (www.kochgallery.com). The 4th floor features absorbing installations at **Stephen Wirtz Gallery** (www.wirtzgallery.com) plus social commentary assemblage at **Steven Wolf Fine Art** (www.stevenwolffinearts.com). Stop on the 3rd floor for museum-piece modern photography at **Fraenkel Gallery** (www.fraenkelgallery.com), and end with an exclamation on the 2nd floor among the graphic statement pieces at **Mark Wolfe Contemporary** (www.wolfecontemporary.com).

## ◎ 77 GEARY

**77 Geary St; admission free;** ☼ **most galleries 10:30am-5:30pm Tue-Fri, 11am-5pm Sat;** 🚌 **F, J, K, L, M, N, 5, 7, 38, 71;** ◉ **Montgomery**

Step out of the elevator and your usual frame of reference on the 2nd floor, where you'll discover the Bay Area's next art star among the constellation of white-hot painters at **Marx & Zavattero** (www.marxzav.com), raise an eyebrow at provocative think-pieces at **Rena Bransten Gallery** (www.renabranstengallery.com) and strike up conversations over the folk and political art at **Togonon Gallery** (www.togonongallery.com). On the mezzanine, don't miss the seductive minimalism at **Patricia Sweetow Gallery** (www.patriciasweetowgallery.com). First Thursdays and openings bring artist appearances, collector buying frenzies and other artistic hijinks fueled by cheap white wine.

## ◎ AP HOTALING WAREHOUSE

**451-455 Jackson St;** 🚌 **10, 12, 15**

The snappiest comeback in SF history was a retort after Hotaling's 1866 whiskey warehouse survived the 1906 fire: 'If, as they say, God spanked the town/For being over-frisky,/Why did He burn His churches down/And spare Hotaling's whiskey?' So reads the plaque on the front of this spirited storefront. But while visiting amateur theologists may debate the particulars over whiskey drinks at Rye (p98), the answer is obvious to locals: if ever a deity deliberately preserved Italianate architecture and devilish fire-water, that god must surely be San Franciscan.

## FOLK ART INTERNATIONAL

☎ 392-9999; www.folkartintl.com;
140 Maiden Lane; ⏱ 10am-6pm
Tue-Sat; 🚌 30, 38; 🚋 Powell-Mason,
Powell-Hyde

Squeeze the Guggenheim spiral
into a brick box with a sunken
Romanesque archway and there
you have Frank Lloyd Wright's
1949 Circle Gallery Building,
which since 1979 has been the
home of Folk Art International.
Strategically located in niches
along the ramp is a carefully
curated collection of Thai neck
cuffs and pre-Columbian fertility
figurines that casually command
the entire room.

## GALLERY PAULE ANGLIM

☎ 433-2710; www.gallerypauleanglim
.com; 14 Geary St; admission free;
⏱ 10am-5:30pm Tue-Fri, 10am-5pm
Sat; 🚌 F, J, K, L, M, N, 5, 7, 38, 71;
🚇 Montgomery

The doyenne of downtown
stocks conceptual conundrums
like Paul Kos' mighty pawn made
of smaller pawns, and collectors' favorites like Tony Oursler's
video projections of rolling eyes
and upside-down grimaces. But
don't overlook the backroom
gallery that features SF upstarts:
Ala Ebtekar's miniatures of fallen
soldiers filling the margins of
ancient prayer scriptures, and
Clare Rojas' modern cautionary

Ramp it up at Folk Art International

tale of a woman scaring off a man with flowers.

### TRANSAMERICA PYRAMID & REDWOOD PARK
**600 Montgomery St; admission free;**
**9am-6pm Mon-Fri; 1, 15, 41;**
**California**

Despite the rants of Union Square conspiracy theorists, the aliens have not just landed in a redwood grove. This 1972 rocket ship of a building inspired *Star Wars* sets and defines San Francisco's quirky skyline, and though there's no public access to the pyramid's swaying tip, you can still get vicariously queasy in the virtual-reality viewing room. A transplanted California redwood grove has taken root in the remains of whaling ships below, generously shading tai chi practitioners, meditating stockbrokers and summertime SF Jazz Festival performers.

# SHOP

### BRITEX FABRICS
*Fabric & Craft Supplies*
**392-2910; www.britexfabrics.com;**
**146 Geary St; 10am-6pm Mon-Sat;**
**2, 30, 38, 45; Powell-Mason,**
**Powell-Hyde**

Four floors of fabulous fashion drama put *Project Runway* to shame. First floor: designers bicker over who saw the acid-yellow silk jersey first. Second floor: glam rockers dig through a velvet

goldmine. Third floor: Hollywood stylists squeal over '60s Lucite buttons. Top floor: fake fur flies and remnants roll as costumers prepare for Burning Man, Halloween and your average SF weekend.

### JAPONESQUE GALLERY
*Home Design & Art*
**391-8860; 824 Montgomery St;**
**10:30am-5:30pm Tue-Fri, 11am-5pm**
**Sat; 10, 12, 15**

*Wabi-sabi* is not something you smear on sushi, but a fine appreciation for organic forms and materials that you can experience first-hand at Japonesque. Owner Koichi Hara stocks traditional antique Japanese bamboo baskets and earthenware, alongside the mod fluidity of Ruth Rhoten's molten silver vases and the chiseled good looks of Hiromichi Iwashita's rough-hewn panels covered in sleek graphite.

### MARGARET O'LEARY
*Women's Clothing*
**391-1010; www.margaretoleary.com;**
**1 Claude Lane; 10am-5pm Tue-Sat;**
**1, 15; California**

Ignorance of the fog is no excuse in San Francisco – but should you confuse SF for LA (the horror!) and neglect to pack the obligatory sweater, Margaret O'Leary will sheathe you in knitwear, no questions asked. The San Francisco designer's specialties are whisper-light cardigans with an urban edge in ultrasoft wool, cashmere or eco-minded bamboo yarn.

### WESTFIELD SAN FRANCISCO CENTRE *Shopping Mall*

☎ 512-6776; www.westfield.com/sanfrancisco; 865 Market St; ⏲ 9:30am-9pm Mon-Sat, 10am-7pm Sun; 🚌 F, J, K, L, M, N, 5, 7, 21, 71; 🚋 Powell-Mason, Powell-Hyde; Ⓜ Powell Street; ♿ ⓦ

Wait, is this New Jersey? Sure looks like it inside this nine-level chain-store city, with Bloomingdale's and Nordstrom plus 400 other national and international retailers and a movie theater. Best/only reasons to brave this behemoth: post-holiday sales, a gourmet food court with

healthy eats on the go, and a masochistic shopping streak not satisfied by Madame S & Mr S Leather (p109).

# 🍴 EAT

### 🍴 AQUA
*Californian Seafood* $$$

☎ 956-9662; www.aqua-sf.com; 252 California St; ⏲ lunch Mon-Fri, dinner daily; 🚌 F, J, K, L, M, N, 5, 6, 7, 15, 21, 31, 71; Ⓜ Montgomery

The prix-fixe business lunch is a sweet deal for three to seven distinct seasonal pleasures in chef Laurent Manrique's landmark of inventive seafood dining – a perky little tandoori hamachi with grapefruit, say, or the drool-inducing tombo tuna with bacon and

## YANKING OUR CHAIN STORES

San Franciscans are resolutely anti–chain-store, blocking the creep of downtown retail stores into neighborhoods with city resolutions and zoning restrictions – and yet this city has spawned a couple of notable retail megaliths.

Young Levi Strauss arrived in San Francisco in 1850, bringing fashion sense to the gold rush. He noticed that gold prospectors needed sturdy pants to pocket their finds, so he made his from tough French sailcloth from Nîmes ('de Nîmes') and devised copper-riveted pockets with local tailor Jacob Davis. Levi's denim became the local casual uniform, and in 2008 an original pair of miner's Levi's jeans from 1890 spattered with mud and candle wax sold for $36,099 on eBay, the Bay Area–based auction website.

The multifaceted, multinational Gap/Old Navy/Banana Republic clothing juggernaut started out in San Francisco as a single Gap store selling youthful wardrobe basics, and within a year had made $2 million. The retail formula was applied nationwide in the 1970s, to higher-end Banana Republic in the '80s, and to cheaper, trendier Old Navy in 1994. But in nonconformist San Francisco, the Gap at the corner of Haight and Ashbury struggled to keep its front windows intact until it closed in defeat in 2007, and the company's hipster-aimed ads remain a favorite target for snarky vandalism. Read one recent addendum to a 'Peace. Love. Gap.' bus shelter ad: 'It's Peace Love & Understanding, you corporate tools.'

truffle oil – but you may need a venture capitalist to finance the seasonal tasting menu at dinner.

### 🍴 BAR CRUDO *Seafood* $$

☎ 956-0396; www.barcrudo.com; 603 Bush St; ⏱ 6-10:30pm Mon-Thu, 6-11pm Fri & Sat; 🚌 1, 30, 45; 🚋 California

An international idea that's pure California: choice morsels of Californian *crudi*, local seafood served raw Italian-style with pan-Asian condiments and Belgian beers. Stick to the pilsners for delicate raw Hawaiian kampachi served with Asian pear and mustard oil, and graduate to darker ales with gingery yellowfin tuna with Thai fish sauce and spring onion.

### 🍴 BOCADILLOS *Small Plates* $

☎ 982-2622; www.bocasf.com; 710 Montgomery St; ⏱ 7am-10pm Mon-Wed, 7am-10:30pm Thu-Fri, 5-10:30pm Sat; 🚌 15, 45

SF had its flirtation with Spanish tapas, but now the foodies are agog for just-right Basque bites of juicy lamb-burger, crunchy BLT and, for the adventurous eater, savory braised tripe. Mix and match two to three small dishes for lunchtime fine dining that won't break the bank.

### 🍴 BOXED FOODS *Californian* $

☎ 981-9376; www.boxedfoodscompany .com; 245 Kearny St; ⏱ 8am-3pm Mon-Fri; 🚌 1, 15; 🚋 California; Ⓥ

By thinking outside the box with organic, seasonal ingredients, Boxed Foods has cured the common lunch. In season, the zesty strawberry salad with mixed greens, walnuts and tart goat cheese will compete for your affections with the BLT, a drool-worthy sandwich with thick, crunchy applewood-smoked bacon. Enjoy in the tiny seating nook in back or savor in the Transamerica Pyramid redwood grove (p70).

### 🍴 FARMERBROWN
*California Soul Food* $$

☎ 409-3276; www.farmerbrownsf.com; 25 Mason St; ⏱ restaurant 5pm-midnight, bar 5pm-2am, brunch 10am-3pm Sun; 🚌 F, J, K, L, M, N, 5, 7, 21, 71; 🚋 Powell-Mason, Powell-Hyde; Ⓜ Powell Street

Follow cool-cat crowds around a sketchy corner into this mellow, repurposed-tin-shack soul-food joint. Tingling, spicy mac 'n' cheese and smoky, satisfying barbecue are chef Jay Foster's down-home signatures, with ingredients sourced from local, organic and African American family farms. Weekday happy hours from 5pm to 7pm are thronged for cayenne-rimmed margaritas served in Mason jars.

### 🍴 KOKKARI *Mediterranean* $$

☎ 981-0983; www.kokkari.com; 200 Jackson St; ⏱ 5:30-10pm Mon-Thu, 5:30-11pm Fri, 5-11pm Sat; 🚌 10, 12, 15; Ⓥ

This is one Greek restaurant where you'll want to lick your plate instead of break it, with starters like grilled lamb-tongue souvlaki drizzled with mustard vinaigrette and a lamb-and-eggplant moussaka as rich as the Pacific Stock Exchange. Reserve ahead to avoid waits, or make a meal of hearty Mediterranean appetizers at the bar.

### 🍴 MICHAEL MINA
*Californian* $$$

☎ 397-9222; www.michaelmina.net; 335 Powell St; 🕐 5:30-10pm; 🚃 F, J, K, L, M, N, 30, 38; 🚋 Powell-Mason, Powell-Hyde; 🚇 Powell Street
Inventive trio dishes offering creative variations on an ingredient have been much copied – especially the tuna tartare triplet and heirloom tomato troika – but never replicated, even in Mina's own empire of 14 restaurants. To sample Mina's trios without a triple-figure bill, try the bar-menu variations on Liberty Farms duck or Elysian Fields Farm lamb.

### 🍴 MIXT GREENS
*Sustainable Salads* $

☎ 433-6498; www.mixtgreens.com; 120 Sansome St; 🕐 10:30am-3pm Mon-Fri; 🚃 F, J, K, L, M, N, 5, 6, 7, 15, 21, 31, 71; 🚇 Montgomery; Ⓥ
No, the Grateful Dead isn't getting back together – those ponytailed stockbrokers lined up out the door are here for generous organic

salads with mango and seared sushi-grade tuna. Grab a stool or get yours to go in a compostable corn container to enjoy bayside at the Ferry Building (p59).

## 🍸 DRINK

### 🍸 BLUE BOTTLE COFFEE COMPANY *Café*

☎ 510-653-3394; www.bluebottlecoffee .net; 66 Mint St; 🕐 7am-7pm Mon-Fri, 8am-6pm Sat, 8am-4pm Sun; 🚃 F, J, K, L, M, N, 5, 7, 21, 71; 🚋 Powell-Mason, Powell-Hyde; 🚇 Powell Street
Don't mock SF's coffee geekiness until you try a superior fairtrade organic drip that bubbles and spurts through the madscientist glass tubes of Blue Bottle's $20,000 coffee siphon. This coffee microroaster gets crafty with ferns drawn on cappuccino foam and bittersweet mocha with the power to cure broken hearts. Expect a wait and $4 for your fix.

### 🍸 CAFFE AMICI *Café*

☎ 391-3241; 155 Montgomery St; 🕐 7am-5pm Mon-Fri, 7am-4pm Sat; 🚃 1, 15, 30, 45; 🚇 Montgomery
Did you leave your heart in San Francisco? Not to worry: there's another waiting for you at Amici, drawn in foam on your cappuccino. While neighborhood office jockeys get theirs to go, sip yours from a hand-painted Italian cup with a gooey chocolate chip cookie.

### ▼ EMPORIO RULLI *Café*
☎ 923-6464; www.rulli.com; 333 Post St; ⏱ 7:30am-7pm; 🚌 F, J, K, L, M, N, 30, 38; 🚋 Powell-Mason, Powell-Hyde; ⓟ Powell Street

Ideal people-watching spot in a glass box perched atop Union Square, with excellent espresso and a wide range of pastries to fuel yourself up for your next round of shopping, plus wine by the glass afterward. Grab outdoor seats at the risk of being mocked by mimes.

### ▼ GOLD DUST LOUNGE
*Dive Bar*
☎ 397-1695; 247 Powell St; ⏱ 7am-2am; 🚌 F, J, K, L, M, N, 30, 38; 🚋 Powell-Mason, Powell-Hyde; ⓟ Powell Street

When you wake up hoarse from singing show tunes with aloha-shirted cowboys, you'll know you've been Gold Dusted. Barbary Coast bordello decor, throwback prices on Irish coffee and well drinks and cheerfully inauthentic Dixieland jazz, all in the heart of downtown.

### ▼ IRISH BANK *Pub*
☎ 788-7152; www.theirishbank.com; 10 Mark Lane; ⏱ 11:30am-2am; 🚌 1, 15, 30, 45; 🚋 California

Perfectly pulled pints and thick-cut fries with malt vinegar, plus juicy burgers, brats and anything else you could possibly want with lashings of mustard, with the pos-

Gold Dust Lounge – it's the bar, the bar with the Midas touch…

sible exception of your ex. Pull up a church pew and chat with Irish owner Ronan, a former employee who bought the place off his boss.

### ☒ JOHN'S GRILL *Noir Bar*
☎ 986-0069; 63 Ellis St; ☺ 11am-10pm Mon-Sat, noon-10pm Sun; ☒ F, J, K, L, M, N, 5, 7, 21, 71; ☒ Powell-Mason, Powell-Hyde; ☺ Powell Street
'She was a real gone gal, see, and we coulda had something – but she was on the grift, looking for a stoolie, and I wasn't shootin' her kinda pool.' Could be the martinis, the low lighting or the Maltese Falcon statuette upstairs, but Dashiell Hammett's favorite bar lends itself to hardboiled tales of lost love and true crimes, confessed while chewing toothpicks.

### ☒ REDWOOD ROOM
*Cocktail Lounge*
☎ 929-2372; www.clifthotel.com; 495 Geary St; ☺ 5am-2am Sun-Thu, 4pm-2am Fri & Sat; ☒ 2, 3, 4, 27, 38; ☒ Powell-Mason, Powell-Hyde
This landmark deco bar got the Philippe Starck treatment, complete with trippy 3-D moving plasma portraits on the redwood walls and celebrities flanked by faux-tanned entourages. Add throngs of straight couples dressed for cocktails lined up behind the velvet rope, and you might think LA migrated north. Go on weeknights, when the wait for

your lychee martini is blessedly brief and the staff more relaxed.

### ☒ TUNNEL TOP *Dive Bar*
☎ 986-8900; www.tunneltop.com; 601 Bush St; ☺ 5pm-2am Mon-Sat; ☒ 1, 30, 45; ☒ California
Like stowing away in the hold of a ship, only with better hooch. The exposed beams and rickety balcony always seem about ready to give, so patrons batting eyes at one another across this crowded room get the added thrill of flirting with disaster. If this place does cave in, you might find yourself in a compromising position atop customers at the notorious massage parlor downstairs.

##  PLAY
### ☒ COMMONWEALTH CLUB
*Lectures*
☎ 597-6700; www.commonwealthclub .org; 2nd fl, 595 Market St; ☒ F, J, K, L, M, N, 5, 6, 7, 15, 21, 31, 71; ☺ Montgomery
The nearest thing to blood sport in the Bay Area are the debates that rage before, sometimes during, and after panel discussions at the Commonwealth Club. Whether the topic is food politics or nuclear proliferation, odds are you'll have to take the discussion outside after the ceremonial cheese and crackers, and over to House of Shields for a resolution over Scotch.

# >CHINATOWN

In Chinatown's historic back alleys, a slight breeze carries traces of temple incense, mahjong-tile clatter, and the plaintive notes of the *qin* (Chinese fiddle). But don't be fooled by this serene setting. In the 1849 gold rush, Mexican, American, European, African American and Chinese miners hustled, gambled and snored here side by side – and women who entered these alleyways instantly surrendered their reputations.

When gold prices came crashing down in the 1850s, miners down on their luck turned irrational resentments on the comparatively better-off service-based economy of Chinatown. In 1870, San Francisco began restricting housing and employment for anyone born in China, creating tough competition for honest work in increasingly cramped quarters. Meanwhile, white landlords, police and even mayors pocketed proceeds from Chinatown brothels, opium dens and bootlegging operations. Officials planned to relocate the Chinese community after the 1906 fire – but the Chinese consulate, temples and rifle-toting Chinatown merchants convinced the city otherwise.

Instead, Chinese businesses attracted a new clientele with tchotchkes for tourists, beer for Beat poets and tapioca bubble tea for teens. Today it's an economic boon to SF, yet Chinatown remains the most densely populated US urban area outside Manhattan, with many residents scraping by on $10,000 a year. Chinatown is no mere attraction: it's a 22-block tribute to astounding resilience.

## CHINATOWN

### 👁 SEE
Chinese Historical
  Society.............................1  B4
Dragon Gate .....................2  C6
Good Luck Parking
  Garage............................3  B2
Old St Mary's Church &
  St Mary's Park ...............4  C5
Portsmouth Square.........5  C4
Ross Alley ........................6  C4
Spofford Alley ................7  C4
Waverly Place .................8  C4

### 🛍 SHOP
China Bazaar ...................9  C5
Clarion Music Center ....10  C5
Far East Flea Market.....11  C4
Golden Gate Fortune
  Cookie Company .......12  C3

### 🍴 EAT
Chef Jia's.......................13  C3
City View .......................14  D4
House of Nanking.........15  C3

Jai Yun ..........................16  D4
Yuet Lee.........................17  B2

### 🍸 DRINK
EZ5................................18  D4
Li Po Cocktails ..............19  C4
Red Blossom Tea
  Company ...................20  C4
Rosewood......................21  B2

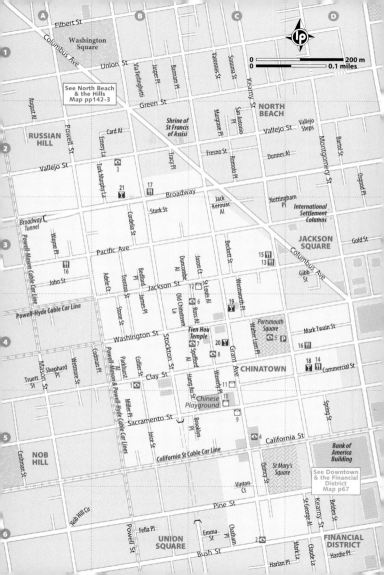

# 👁 SEE

## 📷 CHINESE HISTORICAL SOCIETY

☎ 391-1188; www.chsa.org; 965 Clay St; adult/senior & student/child $3/2/1, 1st Thu of month free; 🕐 noon-5pm Tue-Fri, 11am-4pm Sat; 🚌 1, 9, 30, 45; 🚃 California, Powell-Mason, Powell-Hyde; ♿

Wonder what it was like to be Chinese in the US during the gold rush, transcontinental railroad construction, the Roaring '20s or the Beat heyday? The nation's largest Chinese American historical institute helps you picture it with intimate vintage photos of Chinatown by Ansel Adams acolyte Benjamin Chinn, mining tools and other gold rush artifacts, and exhibits exploring Chinese stereotypes in advertisements and movies. Art shows are held across the courtyard in this 1932 landmark, built as Chinatown's YWCA by architect Julia Morgan of Hearst Castle fame.

## 📷 DRAGON GATE

**Intersection of Bush St & Grant Ave;** 🚌 1, 15, 30, 45; 🚃 California; ♿ 🚻

A noble sentiment rises above the chaos of kitschy Grant Ave trinket shops: 'Everything in the world is in just proportions' proclaims the plaque atop this graceful archway donated by Taiwan in 1970. The signature 'Chinatown Deco' look of the dragon lamps and pagoda roofs beyond this gate was in-

novated by forward-thinking Chinatown businessmen led by Look Tin Ely in the 1920s, transforming Grant from a playground for alcoholics into a stomping ground for shopaholics.

## 📷 GOOD LUCK PARKING GARAGE

**735 Vallejo St;** 🚌 1, 9, 15, 30, 45; 🚃 California, Powell-Mason, Powell-Hyde; 🅿 ♿

You'd be lucky to find parking anywhere near Chinatown, but a free space in the Good Luck Parking Garage brings double happiness. Each parking spot comes with fortune-cookie wisdom stenciled onto the asphalt: 'You have already found your true love. Stop looking.' Or 'You are only starting on your path to success.' These car-locating omens are brought to you by West Coast artists Harrell Fletcher and Jon Rubin, who also gathered the photographs of local residents adorning the garage archways like multicultural heraldic emblems.

## 📷 OLD ST MARY'S CHURCH & ST MARY'S PARK

☎ 288-3800; www.oldsaintmarys.org; 660 California St; 🚌 1, 9, 15, 30, 45; 🚃 California, Powell-Mason, Powell-Hyde; ♿ 🚻

Built by an Irish immigrant entrepreneur determined to give San Francisco some religion in 1854, St Mary's offered confessionals

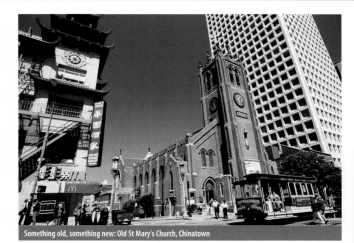
Something old, something new: Old St Mary's Church, Chinatown

conveniently located alongside the brothels of Grant Ave. The 1906 fire destroyed one of the district's biggest bordellos directly across from the church, making room for a park where skateboarders stealthily ride handrails while Beniamino Bufano's 1929 statue of Sun Yat-sen keeps a lookout.

### PORTSMOUTH SQUARE
**733 Kearny St; 🚌 1, 9, 15, 41, 45; 🚋 California; 🅿 ♿ 👣**
The action begins at first light in Chinatown's living room, where tai chi practitioners greet the dawn with open arms. Tea-drinkers under the pedestrian bridge are interrupted by the mad dash of toddlers to the slides once morning

preschool lets out. In the afternoon, the bronze replica of the Goddess of Democracy statue made by 1989 Tiananmen Square protesters casts a long shadow across the square, but chess players intent on their game hardly notice (political metaphor? you decide). Summer and Chinese New Year brings the **night market** ( 🕙 6-11pm Jul-Oct), featuring Chinese opera, calligraphy demonstrations and cell-phone charms for better reception.

### ROSS ALLEY
**🚌 1, 9, 30, 45; 🚋 Powell-Mason, Powell-Hyde; 👣**
Walk through Ross Alley past murals of people walking through

Ross Alley, and you've entered Chinatown's kaleidoscope of past and present. SF's oldest alley has been called Mexico, Spanish and Manila St after the women who staffed back-parlor brothels until most perished behind locked iron-clad doors in the 1906 fire. These days Ross Alley is occasionally pimped out for Hollywood flicks, including *Karate Kid II* and *Indiana Jones and the Temple of Doom*.

### ☺ SPOFFORD ALLEY

🚌 1, 9, 30, 45; 🚋 California, Powell-Mason, Powell-Hyde; ♿
Stop and listen to a Chinatown symphony: the clatter of mahjong tiles slapped down by octogenarians at senior centers, beauticians gossiping indiscreetly over the din of their blow-dryers, and a Chinese orchestra pausing for a soulful solo on the *erhu* (two-stringed fiddle). Only after shadows and silence fall can you fathom the 1920s bootlegging turf wars waged here, or Dr Sun Yat-sen planning a people's revolution to overthrow China's Manchu monarchy at number 36.

### ☺ WAVERLY PLACE

🚌 1, 9, 30, 45; 🚋 California, Powell-Mason, Powell-Hyde; ♿
To see Chinatown's crowning glory, look up at the painted balconies festooned with flags and lanterns along Waverly Place. There was no place to go but up back at the

beginning of the 20th century, due to restrictions on the expansion of Chinatown – so family associations and temples were built right on top of the barber shops and laundries lining this street. The **Tien Hou Temple** (admission free, donation appreciated; ⏰ vary) atop 125 Waverly Place was built in 1852, and the altar miraculously survived the 1906 earthquake and fire to become a symbol of community endurance.

# 🛍 SHOP

### ☐ CHINA BAZAAR

*Gifts & Souvenirs*
☎ 391-6369; 667 Grant Ave; ⏰ 10am-10pm; 🚌 1, 9, 30, 45; 🚋 California, Powell-Mason, Powell-Hyde
The vintage marquee with frolicking pandas boasts '1000s of Unique and Fun Items,' but that's an understatement. Wire racks are perilously overloaded here with bargain novelty items in no discernable order, except for the aisle of oversized piggy banks and the tiki section crammed with dashboard hula dancers and Easter Island swizzle sticks. The upstairs toy section is incongruously department-store-priced, but the bargain basement is practically a giveaway.

### ☐ CLARION MUSIC CENTER

*Musical Instruments*
☎ 391-1317; www.clarionmusic.com; 816 Sacramento St; ⏰ 11am-6pm Mon-Fri,

9am-5pm Sat; 🚌 1, 9, 30, 45; 🚋 California, Powell-Mason, Powell-Hyde
With this impressive range of Chinese *erhus,* African congas, Central American marimbas and gongs galore, you could become your own multiculti one-man band. Check the website for concerts, workshops and demonstrations by master musicians.

### 📷 FAR EAST FLEA MARKET
*Gifts & Souvenirs*
☎ 989-8588; 729 Grant Ave; ⏲ 10am-10pm; 🚌 1, 9, 30, 45; 🚋 California, Powell-Mason, Powell-Hyde; ♿
The shopping equivalent of crack, this bottomless store is suspiciously cheap and certain to make you giddy and delusional. Of course you have room in your carry-on for a teapot disguised as an eggplant! Your office cubicle is crying out for a guillotine-ready Marie Antoinette bobblehead doll! No one in your extended family should be denied a paper butterfly kite with matching parasol! Step away from the 98-cent Golden Gate Bridge snow globes while there's still time…

### 📷 GOLDEN GATE FORTUNE COOKIE COMPANY
*Fortune Cookies*
☎ 781-3956; 56 Ross Alley; admission free; ⏲ 9am-8pm; 🚌 1, 9, 30, 45; 🚋 Powell-Mason, Powell-Hyde
You too can say you made a fortune in San Francisco after visiting this bakery, where fortune cookies are stamped out on old-fashioned presses and folded while hot – just as they were back in 1909, when they were invented for the Japanese Tea Garden (p175). But to get really lucky, pick up a bag of the risqué 'French' fortune cookies for that special someone.

# 🍴 EAT

### 🍽 CHEF JIA'S *Hunan*                     $
☎ 398-1626; 925 Kearny St; ⏲ 10am-10pm Sun-Thu, 10am-10:30pm Fri & Sat; 🚌 9, 15, 41, 45; Ⓥ ♿
Your choice of classic chicken, pork and squid and/or green beans, eggplant or yams inevitably arrives in a brown sauce – vinegary Hunan-style, peppery black bean or savory-salty oyster sauce – but never mind how it looks, it's plenty tasty. Dishes are so generous that one will feed two famished Grant Ave shoppers, but don't neglect the sublime onion cakes with peanut sauce.

### 🍽 CITY VIEW *Dim Sum*                     $
☎ 398-2838; 662 Commercial St; ⏲ lunch; 🚌 1, 10, 41
Take your seat in a sunny dining room and your pick from carts loaded with delicate shrimp and leek dumplings, tangy spare ribs, garlicky Chinese broccoli and other tantalizing, ultrafresh flavors that make dim sum seem like your best lunch idea yet. Time your arrival before or after the lunch rush, so

you can avoid having to flag down speeding carts or sitting downstairs with a view of the surreal Astroturf Zen garden under the stairs.

### 🍴 HOUSE OF NANKING
*Shanghai* $$

☎ 421-1429; 919 Kearny St; 🕐 lunch Mon-Sat, dinner nightly; 🚌 1, 15, 41; ♿ 🅥 ♨

Like older sisters, staff here are bossy because they know what's best for you. Meekly suggest an interest in seafood, nothing deep-fried, perhaps some greens – and snap, your menu is gone and the order already on its way to the kitchen. Within minutes, you'll be devouring pan-seared scallops,

Get Shanghai'ed at House of Nanking

minced squab lettuce cups and spicy braised long beans. Come prepared to wait, and bearing cash.

### 🍴 JAI YUN *Shanghai* $$

☎ 981-7438; www.menuscan.com /jaiyun; 680 Clay St; 🕐 dinner Fri-Wed; 🚌 1, 9, 15, 30, 45; 🚃 Powell-Mason, Powell-Hyde; ♨

'Hello? When? How many? $55, $65 or $75? OK, see you!' That's how your reservation and menu consultation will play out at Jai Yun, where Chef Nei serves 15- to 20-course Shanghai-style, market-fresh feasts by reservation only. There's no menu, since the chef creates the bill of fare based on what's fresh that day – but fingers crossed, your menu will include tender abalone that drifts across the tongue like a San Francisco fog; lacy, translucent slivers of pickled lotus root; housemade rice noodles with cured pancetta; and mung beans with sesame oil. Never mind that the restaurant has more mirrors than a Bruce Lee movie and more tinsel than Macy's at Christmas – the sophisticated, fascinating flavors will leave you smugly assured in your impeccable taste.

### 🍴 YUET LEE *Chinese* $$

☎ 982-6020; 1300 Stockton St; 🕐 11am-3am Wed-Mon; 🚌 1, 9, 15, 30, 45; 🚃 Powell-Mason, Powell-Hyde; ♿ 🅥 ♨

Like a scene from a Wong Kar-Wai movie, true love and late-night munchies conquer even brusque service and a radioactive green paint job at Yuet Lee. The brash fluorescent lighting isn't especially kind on first dates, but sharing Yuet Lee's legendary crispy salt and pepper crab or smoky-sweet tender roast duck creates a life-long bond.

#  DRINK

### EZ5 *Dive Bar*
☎ 362-9321; 682 Commercial St; ⏱ 4pm-2am Mon-Fri, 6pm-2am Sat; 🚌 1, 10, 41
Need a day off, maybe two? EZ5 obliges at happy hour, when sweet-sour Day Off cocktails are $7 and holiday cheer prevails with tinsel, a hypnotic disco ball and Happy New Year signs well into April. The flush days of the 1980s and '90s never end at EZ5, where you can still play Ms Pac-Man arcade games, groove to DJs spinning vintage vinyl and join a crowd of Web 2.0 engineers for $1 Jell-O shots.

### LI PO COCKTAILS *Dive Bar*
☎ 982-0072; 916 Grant Ave; ⏱ 2pm-2am; 🚌 1, 9, 15, 30, 45; 🚋 Powell-Mason, Powell-Hyde
'The things I feel when wine possesses my soul/I will never tell those who are not drunk,' wrote Tang-dynasty poet Li Po. For like-minded drinkers, there's no better place than these red vinyl booths beloved of Beats, surly philosophers and career alcoholics. Enter the grotto doorway, and if you pass the once-over by the huge golden Buddha by the bar, order your Tsing Tao beer – or if you're feeling bold, a mai tai made with *bai ju* (Chinese rice liquor) that tastes uncannily like white lightning.

### RED BLOSSOM TEA COMPANY *Tea Lounge*
☎ 395-0868; www.redblossomtea.com; 831 Grant Ave; ⏱ 10am-6:30pm Mon-Sat, 10am-6pm Sun; 🚌 1, 30, 45; 🚋 California, Powell-Mason, Powell-Hyde
Think beyond the world of black and green teas to the universe of white teas, herbal infusions and, of course, the signature blossom teas that unfurl in your pot like time-lapse photography of the dahlia garden in Golden Gate Park.

### ROSEWOOD *Cocktail Lounge*
☎ 951-4886; www.rosewoodbar.com; 732 Broadway; ⏱ 5:30pm-2am Wed-Fri, 7pm-2am Sat; 🚌 1, 9, 15, 30, 45; 🚋 Powell-Mason, Powell-Hyde
SF hipsters like their bars just like Chinatown's cops and gangsters of yore preferred their bills – small and unmarked – and this one delivers. Nature takes its course in this discreet, handsome lounge, where the only decor is sleek rosewood paneling and low lighting. The DJ keeps the back room on its feet, and serious flirting transpires on the outdoor patio within the bamboo thicket.

# >HAYES VALLEY, CIVIC CENTER & THE TENDERLOIN

Don't be fooled by its strict beaux-arts formality: San Francisco's Civic Center has a radical streak several city blocks wide. City Hall helped establish gay rights and green politics, and the arts institutions surrounding it ensure San Francisco is never at a loss for inspired ideas. Gale-force wind tunnels can't deter the masses from protests and community gardening projects that leave City Hall's drab plaza echoing with idealism and sprouting with organic vegetables – but when the crowds clear out,

## HAYES VALLEY, CIVIC CENTER & THE TENDERLOIN

the scene isn't so utopian. The gold-leafed City Hall dome gleams above the shopping carts of homeless people below, a visible reminder of the city's stark disparities in wealth.

West of City Hall lies chic Hayes Valley, where Victorian storefronts showcase cutting-edge local designers and upstart chefs. North of City Hall is Polk St, which in the 1950s was gay San Francisco's gritty main drag (in more ways than one). Today Upper Polk has gentrified, but Lower Polk, Hyde and Larkin still feature gay bars, hustlers and funky vintage shops. Vietnam War refugees have brought a family aspect to the neighborhood since the 1970s, but the sketchy area remains crassly yet tenderly known as the 'Loin.

# ◉ SEE

## ◉ ASIAN ART MUSEUM

☎ 581-3500; www.asianart.org; 200 Larkin St; adult/senior/student/child under 13yr $12/8/7/free, after 5pm Thu $5, 1st Tue of month free; ⏲ 10am-5pm Tue-Sun, 10am-9pm Thu; 🚇 F, J, K, L, M, N, 5, 7, 21, 71; ◉ Civic Center; Ⓟ ♿ 👶

Take an escalator ride across oceans and centuries, from racy Rajasthani miniatures to Osamu Tezuka's legendary Japanese manga drawings of Astro Boy – just don't go bumping into those priceless Ming vases. The Asian has worked diplomatic wonders with a rotating collection of 15,000 treasures that bring Taiwan, China and Tibet together, reconcile Pakistan and India, and unite Japan, Korea and China. Linger over a bento box lunch at the downstairs Café Asia, and stick around for the thrill of the unexpected at First Thursday MATCHA nights from

5pm to 9pm, when *soju* cocktails flow, DJs spin Japanese hip-hop and guest acupuncturists assess visitors' tongues.

## ◉ CITY HALL

☎ tours 554-6032, art exhibit line 252-2568; www.ci.sf.ca.us/cityhall; 400 Van Ness Ave; ⏲ 8am-8pm Mon-Fri; 🚇 5, 19, 21, 49; ◉ Civic Center; Ⓟ ♿ 👶 Gilded Age grandeur with avant-garde art in the basement and protesters out front in the organic vegetable garden: yep, sounds like a city hall just right for San Francisco. Construction had already begun in 1906 when the earthquake and fire hit, but a beaux-arts behemoth rose from the ashes. Over the years, the splendid Rotunda has seen it all: sit-ins organized against McCarthy hearings in 1960; the 1978 murder of Supervisor Harvey Milk, the nation's first openly gay elected official; and same-sex newlyweds married with the mayor's approval in 2004 and 2008, after California courts upheld marriage rights. Downstairs are rotating art exhibitions, which have featured visually impaired artists and photo-essays comparing Tehran and California.

### 🖸 FEDERAL BUILDING

**Cnr Mission & 7th St;** 🚌 **F, J, K, L, M, N, 5, 7, 14, 71;** 🚇 **Civic Center**
American tax dollars at work, and for once in a good way. The revolutionary green design of this new government office building by 2005 Pritzker Architecture Prize winner Thomas Mayne conserves energy and eliminates office politicking over corner offices, with 90% of work stations enjoying direct sunlight, natural ventilation and window views (over the Tenderloin, but still).

### 🖸 GLIDE MEMORIAL UNITED METHODIST CHURCH

☎ **674-6090; www.glide.org; 330 Ellis St;** 🕑 **services 9am & 11am Sun;** 🚌 **F, J, K, L, M, N, 27, 31, 38;** 🚇 **Powell Street**
The Glide gospel choir takes the stage beaming in tie-dyed robes and everyone squeezes in closer to make room in the pew for one more – the 1500-plus congregation is GLBT-friendly and warmly welcomes everyone. After the Sunday celebration ends in hearty handshakes and hugs, the activist Methodist church gets to work,

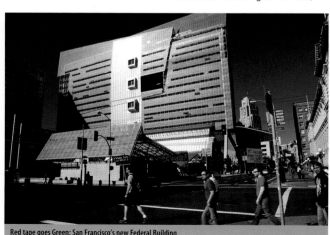

Red tape goes Green: San Francisco's new Federal Building

providing one million free meals a year and homes for 52 formerly homeless families (56 more housing units are in the works).

### ☺ LUGGAGE STORE GALLERY

☎ 255-5971; www.luggagestoregallery .org; 1007 Market St; admission free; ☽ noon-5pm Wed-Sat; 🚍 F, J, K, L, M, N, 5, 7, 71; ⊚ Civic Center

Showing some tenderness in the Tenderloin, the nonprofit Luggage Store has given street artists a gallery platform for more than 20 years and helped launch art-star street satirists Barry McGee, Clare Rojas and Rigo. You'll recognize the place by its graffitied door and a rooftop mural of a terrified kid holding a lit firecracker by Brazilian duo Osgemeos.

### ☺ SAN FRANCISCO ARTS COMMISSION GALLERY

☎ 554-6080; www.sfacgallery.org; 401 Van Ness Ave; ☽ noon-5pm Wed-Sat; 🚍 F, J, K, L, M, N, 5, 42, 47, 49; 🚍 Van Ness; 🅿 ♿

Skip the grueling climb up Coit Tower and broaden your horizons at this ground-level public gallery featuring international perspectives and local talents. A recent Bay Area photography show featured the inevitable through-the-fog shots, but also Sabrina Wong's Portsmouth Square (p79) portraits and David Wilson's pain-

fully funny *Urban Purgatory* series, featuring a BART car crowded with a single doleful businessman repeated in various commuter poses.

### ☺ SAN FRANCISCO PUBLIC LIBRARY MAIN BRANCH

☎ 557-4400; sfpl.lib.ca.us; 100 Larkin St; ☽ 10am-6pm Mon, 9am-8pm Tue-Thu, noon-6pm Fri, 10am-6pm Sat, noon-5pm Sun; 🚍 F, J, K, L, M, N, 5, 7, 21, 71; ⊚ Civic Center; 🅿 ♿ ♿

Besides its eclectic collection of San Franciscans and their beloved books, the SF Main sheds light on favorite local subjects from cooking to civil rights, with the help of a splendid central lightwell and excellent lecture series. Fascinating ephemera exhibits are in the 6th floor Skylight Gallery and the 3rd floor James C Hormel Gay & Lesbian Center, and there are international newspapers in the news-reading room and graphic novels galore in the Teen Zone. Check out the wallpaper made from the old card catalog on the 2nd floor – artists Ann Chamberlain and Ann Hamilton invited 200 San Franciscans to add multilingual running commentary to 50,000 cards.

### ☺ ZEN CENTER

☎ 863-3136; sfzc.org; 300 Page St; ☽ 9:30am-12:30pm & 1:30-4pm Mon-Fri, 9am-noon Sat; 🚍 6, 7, 21, 22, 71

No, this isn't a spa, but an active spiritual retreat since 1969 for the largest Buddhist community outside Asia. The graceful landmark building was designed by California's first licensed woman architect, Julia Morgan, who also designed Hearst Castle and the Chinese Historical Society (p78). The center is open for visits, meditation and overnight stays for spiritual seekers by prior arrangement. Consult the website for the meditation schedule.

#  SHOP

### 🏠 AZALEA *Clothing*
☎ 861-9888; www.azaleasf.com; 411 Hayes St; 🕑 11am-7pm; 🚌 5, 21, 42, 47, 49

Shopping these fashion-forward racks is like getting one of those head-to-toe reality show makeovers, only without the humiliation – there's even a mani-pedi station. Load up on ultrasoft James Perse tees and dark, flattering Naked denim, raid the sales rack for statement pieces by Rag & Bone and Sonia Rykiel, and don't hesitate to ask staff for their opinion – they're diplomatic and not pushy.

### 🏠 DARK GARDEN *Corsets*
☎ 431-7684; www.darkgarden.com; 321 Linden St; 🕑 11am-7pm Mon-Sat, 11am-5pm Sun; 🚌 6, 7, 21, 71

Not sure what to wear to the Folsom Street Fair (p28) or a fancy-dress Victorian wedding? Dark Garden might have your answer, as long as you're patient about lacing and not prone to gasping. Corsets are made to order and surprisingly comfortable, especially the vampy velvet numbers.

### 🏠 FLAX *Art Supplies*
☎ 552-2355; flaxart.com; 1699 Market St; 🕑 9:30am-7pm Mon-Sat; 🚌 J, K, L, M, N, 7, 71; 🅿 ♿ 🚻

People who swear they lack artistic flair suddenly find it at Flax, where an entire room of specialty papers, racks of luscious paint colors and a wonderland of hot-glue guns practically make the collage for you. Home decor makeovers and kid-art projects start here, and the vast selections of pens and journals are novels waiting to happen.

### 🏠 FLIGHT 001
*Luggage & Travel Supplies*
☎ 487-1001; www.flight001.com; 525 Hayes St; 🕑 11am-7pm Mon-Sat, 11am-6pm Sun; 🚌 5, 21

If anything could make you less cranky about flying SFO–JFK in the no-liquids, no-legroom era, it's Flight 001. Their Jet Comfort Kit is first class all the way, with earplugs, sleep mask, booties, neck rest, candy and cards. For

HAYES VALLEY, CIVIC CENTER & THE TENDERLOIN

**Carry on shopping at Flight 001 (p89)**

jet-set friends, pick up a rubber alarm clock, pocket poker or luggage tags that boldly state what everyone is thinking at baggage claim: 'Hands off my bag.'

### GIMME SHOES *Shoes*
☎ 864-0691; www.gimmeshoes.com; 416 Hayes St; ⏰ 11am-7pm Mon-Sat, noon-6pm Sun; 🚌 5, 21, 42, 47, 49
The nemesis of recovering shoe fetishists. Those round-toed, strappy red suede Chie Mihara heels are worthy of Dorothy in Oz, but did you see those sweet chocolate-brown, button-closure Repetto flats on the 40–60% off rack? Men deliberate between Paul Smith distressed leather oxfords and SpiderManly rubber-webbed sneakers by Alexander McQueen for Puma.

### ISOTOPE *Comics*
☎ 621-6543; www.isotopecomics.com; 326 Fell St; ⏰ 11am-7pm Tue-Fri, 11am-6pm Sat & Sun; 🚌 6, 7, 21, 71; ♿ 🚻
The toilet seats signed by famous cartoonists over the front counter show just how seriously Isotope takes comics. Newbies tentatively flip through Daniel Clowes and Joe Sacco in the graphic novel section, while fanboys load up on a specific superhero or publisher and head upstairs to loiter in the lounge with local cartoonists.

## ☐ KAYO BOOKS *Books*

☎ 749-0554; www.kayobooks.com;
814 Post St; ◷ 11am-6pm Thu-Sat or by
appointment; 🚌 2, 3, 27, 38, 76
Juvenile delinquents will find an
entire section dedicated to their
life stories at Kayo Books, where
vintage pulp ending in exclamation points (eg *Girls Out of Hell!*
and the more succinct *Wench!*)
earned a John Waters endorse-
ment on NPR. You might find a
first edition Dashiell Hammett
noir, or an underappreciated classic like *Women's Medical Problems*
in the Bizarre Nonfiction section.

## ☐ LAVISH
*Children's Clothing & Gifts*
☎ 565-0540; www.shoplavish.com;
540 Hayes St; ◷ 11am-7pm Mon-Sat,
11am-6pm Sun; 🚌 5, 21; ♿
Adults are always cooing baby
talk to the merchandise here. To
be fair, the Jellycat blue elephant
is indeed fuzzy-wuzzy, the brown
organic cotton onesie with the
orange tree emblem by SF's own
Speesees is admittedly cuddly-
wuddly, and the front features
dainty necklaces, letterpress note
cards and other too-cute, widdle-
bitty things. Don't worry, you'll
snap out of it eventually.

## ☐ LOTUS BLEU *Home Design*
☎ 861-2700; www.lotusbleudesign
.com; 327 Hayes St; ◷ 11am-6pm Tue-

Fri, 11am-7pm Sat, noon-5pm Sun; 🚌 5,
21, 42, 47, 49
French whimsy, Vietnamese
design and a San Franciscan
love of splashy color make this
tiny design boutique the kind of
place you'll wish you could stuff
in your suitcase, enthusiastic staff
and all – but you might settle for
linen pillows with psychedelic
blooms, French striped canvas
teddy bears and pop-art lacquer
candleholders.

## ☐ MAC *Clothing*
☎ 863-3011; 387 Grove St; ◷ 11am-
7pm Mon-Sat, noon-6pm Sun; 🚌 5, 21,
42, 47, 49; Ⓟ ♿
When in doubt about what to
wear to an SF occasion, here's
your answer: structured looks
from Belgian minimalist Dries Van
Noten to outdress anyone at City
Hall, and Tsumori Chisato's gos-
samer layers of silk crepe that float
up the Opera House steps. Trust
staff to style you, point out steals
on the 40–75% off sales rack,
and get any purchase tailored
efficiently and impeccably.

## ☐ NANCY BOY
*Body & Bath Products*
☎ 552-3802; www.nancyboy.com;
347 Hayes St; ◷ 11am-6pm Mon-Fri,
11am-7pm Sat & Sun; 🚌 5, 21, 42, 47, 49
All you closet pomaders and
after-sun-balmers: wear products

NEIGHBORHOODS

HAYES VALLEY, CIVIC CENTER & THE TENDERLOIN

with pride, without becoming a cosmetics conglomerate dupe. This clever SF grooming company knows you'd rather pay for the product than ads featuring the Beckhams, and delivers effective plant-based products tested on boyfriends, never animals.

### PEACE INDUSTRY *Rugs*
☎ 255-9940; www.peaceindustry.com; 539 Octavia St; ⏰ 10am-6pm Mon-Fri, 11am-6pm Sat, 11am-5pm Sun; 🚌 5, 21; ♿

Iranian cooperative-made felted wool rugs set a mod mood with spongy, ticklish texture underfoot. Get back to nature with a dewdrop pattern in off-white and brown wool, go arty with Ruth Asawa–inspired glowing red and orange orbs, or opt for Op Art black-and-white swirls.

### RESIDENTS APPAREL GALLERY *Clothing*
☎ 621-7718; www.ragsf.com; 541 Octavia St; ⏰ noon-7pm Mon-Sat, noon-5pm Sun; 🚌 5, 21

Pull off eclectic SF chic with your pick of local designers at design-school prices. Score a hit at the San Francisco International Film Festival in a $59 Sho Sho dress emblazoned with screen legend Anna May Wong's face and the Chinese character for 'rebel,' or blend in with Clarion

Alley graffiti in a limited-edition, $36 T-shirt screenprinted with Mission power lines by My Windup Bird.

# 🍴 EAT

### 🍴 BAR JULES *Californian*          $$
☎ 621-5482; www.barjules.com; 609 Hayes St; ⏰ lunch Wed-Sat, dinner Tue-Sat, brunch Sun; 🚌 5, 21

Small, local and succulent is the credo at this corridor of a neighborhood bistro. The short daily menu thinks big with flavor-rich, sustainably minded pairings like local duck breast with farro, an abbreviated but apt local wine selection, and the dark, sinister 'chocolate nemesis.' There are no reservations and waits are a given – but so is simple, tasty food.

### 🍴 BRICK *Californian*          $$
☎ 441-4232; www.brickrestaurant.com; 1085 Sutter St; ⏰ 5-10pm Sun-Thu, 5-11pm Fri & Sat, late night menu 10pm-midnight Thu, 11pm-1am Fri & Sat, bar 5pm-2am; 🚌 1, 19, 38, 47, 49

Brick upgrades late-night snacks from pizza slices to baked local Red Hawk cheese with eggplant caponata spread, and from greasy burgers to local Meyer Ranch burgers with pickled onions and Gruyère. Noshers and drinkers converge on the bar for smaller plates at lower prices.

**Raj Patel,**
*SF foodie and author,* **Stuffed and Starved: The Hidden Battle for the World Food System**

**Why consider sustainability in food-abundant SF?** Precisely because it's so easy to do. San Francisco is America's food capital, and a great crash course in how lovely it can be to eat sustainably, locally and seasonally. If you eat McDonald's here, you've wasted one of the best reasons for being in San Francisco. **How can you tell it's sustainable?** Waitstaff in San Francisco are unusually knowledgeable, and they're going to care more about you if you care more about what they serve. So ask: Is this in season? Where did it come from? Which farm? Is it organic? What sort of conditions was it raised in? **Favorite foodie landmarks:** An organic vegetable garden was set up in front of City Hall by a group of artists and Slow Food, and the harvest goes to homeless shelters. Heart of the City Farmers Market (p94) is a lively, multiracial space that crosses income levels, and really shows you San Francisco.

## 🍴 FISH & FARM

*Sustainable Seafood & Californian*                $$

☎ 474-3474; www.fishandfarmsf.com; 339 Taylor St; 🕙 5-10pm; 🚌 2, 3, 4, 27, 38; 🚋 Powell-Mason, Powell-Hyde

Eco-comfort food bound to improve your mood and the planet, featuring organic produce, sustainable seafood and humanely raised meats sourced within 100 miles of San Francisco. White Brentwood corn and organic sweet onions make a silky, sensational soup, while roasted Monterey Bay sardines with cherry tomatoes set off fireworks of flavor. Housemade pickles and preserves keep the menu lively even in winter, and cocktails with organic fruit help the conversation keep pace.

## 🍴 HEART OF THE CITY FARMERS MARKET

*Farmers Market*                $

☎ 558-9455; United Nations Plaza; 🕙 7am-5pm Sun & Wed year-round; 🚌 F, J, K, L, M, N, 5, 7, 21, 71; 🚇 Civic Center

On other days, United Nations Plaza is an obstacle course of skateboarders, Scientologists and raving self-talkers, plus a few crafts stalls – but every Sunday and Wednesday, local producers show up with sustainably sourced California produce at bargain prices.

## 🍴 JARDINIÈRE

*Sustainable Californian*                $$

☎ 861-5555; www.jardiniere.com; 300 Grove St; 🕙 dinner; 🚌 5, 21, 42, 47, 49

Opera arias can't compare to high notes hit by James Beard Award–winning chef Traci des Jardins – think succulent bites of diver-caught scallops, organic melon and Tsar Nicoulai caviar. Anything chocolate on pastry chef Ellie Nelson's dessert menu is a serotonin rush that will leave you fanning yourself like a diva. All ingredients are local, sustainable and seasonal, and cocktails and bar noshes in the lounge make post-opera dish sessions truly delicious.

## 🍴 LAHORE KARAHI

*Pakistani*                $

☎ 567-8603; www.lahorekarahirestaur ant.com; 612 O'Farrell St; 🕙 5-11pm Mon, 11am-11pm Tue-Sun; 🚌 3, 4, 38; 🚋 Powell-Mason, Powell-Hyde

Only one thing could induce relatively sane San Franciscans to brave merciless fluorescent lighting and risky business propositions in the gritty Tenderloin: succulent tandoori chicken with a hint of seared smokiness. Of all the linoleum-floored Pakistani tandoori joints this side of Geary, Lahore Karahi wins the loyalty of theater-goers and streetwalkers alike for consistency, cleanliness and cheapness with a side of good cheer.

### 🍴 MILLENNIUM
*Sustainable Vegan & Vegetarian* $$

☎ 345-3900; www.millenniumrestaurant.com; 580 Geary St; 🕙 dinner; 🚌 27, 38; **V**

Three words you're not likely to hear together outside these doors describe the menu: opulent vegan dining. GMO-free and proud of it, with wild mushrooms and organic fruit featuring in sexy seasonal concoctions. Reserve ahead for monthly themed feasts, especially aphrodisiac dinners and vegetarian Thanksgiving.

### 🍴 PAGOLAC
*Vietnamese* $$

☎ 776-3234; 655 Larkin St; 🕙 5-10pm Tue-Sun; 🚌 5, 19, 31; ♿ 👶

Right in the hard heart of the Tenderloin is this inviting nook that's all warm wood, candlelight, sublime sugarcane shrimp and barbecued chicken, and generous bowls of *pho* (rice noodles) with rare steak slices as extravagantly beefy as a Polk St men's bar.

### 🍴 SAIGON SANDWICH SHOP
*Vietnamese Sandwiches* $

☎ 475-5698; 560 Larkin St; 🕙 6:30am-5:30pm; 🚌 5, 19, 31; ♿ 👶

Consider it frontier justice for the indecisive: order your $2.50 *banh mi* sandwich when the lunch ladies of the Saigon call you, or you'll get skipped. Think quickly, and score a baguette piled high with your choice of pork, chicken, meatball or tofu, plus housemade pickled carrots, onion, jalapeños, cilantro and mayo.

### 🍴 SUPPENKÜCHE *German* $$

☎ 252-9289; www.suppenkuche.com; 525 Laguna St; 🕙 5-10pm daily, brunch Sun; 🚌 7, 21, 71

Doesn't matter if you're caught in fog without a jacket or a Mahler symphony with a hangover: Suppenküche's German comfort food will put things right. Blissfully buck small-plate trends with berry-studded inch-thick pancakes and farmer's omelets that deserve their own zip codes, and get a new lease on life with sausages and pickles.

### 🍴 TU LAN *Vietnamese* $

☎ 626-0927; 8 6th St; 🕙 11am-9pm Mon-Sat; 🚌 F, J, K, L, M, N, 5, 7, 21, 71; 🚇 Civic Center

Get a whiff of what's cooking and you won't mind waiting on the sketchiest stretch of sidewalk in SF, the surly service or dingy linoleum. The menu requires further translation: 'tomato sauce prawn' is a succulent stir-fry with tomatoes, onions and hot peppers, and

'VN chicken curry' means chicken, potatoes and peppers in a velvety, savory-sweet yellow curry sauce. One dish under $10 feeds two starving artists.

**ZUNI CAFÉ** *Californian* $$
☎ 552-2522; 1658 Market St; ☀ 11:30am-midnight Tue-Sat, 11am-11pm Sun; ☒ F, J, K, L, M, N, 5, 6, 7, 71

Zuni has been reinventing basic menu items as gourmet staples since 1979. Reservations and fat wallets are necessary, but see-and-be-seen seating is a kick and the food beyond reproach: organic beef burgers on focaccia with matchstick fries, Caesar salad with house-cured anchovies,

crispy roasted free-range chicken with horseradish mashed potatoes, and impeccable chocolate pudding.

# DRINK

**ABSINTHE** *Fine Spirits*
☎ 551-1590; www.absinthe.com; 398 Hayes St; ☀ 11am-midnight Tue-Wed & Sat, 11:30am-midnight Thu-Fri, 11am-10pm Sun, bar open until 2am Thu-Sat; ☒ 5, 21, 42, 47, 49

Let the spirits move you to a sidewalk table on Thursdays between 6pm and 9pm for happy-hour prices on the featured hooch – Scotch, brandy, Italian bitters, even the signature green devil – in

Californian cuisine cooks at Zuni Café

cocktails or flights. The venerable cheese plate, burger and West Coast oysters are standout bar bites.

### ☒ BOURBON & BRANCH
*Speakeasy*

☎ 346-1735; www.bourbonandbranch .com; 501 Jones St; ☿ 6pm-2am Wed-Sat; 🚌 19, 38, 47, 49

'Don't even think of asking for a cosmo' reads one of many House Rules at this revived speakeasy, complete with secret exits from its Prohibition-era heyday. For drop-in top-shelf gin and bourbon cocktails, tell the bouncer you're here for the Library, and you'll be led through a bookcase and possibly asked for the password ('books'). Reservations are required for front-room booths, and worth it for hot dates without the usual bar din.

### ☒ CAV WINE BAR *Wine Tasting*

☎ 437-1770; www.cavwinebar.com; 1666 Market St; per class about $50 or by order; ☿ 5:30-11pm Mon-Thu, 5:30pm-midnight Fri & Sat; 🚌 F, J, K, L, M, N, 5, 7, 71

Let your palate rack up frequent flier miles with Cav wine flights to specific growing regions, or assemble your own taste tests with 40 wines by the glass – most are priced in the single digits, with 2.5oz tastes at half the price.

Get whisked away to the island of Sardinia with a free-spirited Vermentino, down to Chile for a sultry cab with hints of coffee, and back to the Bay for Zin with cinnamon backsass.

### ☒ HEMLOCK TAVERN *Dive Bar*

☎ 923-0923; www.hemlocktavern.com; 1131 Polk St; ☿ 4pm-2am; 🚌 2, 3, 4, 19, 38, 47, 49

When you wake up tomorrow with peanut shells in your hair and someone else's mascara on your armpit, you'll know it was another successful, near-lethal night at the Hemlock. Blame it on cheap drink at the oval bar, pogo-worthy punk rock in the back room, and free peanuts in the shell to eat or throw at the infamously difficult Trivia Night. Weekday nights and even literary readings are anything but staid among this motley crowd of San Franciscans.

### ☒ MOMI TOBY'S REVOLUTION CAFÉ *Café & Art Bar*

☎ 626-1508; www.momitobys.com; 528 Laguna St; ☿ 7:30am-10pm Mon-Fri, 8am-10pm Sat & Sun; 🚌 7, 21, 71

No internet connections at this old-school bohemian café: just musicians and artists running the espresso machine and poets scribbling furiously in the corner until the afternoon switchover from coffee to wine by the glass. Take in the sun outdoors or grab a window seat to eavesdrop on first dates and conspiracy theories.

### ▼ RYE *Cocktail Lounge*
☎ 474-4448; 688 Geary St; ⏱ 5:30pm-2am Mon-Fri, 7pm-2am Sat & Sun; 🚌 38; 🚋 Powell-Mason

It's the type of place where the bartender is called a mixologist, and earns the title. Come early to grab a mod pod with your entourage in the sunken lounge, drink something challenging involving dark rum or juniper gin, and leave before the smoking cage overflows and someone gets burned.

# ⭐ PLAY

### ⭐ AMERICAN CONSERVATORY THEATER *Theater*
ACT; ☎ 749-2228; http://act-sf.org; 415 Geary St; 🚌 2, 3, 4, 27, 38; 🚋 Powell-Mason, Powell-Hyde

Shows destined for London or New York must first pass muster at the turn-of-the-century Geary Theater, which has hosted ACT's landmark productions of Tony Kushner's *Angels in America* and Robert Wilson's *Black Rider,* featuring a libretto by William S Burroughs and music by the Bay Area's own Tom Waits.

### ⭐ AUNT CHARLIE'S
*Drag Dive Bar*
☎ 441-2922; www.auntcharlieslounge .com; 133 Turk St; ⏱ 9am-2pm; 🚌 F, J, K, L, M, N, 5, 7, 21, 71; 🚇 Powell Street

Like any lady of mystery, Aunt Charlie prefers her drinks cheap and potent, her flings likewise, and lights dim enough to disguise 5 o'clock shadows. Wednesdays bring anything-can-happen tranny diva extravaganzas and Thursdays pack the hallway-sized dance floor with art-school gays grooving on '80s retro techno.

### ⭐ CRAFT GYM *Craft Classes*
☎ 702-5700; www.craftgym.com; 1452 Bush St; 3hr workshop $45-95; 🚌 2, 19, 47, 49, 76

Banish those distant memories of lumpy scarves or mangled origami that left you convinced you were born with ten thumbs. These classes teach you how to make things you would actually want to use, like stencil-etched beer glasses, a silver ID bracelet or your own signature lip balm. If you want an SF souvenir done right, DIY.

### ⭐ DAVIES SYMPHONY HALL
*Classical Music*
☎ 864-6000; www.sfsymphony.org; 201 Van Ness Ave; tickets from $20; ⏱ box office 10am-6pm Mon-Fri, noon-6pm Sat; 🚌 F, J, K, L, M, N, 5, 21, 47, 49; ♿

Michael Tilson Thomas conducts on the tips of his toes and keeps the audience on the edge of its seat through Poulenc, Beethoven or Mahler, and throws experimental music onto most programs to keep everyone guessing. Don't miss pre-show talks, where 'MTT' explains exactly what makes each piece exciting and relevant. New Yorkers complain that MTT's direction makes their symphony scene seem tame by comparison, and guess what: they're right. Get tickets in advance or chance a matinee anytime September to May.

### ☆ EDINBURGH CASTLE PUB
*Literary Events & Live Music*
☎ 885-4074; www.castlenews.com; 950 Geary St; ⏲ 5pm-2am; 🚍 19, 38, 47, 49
The town's finest monument to drink, complete with dart boards, pool tables, stages for rock bands and raucous literary readings. Photos of bagpipers, the *Trainspotting* soundtrack on the jukebox, occasional appearances by Irvine Welsh and a service delivering vinegary fish and chips in newspaper are all the Scottish authenticity you could ask for, short of haggis.

### ☆ EXIT THEATER
*Experimental Theater*
☎ 673-3847; www.sffringe.org; 156 Eddy St; tickets $10-20; ⏲ box office 30min before shows; 🚍 F, J, K, L, M, N, 5, 7, 21, 71; Ⓟ Powell Street; ♿

Other towns have their multiplexes and musicals, but boho SF has a triple-stage experimental theater venue. The Exit is home to avant-garde productions year-round and SF's Fringe Festival, which recently featured *Tenderloin Christmas Hustler* in lieu of *A Christmas Carol*, and upstaged faux-urban *Rent* with *Lost and Found in the Mission*, a musical based on scraps of paper found on Mission streets.

### ☆ GREAT AMERICAN MUSIC HALL *Live Music*
☎ 885-0750; www.gamh.com; 859 O'Farrell St; tickets $12-35; ⏲ box office 10:30am-6pm Mon-Fri, until 9pm weekday show nights, 6-9pm weekend show nights; 🚍 19, 38, 47, 49; ♿
This opulent former bordello on a sketchy block is full of surprises: rockers Black Rebel Motorcycle Club playing acoustic, Nick Lowe jamming with Ry Cooder, and San Francisco's favorite Brazilian-ska-punk band Bat Makumba. Arrive early to claim front-row balcony seats with a pint and a passable burger or find standing room downstairs by the stage.

### ☆ RICKSHAW STOP *Live Music*
☎ 861-2011; www.rickshawstop.com; 155 Fell St; tickets $7-12; ⏲ 6pm-2am; 🚍 5, 21, 42, 47, 49
Noise-poppers, eccentric rockers and crafty DJs cross-pollinate hemispheres with something for everyone: bad-ass bhangra

nights, Latin explosion bands, 'homofabulous' Rebel Girl for the ladies on third Saturdays and bouncy Cockblock on second Saturdays.

## ☆ SAN FRANCISCO BALLET
*Ballet*

☎ info 861-5600, tickets 865-2000; www.sfballet.org; tickets $7-100

The USA's oldest ballet company is exceedingly sprightly, performing over 100 shows annually nationally and abroad from classic *Swan Lake* to modern Mark Morris. The company performs mostly at the War Memorial Opera House (right) from January to May, with occasional shows at the Yerba Buena Center for the Arts (p108). Half-price senior, military and student tickets are sometimes available.

## ☆ WAR MEMORIAL OPERA HOUSE *Opera*

☎ 864-3330; www.sfopera.com; 301 Van Ness Ave; ⊗ box office 10am-6pm Mon-Fri; 🚌 F, J, K, L, M, N, 5, 21, 47, 49; ♿

Ever since the gold rush, SF has been obsessed with opera – and in 2008, a stockbroker donated $40 million to keep the SF Opera in good voice under hot young Tuscan director Nicola Luisotti, and commission more original operas like *Dead Man Walking* and

Local boy Michael Franti makes good (music) at the Warfield

Amy Tan's *The Bonesetter's Daughter*. Book early for the September to December season, or score standing-room tickets two hours before performances and hang out with the die-hard opera buffs until doctors on call clear out at intermission.

## ⭐ WARFIELD
*Live Music & Comedy*
☎ 775-7722; www.ticketmaster.com; 982 Market St; ⌚ box office at the

Fillmore 10am-4pm Sun, 7:30-10pm show nights; 🚍 F, J, K, L, M, N, 5, 6, 7, 21, 31, 71; Ⓜ Powell Street; ♿

Big acts with an international following line up to play this old vaudeville theater: balcony-shaking rockers like Patti Smith, Iggy Pop and The Killers, danceable groovers Dandy Warhols and Alison Moyet, and thinking-person's comedians like Jim Gaffigan and hometown favorite Margaret Cho.

NEIGHBORHOODS

HAYES VALLEY, CIVIC CENTER & THE TENDERLOIN

# >SOMA

Biotech start-ups, solar-powered baseball, S&M clubs, iPod conferences, warehouse sweatshops and new media art galleries: SoMa (South of Market) seems like the invention of a city planner who secretly wanted to be a science-fiction novelist. The dot-com boom exploded and fizzled in live/work lofts around 3rd St, and skyscrapers have sprung up in Mission Bay along 5th St to accommodate a biotech boom that has yet to actually begin. Fourth St is dominated by Moscone Center, host of Macworld and other tradeshows where techies try to outdo one another for sheer novelty, not unlike trendy neighborhood restaurants and leather-daddy bars.

SoMa specializes in crazy schemes with the occasional flash of brilliance. DJ sets, drag show extravaganzas and fetish fests erupt and disappear overnight. By day, SoMa was once a warehouse party waiting to happen, but the Yerba Buena arts district that has popped up around SFMOMA has finally exposed SF's arty outrageousness to broad daylight.

## SOMA

### 👁 SEE
California Historical
  Society Museum..........1 D1
Cartoon Art Museum.....2 D1
Catharine Clark Gallery..3 D1
Contemporary Jewish
  Museum ......................4 D1
Electric Works ...............5 B4
Hosfelt Gallery .............6 C3
Museum of Craft &
  Folk Art.......................7 D2
Museum of the African
  Diaspora .....................8 D1
New Langton Arts.........9 B5
San Francisco Museum
  of Modern Art...........10 D2
Yerba Buena Center
  for the Arts...............11 D2
Zeum .........................12 D2

### 🛍 SHOP
General Bead................13 B4
Jeremy's .....................14 F3
Madame S & Mr S
  Leather.....................15 C5

### 🍴 EAT
Coco500.......................16 E4
Patisserie Philippe ......17 D6
Salt House ...................18 E1
Split Pea Seduction......19 C3

### 🍸 DRINK
111 Minna....................20 E1
City Beer Store &
  Tasting Room ...........21 B4
Eagle Tavern ...............22 B6
House of Shields...........23 D1

### ⭐ PLAY
Annie's Social Club.......24 D3
AsiaSF..........................25 B5
AT&T Park ...................26 G3
Cat Club ......................27 B4
EndUp .........................28 D4
Hotel Utah...................29 E3
Mezzanine...................30 C2
Slim's ..........................31 B5
Stud .............................32 B5

Please see over for map

# SEE

## CALIFORNIA HISTORICAL SOCIETY

☎ 357-1848; www.californiahistorical society.org; 678 Mission St; adult/senior & student/child under 5yr $3/1/free; 🕐 noon-4:30pm Wed-Sat; 🚋 F, J, K, L, M, N, 7, 14, 71; 🚇 Montgomery
More colorful flashbacks than a hippie at a Dead show, with wall-to-wall ephemera ranging from political campaign propaganda throughout California history to Gene Anthony's photographs of 1967 Be-Ins at Golden Gate Park. Reserve ahead for seasonal historical walking tours, ranging from the Mission to Ocean Beach.

## CARTOON ART MUSEUM

CAM; ☎ 227-8666; www.cartoonart.org; 655 Mission St; adult/senior & student/child 6-12yr/child under 5yr $6/4/2/free; 🕐 11am-5pm Tue-Sun; 🚋 F, J, K, L, M, N, 6, 7, 14, 21, 31, 71; 🚇 Montgomery
Comics fans need no introduction to this museum founded on a grant from Bay Area cartoon legend Charles M Schultz (Peanuts), featuring mainstream superheroes plus indie strips by longtime Haight resident R Crumb (Mr Natural) and East Bay graphic novelists Daniel Clowes (Ghostworld), Gene Yang (American Born Chinese) and Adrian Tomine (Optic Nerve). Far more than a laugh riot, the CAM

hosts classes on cartooning and drawing with kids, exhibits on political cartoons and family days at Pixar Studios. Openings are rare opportunities to mingle with comics legends, animation studio heads and obsessive collectors.

## CATHARINE CLARK GALLERY

☎ 399-1439; www.cclarkgallery.com; 150 Minna St; 🕐 10:30am-5:30pm Tue-Fri, 11am-5:30pm Sat; 🚋 F, J, K, L, M, N, 7, 14, 71; 🚇 Montgomery
No material is too political or risqué at San Francisco's most cutting-edge gallery: witness Kara Maria's psychedelic candy-colored paintings combining Iraq war footage and porn, Chester Arnold's poignant paintings of California's natural disasters or Packard Jennings' instructional pamphlets for converting cities into wildlife refuges.

## CONTEMPORARY JEWISH MUSEUM

☎ 655-7800; www.jmsf.org; 736 Mission St; adult/senior & student/child $10/8/free; 🕐 1-8:30pm Thu, 11am-5:30pm Fri-Tue; 🚋 5, 7, 14, 30, 31, 38, 45, 49, 71, 91; 🚇 Powell Street
Daniel Liebskind's 2008 blue steel-and-brick building incorporates the facade of the 1881 Jesse Street Power Substation and the shape of the Hebrew word l'chaim ('to

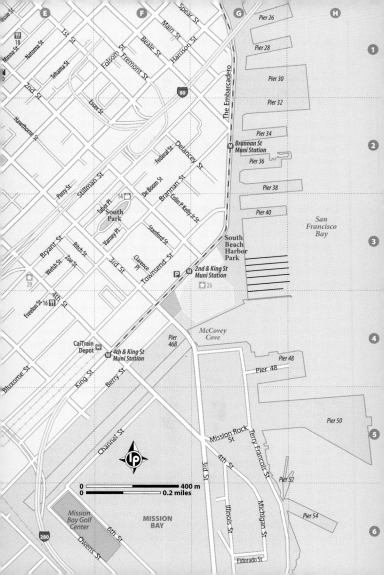

life') – a fine idea in theory, though perhaps best appreciated from a helicopter. But inside, the space and collections are most illuminating, from soundscapes based on the Hebrew alphabet by the likes of Lou Reed and Laurie Anderson to Marc Chagall's backdrops for 1920s Russian Jewish theater.

### ⊙ ELECTRIC WORKS

☎ 626-5496; www.sfelectricworks.com; 130 8th St; admission free; ☼ 10am-6pm Mon-Fri; 🚌 F, J, K, L, M, N, 5, 7, 14, 71; ⊕ Civic Center

Lightbulb moments are a given at the Electric Works, with limited-edition gift selection priced for starving artists and print editions benefiting nonprofits. In the gallery/printmaking studio that calls itself 'The Land of Yes,' anything is possible – including Michelle Blade's cruise-ship tours to enlightenment, Paul Madonna's watercolor odes to a psychedelic cupcake and Sandow Birk's modern *Inferno* starring traffic-jammed LA as Hell and San Francisco as foggy Purgatory.

### ⊙ HOSFELT GALLERY

☎ 495-5454; www.hosfeltgallery.com; 430 Clementina St; ☼ 11am-5:30pm Tue-Sat; 🚌 F, J, K, L, M, N, 27, 30, 45; ⊕ Powell Street

Closer looks are rewarded at Hosfelt, where the gallery program highlights dreamy, meticulously

detailed interior worlds. Chris Ballantine redraws suburbia as one giant skate park and parking lots as Zen gardens, and Marco Maggi covers the floor with sheaves of office paper carved into delicate tendrils that gallery visitors tiptoe through barefooted.

### ⊙ MUSEUM OF CRAFT & FOLK ART

☎ 227-4888; www.mocfa.org; 51 Yerba Buena Lane; adult/senior/child $5/4/free; ☼ 11am-6pm Tue-Fri, 11am-5pm Sat & Sun; 🚌 F, J, K, L, M, N, 7, 14, 21, 71; ⊕ Montgomery

Amazing handiwork becomes all the more impressive once you learn the personal back-stories of the artisans, from the Shaker women behind sublime woodworking to contemporary artists reinventing *parols* (Filipino paper lanterns). Don't miss trunk shows of contemporary California glassblowers, woodworkers and jewelers, or hands-on workshops at family activity days.

### ⊙ MUSEUM OF THE AFRICAN DIASPORA

MoAD; ☎ 358-7200; www.moadsf .org; 685 Mission St; adult/senior & student/child under 13yr $10/5/free; ☼ 10am-6pm Mon & Wed-Sat, noon-5pm Sun; 🚌 F, J, K, L, M, N, 7, 14, 71; ⊕ Montgomery; ♿

A regal couple by Nigerian British sensation Chris Ofili, collaged

A complex history is celebrated at the Museum of the African Diaspora

portraits of Harlem jazz greats by Romare Bearden, a family portrait set within an Aunt Jemima syrup ad by San Franciscan Hank Willis Thomas: MoAD has assembled a standout cast of characters to tell the epic story of the African Diaspora, with an emphasis on contemporary art.

🎞 **NEW LANGTON ARTS**

☎ 626-5416; www.newlangtonarts.org; 1246 Folsom St; admission free; ✷ noon-6pm Tue-Sat; 🚌 F, J, K, L, M, N, 12, 19; 🚇 Civic Center

Strange is the norm at New Langton, where artists have done odd and occasionally unprintable things since 1975. This nonprofit is where Tony Labat hung disco balls from their anatomical namesakes, Felipe Dulzaides created billboards of surveillance-camera photos and OPENrestaurant collective staged a free meal and open bar using only ingredients grown within city limits of SF, Oakland and Berkeley.

🎞 **SAN FRANCISCO MUSEUM OF MODERN ART**

SFMOMA; ☎ 357-4000; www.sfmoma .org; 151 3rd St; adult/senior/student/ child $10/$7/$6/free, Thu half-price, 1st Tue of month free; ✷ 11am-6pm Mon-Tue & Fri-Sun, 11am-9pm Thu; 🚌 F, J, K, L, M, N, 7, 14, 71; 🚇 Montgomery

Mario Botta's light-filled brick box is topped with what looks like a

NEIGHBORHOODS

SOMA

glass sundial, but the contemporary art shows here reveal more about the times we're living through than any clock. Since its 1995 relaunch coincided with the tech boom, SFMOMA became an early champion of new media art, from Matthew Barney's poetic videos involving industrial quantities of Vaseline to Olafur Eliasson's outer-space light installations. Don't miss SFMOMA's astounding photography collection, with works spanning from 19th-century daguerreotypes to modern greats: Ansel Adams, Daido Moriyama, Diane Arbus, Edward Weston, William Eggleston and Dorothea Lange.

### ⓒ YERBA BUENA CENTER FOR THE ARTS

☎ 978-2787; www.ybca.org; 700 Howard St; gallery adult/senior & student $7/5, 1st Tue of month free, performances $15-50; ⏱ gallery noon-5pm Tue, Wed & Fri-Sun, noon-8pm Thu; 🚊 F, J, K, L, M, N, 7, 14, 71; ⓞ Powell Street

Eccentricity stretches around the block as throngs of artists and dreamers line up for openings to ambitious shows of irreverent Nordic art, Vietnamese collage and especially the triennial Bay Area Now survey of emerging art stars. Performances are white-hot, featuring hip-hop greats like Mos Def, Marcus Shelby's celebrated

jazz opera for Harriet Tubman and an entire season of performances by West Coast modern innovators Liss Fain Dance.

### ⓒ ZEUM

☎ 777-2800; www.zeum.org; 221 4th St; adult/student/child $7/6/5; ⏱ 11am-5pm Wed-Sun; 🚊 F, J, K, L, M, N, 30, 45; ⓞ Powell Street; ♿

No velvet ropes or hands off here: kids have the run of the place, with high-tech displays that double-dare them to make their own music videos, claymation movies and soundtracks. Jump right into a live-action video game, sign up for workshops with the Bay Area's superstar animators or hop a ride on the restored Looff carousel ($2 for two rides).

## 🛍 SHOP

### 🛍 GENERAL BEAD
*Beads & Jewelry*

☎ 621-8187; www.genbead.com; 637 Minna St; ⏱ 10am-5pm Tue-Sat, noon-5pm Sun; 🚊 F, J, K, L, M, N, 12, 19; ⓞ Civic Center

This place sorts out jump-ring rookies from the DIY jewelry pros with an arcane ordering system involving golf pencils, forms and rows of boxes behind the counter that only the bead-bedecked staff with bejeweled calculators can access. The bulk bead shopping upstairs is easier and cheaper –

though 74 necklaces later, you might find yourself wondering how it all got started.

### JEREMY'S
*Discount Designer Clothing*

☎ 882-4929; 2 South Park Ave; ⌚ 11am-6pm Mon-Sat, 11am-5pm Sun; 🚊 N, 10, 15, 30, 76

Shhhh…don't tell SF fashionistas who revealed their secret, or Lonely Planet will be threatened by stiletto-wielding socialites. Some of Jeremy's women's and men's clothing comes from photo shoots, so the selection of couture gowns is best for sizes zero to four and men's shirts are sometimes smudged with makeup, but it's hard to complain about $200 to $300 Vera Wang wedding dresses and $40 Prada wallets. Check that half-off shiny blue Marc Jacobs jacket to be sure it's not missing a button, because all sales are final.

### MADAME S & MR S LEATHER *Fetish Supplies*

☎ 863-9447; www.madame-s.com; 385 8th St; ⌚ 11am-7pm; 🚊 F, J, K, L, M, N, 12, 19; Ⓜ Civic Center

An S&M superstore that outsizes Home Depot features aisles of suspension stirrups, latex hoods and for your favorite consenting adult, a chrome-plated chastity belt (male and female). If you've been a very bad puppy, there's

an entire department of leashes to keep you in line, and you can select your punishment of choice in Dungeon Furniture.

## 🍴 EAT

### 🍴 COCO500 *Californian* $$

☎ 543-2222; www.coco500.com; 500 Brannan St; ⌚ 11:30am-10pm Mon-Thu, 11:30am-11pm Fri, 5:30-11pm Sat; 🚊 L, N, 10

Casual, boldly creative and no stranger to breakthroughs, not unlike the Web 2.0 and biotech startups celebrating birthdays and patents over lunch here. Business goes down easier with Loretta Keller's specialties from the wood-fired oven, like truffled squash blossom flatbreads and pizza with salami and garlic confit. Linger over sides of ultrafresh organic veggies from the 'California dirt' section of the menu and inventive cocktails with fresh-squeezed organic fruit juices.

### 🍴 PATISSERIE PHILIPPE *Bakery* $

☎ 558-8016; www.patisseriephilippe .com; 655 Townsend St; ⌚ 8am-6pm Mon-Fri, 8am-5pm Sat; 🚊 N, T, 19, 42

Pastries lighter than air that won't leave a dent your wallet. Come for the impeccable ham-and-cheese croissant or classic quiche Lorraine, but ignore that European glass counter or you'll skip straight

NEIGHBORHOODS

SOMA

to dessert of tarte tatin loaded with caramelized sweet-tart apples. The secret is top-quality local ingredients, with Meyer lemon delivering tang to tarts and premium butter making that $1 bag of cookies a decadent investment.

### 🍴 SALT HOUSE Californian    $$
☎ 543-8900; www.salthousesf.com; 545 Mission St; 🕑 11:30am-11pm Mon-Thu, 11:30am-midnight Fri, 5:30pm-midnight Sat, 5-10pm Sun; 🚊 F, 5, 7, 9, 10, 14, 38, 71; 🚇 Montgomery

For a business lunch that feels more like a spa getaway, take your choice of light fare like duck confit or yellowfin tuna with beets. Forget the ice tea, and unwind with

wine by the glass and refreshing ginger juleps instead. Service is leisurely, so order that carrot cake with cream-cheese ice cream now.

### 🍴 SPLIT PEA SEDUCTION
*Soup & Sandwiches*    $
☎ 551-2223; www.splitpeaseduction .com; 138 6th St; 🕑 8am-2pm Mon-Fri; 🚊 F, 5, 7, 9, 14, 19, 71; 🚇

Right off Skid Row are unexpectedly healthy, homey $8.50 gourmet soup-and-sandwich combinations, including seasonal soups like potato with housemade pesto with a signature *crosta* (open-faced sandwich), such as cambozola cheese and nectarine drizzled with honey.

Find the flavor at Salt House

# � DRINK

## ☙ 111 MINNA *Art Bar*
☎ 974-1719; www.111minnagallery
.com; 111 Minna St; cover $3-10;
☼ 11am-2am Tue-Fri, 9pm-2am
Sat; 🚍 F, J, K, L, M, N, 7, 14, 15, 71;
Ⓜ Montgomery

The night is young and so is
the crowd of MFA students,
minor MySpace celebrities and
engineers trying to score with
emerging fashion designers.
Front-room art shows feature
decent doodles by surfers and
sanitized street art, handy as
conversation pieces when the
banter flags. Back-room DJs
spin electronica grooves and
flow techno most nights, but
bhangra mash-ups get the party
started Bollywood-style on
weekends.

## ☙ ANCHOR BREWING
*Free Beer Tour*
☎ 863-8350; www.anchorbrewing.com;
1705 Mariposa St; 🚍 19, 22

So here's the deal: Anchor only
offers one public tour a week, on
a weekday, and you have to make
reservations at least a month
in advance. But if you do, you'll
get a 45-minute tour of Anchor's
historic facilities (lots of shiny
copper machines), a crash course
in beer tasting and six half-pints of
different Anchor brews at the end.
For free. Enough said.

## ☙ CITY BEER STORE & TASTING ROOM *Beer Bar*
☎ 503-1033; 1168 Folsom St; ☼ noon-
9pm Tue-Sat, noon-6pm Sun; 🚍 12,
19, 47

Exceptional local and Belgian microbrewed beer with killer cheese
pairings, served in a spiffy brick
bar that'll win over lounge-lizard
friends. The floor's not sticky and
it's not even stinky, so you won't
wake up tomorrow with that eau-
de-brewery smell.

## ☙ EAGLE TAVERN *Leather Bar*
☎ 626-0880; www.sfeagle.com;
398 12th St; ☼ noon-2am; 🚍 F, J, K, L,
M, N, 9, 12

Even if you identify with leather
more as a shoe material than a
modus operandi, there's room for
you among the leather daddies
in the Eagle's back patio. Sunday
afternoons it's a tight squeeze, with
local politicians making the scene
to get in good with the gay/trans
community – SF's answer to kissing
babies. Drink-for-a-cause nights
keep you coming back for more.

## ☙ HOUSE OF SHIELDS *Bar*
☎ 975-8651; www.houseofshields.com;
39 New Montgomery St; ☼ 2pm-2am
Mon-Fri, 7pm-2am Sat; 🚍 F, J, K, L, M, N,
7, 14, 15, 71; Ⓜ Montgomery

Strong drink, live band, small pub:
your ears won't be the only thing
buzzing pleasantly by evening's
end. Grab a booth if you can,

though some suit who just won a big account always seems to beat you to it. At least there's enough Powers Whiskey to go around, and $5 well drinks from 5pm to 9pm weekdays.

#  PLAY

## ☆ ANNIE'S SOCIAL CLUB
*Punk Karaoke*

☎ 974-1585; www.anniessocialclub
.com; 917 Folsom St; ☾ 4pm-2am Mon-Fri, 8pm-2am Sat; 🚌 F, J, K, L, M, N, 12, 27, 30, 45; 🚇 Powell Street
Certain Monday, Friday and Saturday nights call for a punk-rock rendition of ABBA's 'Waterloo,' followed by a heartfelt ballad version of 'Pepper' by the Butthole Surfers. Punk Rock & Schlock Karaoke nights require you to murder songs and throw in some cheeky pogo burlesque, and live punk shows do wonders for flagging street creds – check the website for lineup.

## ☆ ASIASF *Drag Lounge*

☎ 255-2742; www.asiasf.com; 201 9th St; ☾ dinner 6:30-10pm Mon-Wed & Fri, 6-10pm Thu & Sun, 5-10pm Sat, club 10pm-2am daily; 🚌 F, J, K, L, M, N, 14, 19; 🚇 Civic Center
Elsewhere an all-Asian tranny lounge with waitresses that'll make you look thrice might be considered a tad unusual – but this being San Francisco, it's the

food that attracts notice. Look out, ladies, we've got a scene-stealer: the Asia-dilla, a quesadilla with duck, peppers and sundried-cherry crème fraîche.

## ☆ AT&T PARK *Baseball*

☎ 972-2000; http://sanfrancisco.giants
.mlb.com; tickets Mon-Thu from $10, Fri & Sat from $17, premium games from $25; 🚌 L, N, T, 10
The SF Giants – the city's National League baseball team – draw crowds to AT&T Park and its solar-powered scoreboard. Locals annoyed by the park's corporate-merger name changes (from Pac Bell to SBC to AT&T) refer to it as 'Giants Stadium.' Outside the park, the waterfront promenade offers a free view of right field.

## ☆ CAT CLUB *Dance Club*

☎ 703-8965; www.catclubsf.com; 1190 Folsom St; cover after 10pm $5; ☾ 9pm-3am Tue & Thu-Sat; 🚌 F, J, K, L, M, N, 12, 19; 🚇 Civic Center
You never really know your friends until you've seen them belt out A-ha's 'Take On Me' at 1984 Thursday nights with the rest of the euphoric straight/bi/gay/whatever crowd, or perform Rapper's Delight with a lesbian posse at hip-hop Hot Pants the second and fourth Fridays of the month. Goth nights bring out the androgyny and the eyeliner, but otherwise the crowd is eclectic SF.

## ★ ENDUP Dance Club
☎ 646-0999; www.theendup.com; 401 6th St; ⏰ 10pm-4am Mon-Thu, 11pm-11am Fri, 10pm-6am Sat, 6am-4am Sun; 🚌 12, 27, 47

Everyone ends up here sooner or later for Fag Fridays, definitive Sunday tea dances (since 1973!), reggae Saturdays and/or all-star lady DJs at Minx Thursdays that last well into Friday morning rush hour. The location almost under the freeway is off the beaten track, but anyone left on the streets of San Francisco after 3am finds their way here through the mysterious magnetic force of marathon turntablist sessions.

## ★ HOTEL UTAH Live Music
☎ 546-6300; www.thehotelutahsaloon .com; 500 4th St; ⏰ 11:30am-2am Mon-Fri, 6pm-2am Sat & Sun; 🚌 N, 27, 30, 45

Whoopi Goldberg and Robin Williams broke in the stage of this historic Victorian hotel back in the '70s, and the thrill of finding SF's top hidden talents draws crowds to singer-songwriter Open Mic Mondays and obscure bands with promising names: A Decent Animal, Fleeting Trance, Room for a Ghost. Nonconformity is a noble tradition here that dates back to the '50s, when the bartender graciously served Beats, grifters and Marilyn Monroe, but snipped the ties of businessmen when they leaned across the bar.

## ★ MEZZANINE Live Music
☎ 625-8880; www.mezzaninesf.com; 444 Jessie St; 🚌 F, K, L, M, N, S, 5, 7, 9, 14, 71; 🚇 Powell Street

Brag about seeing biggish acts in a smallish place for cover ranging from nada to $15, with Mos Def, Dandy Warhols, Nas, the Slits, and Method Man blowing the roof clean off the Mezzanine.

## ★ SLIM'S Live Music
☎ 255-0333; www.slims-sf.com; 333 11th St; ⏰ 5pm-2am Mon-Sun; 🚌 F, J, K, L, M, N, 9, 12, 47

Rock legends like the Damned, Prince and Elvis Costello and pure entertainment like Dread Zepplin, Tenacious D and Gogol Bordello play all-ages shows, though shorties may get swallowed in the mosh pit. Come early for upstairs seating in the balcony with dinner – the burger and fries aren't shabby.

## ★ STUD Gay Club
☎ 252-7883; www.studsf.com; 399 9th St; cover $5-7; ⏰ 5pm-3am; 🚌 12, 19, 47

Rocking the SF gay scene for more than 40 years yet brimming with youthful vigor, this is the bar equivalent of Viagra. Most nights the Stud makes good on its name with hot gay men on the dance floor – but drag shows here draw San Franciscan crowds more varied than a UN delegation. The crowd is also mixed on '80s nights, the SF euphemism for 'gay, bi-curious and straight with fashion sense.'

# >MISSION

San Franciscans love to show off the Mission as proof of the city's open-mindedness, and are itching for you to ask the obvious: what kind of neighborhood is this, anyway? This is a trick question. Latinos, lesbians, foodies, ravers, career activists, chichi designers, punks, prostitutes and suits all play featured roles in the Mission's ensemble act.

The mission founded here in 1776 shows that the Mission's versatility has deep roots. The ancient murals are by the indigenous Ohlone who built the original mission, the newer basilica shows Spanish-Mexican influence, and in the graveyard are buried early Italian, Scots-Irish and Australian adventurers lured here by gold. Within blocks of this historic spot are some of San Francisco's most forward-thinking ideas: a writing

## MISSION

Please see over for map

program where famous authors help teens with their homework, a gallery showcasing developmentally disabled artists, and murals bringing bright ideas to back alleys.

# SEE

## 826 VALENCIA
☎ 642-5905; www.826valencia.com; 826 Valencia St; ⊙ noon-6pm; 🚌 14, 26, 33, 49; ♿

Avast, ye scurvy scalawags! If ye be shipwrecked without yer glass eye and yer McSweeney's literary anthology, lay down yer doubloons and claim yer booty at this here nonprofit Pirate Store. Below decks, kids be writing tall tales for dark nights asea – and ye can study making magazines and video games and such too, if that be yer dastardly inclination…arr!

## CLARION ALLEY
Btwn 17th & 18th Sts; 🚌 14, 22, 26, 33, 49; ⊙ 16th Street Mission

Only the strongest street art survives in Clarion, where lesser works are peed on or painted over. Very few pieces have lasted years: a trompe l'oeil escalator, Andrew Schoultz's mural of gentrifying elephants displacing scraggly birds, and kung-fu-fighting women anarchists that make Charlie's Angels look like chumps.

## CREATIVITY EXPLORED
☎ 863-2108; www.creativityexplored.org; 3245 16th St; ⊙ 10am-3pm Mon-Wed & Fri, 10am-7pm Thu, 1-6pm Sat; 🚌 J, 14, 22, 33, 49; ⊙ 16th Street Mission

Brave new worlds are captured in celebrated artworks that regularly make the New York art scene – all by developmentally disabled artists. Intriguing themed shows reveal fresh perspectives on themes ranging from love to politics, and openings are wonderful opportunities to meet the artists.

## GALERÍA DE LA RAZA
☎ 206-9242; www.galeriadelaraza.org; 2857 24th St; ⊙ 1-7pm Tue, noon-6pm Wed-Sat; 🚌 9, 27, 33, 48; ⊙ 24th Street Mission

Bold statements need no translation here – witness Salvadoran Victor Cartagena's installation of found ID photos, a group show exploring SF's Latin gay culture, and David Bacon's portraits of indigenous Mexican migrant laborers. On the gallery wall outside is the Digital Mural Project, a billboard featuring slogans like 'Trust Your Struggle' instead of cigarette ads.

## JACK HANLEY GALLERY
☎ 522-1623; www.jackhanley.com; 395 Valencia St; ⊙ 11am-6pm Tue-Sat; 🚌 14, 22, 33, 49; ⊙ 16th Street Mission

Furious scribblers and meticulous daydreamers will relate to Michele

NEIGHBORHOODS

MISSION

Feel the white space at Jack Hanley Gallery (p115)

Blade's metaphysical meteor showers, Keegan McHargue's hyper-doodled dudes sprouting antlers, and Chris Johansen's clueless crowds oblivious to businessmen floating overhead. Collectors buy works before shows open, so see them now before they disappear into Manhattan penthouses.

### MISSION DOLORES
☎ 621-8203; www.missiondolores.org; 3321 16th St; adult/child $3/2, audio tour $5; 🕙 9am-4pm; 🚊 J, 14, 22, 33, 49; Ⓜ 16th Street Mission

The city's oldest building and its namesake, the Mission (originally named Misión San Francisco de Asís) was founded in 1776 and rebuilt in 1782 with conscripted native Ohlone labor in exchange for a meal a day – note the ceiling patterned after Ohlone baskets and an Ohlone mural of a stabbed sacred heart. Today, the modest adobe mission is overshadowed by the adjoining ornate Churrigueresque 1913 basilica with stained-glass windows of St Francis and California's 21 missions.

### PRECITA EYES
☎ 285-2287; www.precitaeyes.org; 2981 24th St; adult/senior & student/child under 12yr from $10/5/2; 🕙 10am-5pm Mon-Fri, 10am-4pm Sat, noon-4pm Sun; 🚊 9, 27, 33, 48

Pack in the sights on Mission mural walking tours led by local artists organized by nonprofit Precita Eyes – you'll cover 75 murals spread out over eight blocks in two hours. The centerpiece is Balmy Alley, where you can still glimpse groundbreaking works by early '70s muralistas.

### ☉ SOUTHERN EXPOSURE
☎ 863-2141; www.soex.org; 417 14th St; admission free; ☽ noon-6pm Tue-Sat; ◻ 12, 22, 27, 33; ⊖ 16th Street Mission

Internationally acclaimed for provocative art exhibitions, this nonprofit gallery is transformed with each new installation: Kamau Patton and Suzy Poling's dazzling installation of light effects fragmented by crystals, mirrors and 3-D lenticulars, or Daniel Nevers' maze of barricades in concrete and thread.

### ☉ WOMEN'S BUILDING
☎ 431-1180; www.womensbuilding .org; 3543 18th St; ◻ J, 14, 26, 33, 49; ⊖ 16th Street Mission

The nation's first woman-owned and -operated community center was housed in 1971 and has housed more than 170 women's organizations. The 1994 *Maestra-Peace* is SF's largest mural, featuring icons of female strength from Mayan and Chinese goddesses to

such modern trailblazers as Rigoberta Menchu, Hanaan Ashrawi and Audre Lorde.

# SHOP

### ◻ ADOBE BOOKS & BACKROOM GALLERY
*Books & Art*

☎ 864-3936; www.adobebooksback roomgallery.blogspot.com; 3166 16th St; ☽ 11am-10pm Sun-Thu, 11am-11pm Fri & Sat; ◻ 14, 22, 33, 49; ⊖ 16th Street Mission

Every book you never knew you needed used and cheap, if you can find it in the obstacle course of sofas, cats, art books and German philosophy. Head to the tiny art gallery in back to discover local artwork at reasonable prices.

### ◻ AQUARIUS RECORDS *Music*
☎ 647-2272; www.aquariusrecords .org; 1055 Valencia St; ☽ 10am-9pm Mon-Wed, 10am-10pm Thu-Sun; ◻ 14, 26, 33, 49; ⊖ 24th Street Mission

When pop seems played out, this is the dawning of the age of Aquarius Records, featuring trippy tropicalia, Swedish 'noise drone filth' and other sonic avalanches. Recent staff favorites include Indonesian guitar-tabla combos, garage-rock-meets-twee-pop Vivian Girls, and perennial honorees John Cale and Alice Cooper.

### BLACK & BLUE TATTOO
*Tattoos*

☎ 626-0770; www.black-n-blue-tattoo
.com; 381 Guerrero St; ☽ noon-7pm;
🚌 14, 22, 26, 33; Ⓜ 16th Street Mission
Take home a permanent reminder
of your SF trip courtesy of this
women-owned and -operated
tattoo parlor. Check out the artists'
work at the shop or online first
for ideas, then book a consultation with the artist whose work
interests you most. Once you've
talked over the design, you can
book your tattoo – you'll need to
show up sober, well-fed and clear-
headed for your transformation.

### CANDYSTORE COLLECTIVE
*Clothing & Accessories*

☎ 863-8143; www.candystorecollective
.com; 3153 16th St; ☽ 9am-6pm Mon-Fri;
🚌 14, 26, 33, 49; Ⓜ 16th Street Mission
Jars of Pixie Stix and tasty little
numbers for men and women by
indie designers. Swingy jersey
dresses by SF designer Deanna
Bratt go from day to night to day
again with nary a wrinkle, and
dark grey denim jeans and jackets
are the latest in stain-resistant Mission bar-crawl menswear.

### COMMUNITY THRIFT
*Vintage Home Design & Clothing*

☎ 861-4910; www.communitythrift
.bravehost.com; 623 Valencia St;
☽ 10am-6:30pm; 🚌 14, 26, 33, 49;
Ⓜ 16th Street Mission

Go ahead and gloat over scoring
major vintage pieces and new
items by local designers, because
every purchase supports local
charities. Price tags induce double-
takes: $6.99 vintage '60s teak can-
dlesticks, $5.99 '80s miniskirts, plus
$4.99 new teacups. Donate your
own unwanted stuff, and show
some love to the Community.

### DEMA
*Women's Clothing – Local Designer*

☎ 206-0500; www.godemago.com;
1038 Valencia St; ☽ 11am-7pm Mon-Fri,
noon-7pm Sat, noon-6pm Sun; 🚌 14, 22,
26, 33, 49; Ⓜ 24th Street Mission
Ride from downtown lunches to
Mission art gallery openings in
vintage-inspired chic by local gal
Dema Grimm. House specialties are
nostalgic bias-cut dresses and tie-
top blouses with buttons that look
like lemondrops. Like any original
designer, Dema's not dirt-cheap,
but you get what you pay for with
looks that yield squealed compli-
ments. Check bins and sale racks
for deals up to 80% off.

### FABRIC8
*Music, Clothing & Accessories –
Local Designers*

☎ 647-5888; www.fabric8.com; 3318
22nd St; ☽ 5-7pm Mon-Fri, 11am-7pm
Sat & Sun; 🚌 14, 26, 33, 49; Ⓜ 24th
Street Mission
Pull into this AstroTurfed-garage-
turned-indie-design-boutique for

**Idexa Stern,**
*Tattoo artist and owner, Black & Blue Tattoo (opposite)*

**Living the alt-culture dream** I came to San Francisco from Germany for the queer culture. I was studying art in Germany, but the curriculum was very traditional – and once I got my first tattoo, I knew I wanted to get behind the needle, and within a couple of years in San Francisco, I'd opened this studio.
**Intuitive tattoos** I believe that tattoos are designs you carry inside you, and my job is to make them visible on the skin. So I do a nonpermanent drawing directly on the skin, not on paper, and we adjust the details from there. I never draw that same design again – it came from that person, and belongs to them.
**From galleries to the streets** I like to take my kids to MH de Young Museum (p178), so we all get inspired to draw together. But for tattoos I collaborate with my clients, who are often artists themselves or inspired by Mission street art

a Mission hipster style overhaul. Rings sprout tiny volcanic geodes, local DJs remix one-hit-wonders from the '80s into hyphy jams, and SF Victorians become mod motifs on limited-edition FloMart T-shirts.

### 📷 GOOD VIBRATIONS
*Adult Toys*
☎ 522-5460; www.goodvibes.com; 603 Valencia St; ◷ noon-7pm Mon-Wed, noon-8pm Thu, noon-9pm Fri, 11am-9pm Sat, 11am-7pm Sun; 🚍 14, 22, 33, 49; Ⓜ 16th Street Mission

'Wait, I'm supposed to put that *where*?' The understanding salespeople in this worker-owned cooperative are used to giving rather, um, explicit instructions, so don't hesitate to ask. Check out the antique vibrators on the back wall, and imagine getting up close and personal with the one that looks like a floor waxer – then thank your stars for SF technology.

### 📷 LITTLE OTSU
*Stationery & Gifts – Local Designer*
☎ 255-7900; www.littleotsu.com; 849 Valencia St; ◷ 11:30am-7:30pm Wed-Sun; 🚍 14, 26, 33, 49; Ⓜ 16th Street Mission

Locally designed, recycled paper stationery printed with soy inks makes eco-smart gifts, especially that phone log for your slacker roommates (hint, hint). Make room for creativity in your schedule with Keri Smith's freeform 'Daily Non-Planner,' and stay in

The paper chase ends at Little Otsu

the pink with checkbook covers made of rosy paint samples.

### 📷 NEEDLES & PENS
*Gifts, Zines & DIY Supplies – Local Makers*
☎ 255-1534; www.needles-pens.com; 3253 16th St; ◷ noon-7pm; 🚍 14, 22, 33, 49; Ⓜ 16th Street Mission

Do it yourself or DIY trying. This scrappy zine/craft/how-to/art gallery delivers the inspiration to create your own magazines, rehabbed T-shirts and album covers. Nab *Dishwasher 'Zine,* Pete Jordan's continuing adventures in pot-scrubbing across all 50 states, and while supplies last, $3 local punk zines by Jay Howell.

### ▢ PAXTON GATE
*Taxidermy, Home Design & Gardening Supplies*

☎ 824-1872; www.paxtongate.com; 824 Valencia St; ☾ noon-7pm Mon-Fri, 11am-7pm Sat & Sun; ☒ 14, 26, 33, 49; ⊕ 16th Street Mission

One-stop-shopping for taxidermy home decor, gardening supplies and wall-to-wall Dada: puppets made with animal skulls, a stuffed mouse dressed like the Pope, a wicked selection of pruning shears and lollipops with worms in them.

### ▢ RAINBOW GROCERY
*Self-Catering & Sustainable Gifts, Body & Bath Products*

☎ 863-0620; www.rainbowgrocery.org; 1745 Folsom St; ☾ 9am-9pm Mon-Sun; ☒ 12, 22, 33, 49, 53; ⊕ 16th Street Mission

The legendary cooperative attracts eco-minded masses with organic, fair-trade products in bulk, a local cheese counter, and hemp-based skincare galore. Take your pick of all-natural locally made products, and there's your gift list and your conscience taken care of in one fell swoop.

### ▢ SUNHEE MOON
*Women's Clothing & Jewelry – Local Designer*

☎ 355-1800; www.sunheemoon.com; 3167 16th St; ☾ noon-7pm Mon-Fri, noon-6pm Sat & Sun; ☒ 14, 22, 33, 49; ⊕ 16th Street Mission

Minding your girlish figure so you don't have to, local designer Sunhee Moon creates flattering stretch denims and wrap dresses to make those curves work for you. You'll never need to wait for a sale, since there's always a 20–30% off rack – leaving a little something to spend on locally designed jewelry.

## 🍴 EAT

### ▯ BAR BAMBINO *Cal-Italian* $$
☎ 741-8466; www.barbambino.com; 2931 16th St; ☾ 11am-11pm Tue-Thu, 11am-midnight Fri & Sat, 4-10pm Sun; ☒ 14, 22, 26, 33, 49, 53; ⊕ 16th Street Mission

Rustic Italian fare at communal tables, right off the freeway. The olive oil tasting is a bit much at $3 to $5 an ounce, but otherwise there's no denying the appeal of this Southern Italian menu highlighting Californian produce: pasta with Mission figs and pancetta, fresh squash blossoms stuffed with sheep's milk ricotta, and pine-nut-studded eggplant polpette, each for under $15.

### ▯ BI-RITE MARKET
*Self-Catering* $

☎ 241-9760; www.biritemarket.com; 3639 18th St; ☾ 9am-9pm Mon-Fri, 9am-8pm Sat & Sun; ☒ J, 14, 26, 33, 49; ⊕ 16th Street Mission

The Tiffany's of groceries, with local artisan cheeses and

chocolates, seasonal dishes whipped up on the premises and organic local fruit displayed like jewels. Across the street is **Bi-Rite Creamery** ( ☎ 626-5600; 3692 18th St; 🕑 11am-10pm Sun-Thu, 11am-11pm Fri & Sat), an organic ice-cream shop, where the salted caramel flavor and housemade hot fudge are worth the wait in line.

### 🍴 DELFINA *Cal-Italian* $$
☎ 552-4055; www.delfinasf.com; 3621 18th St; 🕑 5:30-10pm Mon-Thu, 5:30-11pm Fri & Sat, 5-10pm Sun; 🚌 J, 14, 26, 33, 49; 🚇 16th Street Mission

The one California cuisine restaurant all of SF's picky eaters agree on. The menu is simple, seasonal and sensational: steelhead trout graced with caramelized endive, roast chicken and mashed spuds with royal trumpet mushrooms, and bucatini pasta with local sardines and chili. Reserve ahead and come prepared for a wait.

### 🍴 EL TONAYENSE TACO TRUCK *Mexican* $
☎ 550-9192; parked near 16th St & S Van Ness Ave; 🕑 from 9am; 🚌 14, 49; 🚇 16th Street Mission

The best meal on wheels in SF. Burritos and quesadillas are generous to a fault, but the $1.50 to $2 tacos are the ideal gourmet meal – especially the *al pastor* (marinated roast pork) and *lengua* (beef tongue).

### 🍴 FOREIGN CINEMA
*Californian* $$
☎ 648-7600; www.foreigncinema.com; 2534 Mission St; 🕑 6-10pm Tue-Thu, 6-11pm Fri & Sat, 11am-11pm Sat, 11am-10pm Sun; 🚌 14, 26, 48, 49; 🚇 24th Street Mission; Ⓥ

Reliably tasty dishes like seared scallops with pancetta or pork tenderloin with tart cherries and olives are the main attractions, but Luis Buñuel and François Truffaut provide an entertaining backdrop with movies screened in the courtyard and subtitles you can follow when the conversation lags.

### 🍴 LA TAQUERIA *Mexican* $
☎ 285-7117; 2889 Mission St; 🕑 11am-9pm; 🚌 14, 26, 48, 49; 🚇 24th Street Mission; Ⓥ ♿

Pure burrito bliss. There's no debatable saffron rice, spinach tortilla or mango salsa here – just perfectly grilled meats, flavorful beans and classic tomatillo or mesquite salsa inside a flour tortilla, with optional housemade spicy pickled vegetables and *crema* (crème fraîche). Burritos are a Cal-Mex invention, but Mexico-born Mission foodies claim La Taqueria tastes like home.

### 🍴 MISSION BEACH CAFÉ
*Californian* $$
☎ 861-0198; www.missionbeachcafesf .com; 198 Guerrero St; 🕑 7am-6pm

## BURRITO DOS & DON'TS

> Do have your exact order ready by the time someone behind the counter shouts 'Next!' People in line for burritos are always very hungry – that's why they're here – and liable to turn cannibal on you if they don't get to the counter right quick.
> Don't ask for extra tortilla chips. This is an insult to your burrito.
> Don't overlook the salsa bar, including pickled carrots, onions and jalapeños. Fair warning: if you pile on that stuff marked 'HOT,' your lips will be numb today and buzzing tomorrow.
> Do eat around the sides first. If you attempt a frontal attack, your *carne asada* will turn into downright carnage.
> Do unroll your tinfoil as you eat so you can keep leftovers for breakfast (you know who you are).

Mon, 7am-10pm Tue-Thu, 7am-11pm Fri, 9am-11pm Sat, 9am-10pm Sun; 🚌 J, F, 22, 26, 37, 53
Come for Blue Bottle coffee and housemade pie in the afternoon, and linger over a glass of small-production local wine. Brunches are not to be missed – chef Ryan Scott (of *Top Chef* fame) has a downright naughty way with eggs.

### 🍴 MISSION PIE
*Sustainable Pies* $

☎ 282-1500; www.pieranch.org; 2901 Mission St; 🕑 7am-9pm Mon-Thu, 7am-10pm Fri, 8am-10pm Sat, 8am-9pm Sun; 🚌 14, 49; Ⓜ 16th Street Mission; ⚹
Pie with a purpose: from savory quiche to all-American apple, all purchases support a nonprofit sustainable farm where city kids find out where their food comes from and learn about nutrition and cooking.

### 🍴 PANCHO VILLA *Mexican* $
☎ 864-8840; www.panchovillasf.com; 3071 16th St; 🕑 10am-midnight; 🚌 14, 26, 33, 49; Ⓜ 16th Street Mission
The hero of the downtrodden and burrito-deprived, delivering tinfoil-wrapped meals the girth of your forearm and a worthy condiments bar. The line moves fast going in, and as you leave, the door is held open for you and your newly acquired Pancho's paunch.

### 🍴 RANGE *Californian* $$
☎ 282-8283; www.rangesf.com; 842 Valencia St; 🕑 5:30-10pm Sun-Thu, 5:30-11pm Fri & Sat; 🚌 14, 26, 33, 49; Ⓜ 16th Street Mission
Fine American dining is alive and well within Range. The menu is seasonal Californian, prices reasonable, and style cleverly repurposed industrial chic – think coffee-rubbed pork shoulder

served with microbrewed beer from the repurposed medical supply cabinet.

### 🍴 TARTINE Bakery $

☎ 487-2600; www.tartinebakery.com; 600 Guerrero St; ☽ 8am-7pm Mon, 7:30am-7pm Tue-Wed, 7:30am-8pm Thu-Fri, 8am-8pm Sat, 9am-8pm Sun; 🚊 J, 14, 26, 33, 49; Ⓜ 16th Street Mission; Ⓥ

Lines out the door are to be expected for award-winning pumpkin tea bread, Valrhona double-chocolate cookies, and open-face *croque-monsieurs* (ham-and-cheese sandwiches). Their secret: high-quality butter, not too much sugar, and sunny sidewalk seating for leisurely digestion.

### 🍴 TORTAS LOS PICUDOS Mexican $

☎ 824-4199; 2969 24th St; ☽ 7am-8pm; 🚊 14, 26, 33, 49; Ⓜ 24th Street Mission

Mexico City's signature street food reinvented for San Francisco: sandwiches stuffed with farm-fresh veggies and healthy poached chicken, with optional pickled jalapeños. Wash it down with a strawberry smoothie or fresh-squeezed OJ, and you can skip dinner.

### 🍴 UDUPI PALACE Indian $

☎ 970-8000; www.udupipalaceca.com; 1007 Valencia St; ☽ 11:30am-10pm Mon-Thu, 11:30am-10:30pm Fri-Sun; 🚊 14, 26, 33, 49; Ⓜ 24th Street Mission

Tandoori in the Tenderloin is for novices – at Udupi, SF foodies swoon over the bright, clean flavors of South Indian dosa, a light, crispy pancake made with lentil flour dipped in mildly spicy vegetable *sambar* (soup) and coconut chutney. Don't miss the *medhu vada* (savory lentil doughnuts with *sambar* and chutney) or *bagala bhath* (yogurt rice with cucumber and nutty toasted mustard seeds).

## 🍸 DRINK

### 🍸 AMNESIA Dive Bar

☎ 970-0012; www.amnesiathebar.com; 853 Valencia St; ☽ 6pm-2am; 🚊 14, 26, 33, 49; Ⓜ 16th Street Mission

A teensy bar featuring nightly local music acts that may be playing in public for the first time, so cheer on hardworking bands and shy rappers. Check online for open-mic nights, when you can too take the stage by storm.

### 🍸 CASANOVA Cocktail Lounge

☎ 863-9328; www.casanovasf.com; 527 Valencia St; ☽ 4pm-2am; 🚊 14, 22, 33, 49; Ⓜ 16th Street Mission

A couple of these martinis under the star-shaped lights, and you'll definitely be starry-eyed. The black velvet paintings and plastic fireplace will suddenly strike you as design genius, the DJs serving up grrrl punk, '70s glam and sitar rock worthy of worship, and the monthly kissing contest the best excuse for hooking up since Spin the Bottle.

## ☿ ELIXIR
*Sustainable Cocktail Lounge*
☎ 552-1633; www.elixirsf.com; 3200 16th St; ☿ 3pm-2am Mon-Fri, noon-2am Sat, 11am-midnight Sun; 🚊 14, 26, 33, 39; Ⓜ 16th Street Mission
Drinking is good for the environment at SF's first certified green bar, with your choice of organic, green and even biodynamic cocktails. Invent your own with a consult from the resident mixologist or go with Rancho Ancho No 2, with organic peach and lime juices, 4 Copas organic tequila and ancho chili. Drink-for-a-cause nights encourage imbibing, with proceeds supporting local charities.

## ☿ LATIN AMERICAN CLUB
*Cocktail Lounge*
☎ 647-2732; 3286 22nd St; ☿ 6pm-2am Sun-Thu, 5pm-2am Fri & Sat; 🚊 14, 26, 48, 49; Ⓜ 24th Street Mission
Too spiffy to be a dive, too cheap for high-maintenance dates, just right for killer margaritas and $6 cocktails with friends who still understand you when you slur. Come early to grab window seats and the bartender's attention, but stand often to make sure you still can.

## ☿ LEXINGTON CLUB
*Lesbian Bar*
☎ 863-2052; www.lexingtonclub.com; 3464 19th St; ☿ 5pm-2am Mon-Thu, 3pm-2am Fri & Sat; 🚊 14, 26, 33, 49; Ⓜ 16th Street Mission
Also known as the Hex, because the odds are eerily high that you'll develop a crush on your ex-girlfriend's hot new girlfriend here over strong drink, pinball and tattoo comparisons – go on, live dangerously at SF's most famous/notorious full-time lesbian bar.

## ☿ MEDJOOL *Cocktail Lounge*
☎ 550-9055; www.medjoolsf.com; 2522 Mission St; ☿ 5-10pm Mon-Thu, 5pm-2am Fri & Sat; 🚊 14, 26, 48, 49; Ⓜ 24th Street Mission
The best panorama in town that doesn't involve the Golden Gate Bridge is Medjool's rooftop view of downtown from above old Mission cinema marquees. Go early for sunsets and prime spots by heat lamps, and get your orders in for well-muddled mojitos and tasty Middle Eastern mezze platters.

## ☿ RITUAL COFFEE ROASTERS
*Café*
☎ 641-1024; www.ritualroasters.com; 1026 Valencia St; ☿ 8am-5pm Mon-Sat, 10am-5pm Sun; 🚊 14, 26, 48, 49; Ⓜ 24th Street Mission
House-roasted brews with organic milk and free wi-fi make lines and hovering for a spot among legions

of MacBook users worthwhile. Eavesdrop on group art projects and activist meetings in progress, and you could be privy to kite-flying performance art and the latest antiwar protest.

### WILD SIDE WEST *Lesbian Bar*
☎ 647-3099; 424 Cortland Ave; 🕙 1pm-2am; 🚌 14, 24, 49, 67

The wildest thing about this bar are the plants bursting out of a bathtub in the backyard and the fierce games of Raiders of the Lost Ark pinball indoors – otherwise, it's a mellow scene of women and their occasional male sidekick hanging out on porch swings and striking up the odd banjo tune.

When the fog rolls in, pull up a seat at the sewing machine table by the fireplace and stay awhile.

### ZEITGEIST *Beer Bar*
☎ 255-7505; www.myspace.com/zeitgeistsf; 199 Valencia St; 🕙 9am-2am; 🚌 14, 22, 33, 49; 🕓 16th Street Mission

On balmy Mission nights, all of alternative SF converges here for pitchers at communal picnic tables in the gravel-covered beer garden. Tough lady bartenders dish out sass to bikers who hesitate over the choice of 30 draft beers, and the Tamale Lady usually shows up around 10pm or 11pm to cure stoners' late-night munchies.

Get in the spirit at Zeitgeist

# ⭐ PLAY

## ⭐ BAY AREA VIDEO COALITION
*Film Screenings & Classes*

**BAVC; ☎ 861-3282; www.bavc.org; 2727 Mariposa St; ☽ 9am-8pm Mon-Thu, 9am-6pm Fri, 10am-6pm Sat & Sun; 🚌 12, 22, 27, 33; Ⓜ 16th Street Mission**

So you want to turn your SF adventure into a podcast, video game or full-length documentary? Completely possible, thanks to BAVC (pronounced Bay-Vac). One-day seminars cover video art theory, digital video production techniques and screenwriting essentials.

## ⭐ EL RIO *Bar & Live Music*

**☎ 282-3325; www.elriosf.com; 3158 Mission St; cover $3-8; ☽ 5pm-2am Mon-Thu, 1pm-2am Fri-Sun; 🚌 14, 26; Ⓜ 24th Street Mission**

Where all SF goes to get its groove on to free-form, funky DJ beats from around the world. Regulars of every conceivable ethnicity and orientation mean good company, no judgments and extra fabulousness. Arrive early for prime garden seating, the 'Totally Fabulous Happy Hour' from 4pm to 9pm Tuesday to Friday, and free oysters on the half-shell Fridays at 5:30pm.

## ⭐ ELBO ROOM *Live Music*

**☎ 552-7788; www.elbo.com; 647 Valencia St; cover $5-8; ☽ 5pm-2am; 🚌 14, 26, 33, 49; Ⓜ 16th Street Mission**

Funny name, because there isn't much to speak of in the upstairs stage area on show nights. The calendar is especially strong on jazz, funk and soul, but come before the show if you want to take advantage of $2 pints between 5pm and 9pm.

## ⭐ INTERSECTION FOR THE ARTS *Art & Theater, Jazz & Dance*

**☎ 626-2787; www.theintersection.org; 446 Valencia St; tickets $9-20; 🚌 14, 22, 33, 49; Ⓜ 16th Street Mission**

SF's favorite interdisciplinary art space since 1965 works on many levels, from exciting improvisational jazz, works-in-progress literary readings and experimental theater and dance downstairs to fearless art shows in the upstairs gallery that aren't afraid to take on big ideas like propaganda. The ambidextrous space offers art workshops; check out the website for details.

## ⭐ MAKE-OUT ROOM
*Live Music & Spoken Word*

**☎ 647-2888; www.makeoutroom.com; 3225 22nd St; live music cover $6; ☽ 6pm-2am; 🚌 14, 26, 48, 49; Ⓜ 24th Street Mission**

Between the generous pours and Pabst beer specials, the Make-Out has convinced otherwise sane people to leap onstage and read from their teen journals for Get Mortified nights, and sing along to oddly infectious bands ranging from punk fiddle to ukulele honky-tonk. Velvet curtains and round booths add class to the evening's entertainment, though it's standing-room-only for the popular Progressive Reading Series.

### ⭐ MARSH *Theater & Comedy*
☎ 641-0235; www.themarsh.org; 1062 Valencia St; tickets $15-22; ⏱ shows 8pm Thu-Sun; 🚌 14, 26, 48, 49; Ⓜ 24th Street Mission

A singular breeding ground for SF's comedy and dramatic talent, with one-act, one-person shows, and one-off stagings of works in progress. The audience encircles the performers, so come early for frontal views.

### ⭐ MIGHTY *Dance Club*
☎ 762-0151; www.mighty119.com; 119 Utah St; cover $10; ⏱ 10pm-4am Fri-Sun; 🚌 9, 10, 19, 22, 27, 33, 53, 90; Ⓜ 24th Street Mission

Weekly house parties book high-caliber DJs, yet no one cops an attitude – it's just a Mighty fine time with three long bars, a vast dance floor and a getting-to-know-you balcony.

### ⭐ MISSION CULTURAL CENTER *Art & Classes*
MCC; ☎ 821-1155; www.missioncultural center.org; 2868 Mission St; ⏱ 10am-4pm Tue-Sat; 🚌 14, 26, 48, 49; Ⓜ 24th Street Mission

Samba like you mean it at the MCC or join a class in flamenco, salsa or 'Latin belly dancing' – the teachers are friendly and the crowds of all ages and abilities. If you get an idea for a protest poster from the Mission streets, you can make it happen at the MCC's printmaking studio and workshops.

### ⭐ ODC THEATER
*Dance & Classes*
☎ 863-9834; www.odcdance.org; 3153 17th St; ⏱ box office 2-5pm Wed-Sat, shows 8pm Wed-Sat, 7pm Sun; 🚌 14, 22, 33, 49; Ⓜ 16th Street Mission

Risky and rigorous, the ODC's dance troupe has kept audiences riveted from September to December for the past 30-plus years, and the ODC Theater offers modern dance shows year-round featuring local and international artists. Classes are available in the newly expanded facility; check the website for details.

### ⭐ RITE SPOT CAFÉ *Live Music*
☎ 552-6066; www.ritespotcafe.net; 2099 Folsom St; ⏱ 6pm-2am; 🚌 12, 22, 33

A dive with a difference: it's a supper club with white tablecloths and experimental bands in the corner, from Gypsy jazz to Toshio Hirano (aka the Japanese Jimmie Rodgers). Staff is casual and friendly, though stern with loud talkers during sets.

### ⭐ ROXIE CINEMA *Cinema*
☎ 863-1087; www.roxie.com; 3117 16th St; tickets $8; 🚌 14, 22, 33, 49; 🚇 16th Street Mission

A neighborhood cinema with international clout for helping distribute and launch Hong Kong film *Stateside* and showing controversial films and documentaries banned elsewhere. Film buffs watch this space to see what's next: Matt Groening might show up again to introduce a *Simpsons* film festival, and the audience will probably throw popcorn at the screen during the annual live, audience-participation screening of the Academy Awards.

### ⭐ THEATER ARTAUD
*Dance & Theater*
☎ 626-4370; www.artaud.org/theatre; 450 Florida St; tickets $15-25; 🕑 shows

8pm Tue-Sat, 7pm Sun; 🚌 14, 22, 27, 33, 49; 🚇 16th Street Mission

Traipsing across this stage are local, national and international theater and dance troupes, ranging from one-offs like an audience-input performance by Miranda July to the annual Black Choreographers Showcase.

### ⭐ THEATRE RHINOCEROS
*Theater & Comedy*
☎ 861-5079; www.therhino.org; 2926 16th St; tickets $15-25; 🕑 shows 8pm Wed-Sat, 3pm or 7pm Sun; 🚌 14, 22, 26, 33, 49; 🚇 16th Street Mission

SF's premier queer theater venue and winner of a 2008 GLAAD Award, with original productions ranging from the campy, cross-dressing *Moby Dick, the Musical* to the soul-searching *His Heart Belongs to Me,* about one man's tailspin after the untimely death of his partner.

# >CASTRO

Talk about a makeover: this frumpy Scandinavian-Irish neighborhood became a glamorous symbol of gay freedom when some hippies ditched the Haight for Victorian fixer-uppers with walk-in closets to come out of in style. Within a few years of moving into the place, the Castro's gay community had established businesses and community services, and even elected Harvey Milk as the nation's first gay official.

When a mysterious illness hit the Castro in the early 1980s, loss cast its long shadow over the neighborhood. But the determined intervention of HIV/AIDS activists saved untold lives, establishing global standards for humane, life-saving treatment and prevention. To support this heroic effort, visit Under One Roof (p137) and the Human Rights Campaign (p136).

Today the rainbow flag once again flies high over the neighborhood. The Castro's political muscle makes Schwarzenegger look like a chump, mobilizing GLBT voters nationwide to come out wherever they are and show some Pride at the polls.

## CASTRO

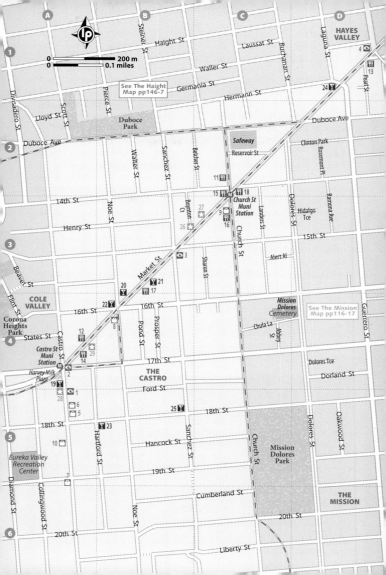

NEIGHBORHOODS

CASTRO

#  SEE

## CASTRO THEATRE

☎ 621-6120; www.thecastrotheatre
.com; 429 Castro St; tickets adult/senior
& child under 12yr $9.50/7; 🚇 F, K, L, M,
24, 33; ♿

The best organ on view in the Castro on a Saturday night, and that's saying something. The mighty instrument rises from the orchestra pit to cheers and whistles, pounding out show tunes until your classic movie or avant-garde film starts. Every night here is audience participation night: singalongs are a given, Ed Wood retro movie trailers bring on the snark, and the crowd chants along with Judy Garland: 'We're not in Kansas anymore!' Seats under the giant chandelier are the last to be filled in this seismic town, but the place gets packed for film fests and showings of *Milk,* starring Sean Penn as SF Supervisor Harvey Milk (filmed right here in the Castro). See also p21.

## F LINE STREETCAR

☎ 673-6844; www.sfmuni.com; adult/
concession $1.50/0.50; ♿ 🚶

All aboard the Pride Express, the most leisurely way to get out and about SF. Hop the refurbished antique streetcar of your desire: whether you prefer the orange Milan model Castro-bound or a green Bostonian headed straight downtown, or might consider going both ways, this is one city where your preference can always be accommodated.

## FEMINA POTENS

☎ 864-1558; www.feminapotens.com;
2199 Market St; 🕑 noon-6pm Thu-Sun;
🚇 12, 22, 33; Ⓜ Church St

---

### SAN FRANCISCO FILM FAVORITES

> *All About Eve* (1950) Bette Davis packs out the Castro Theatre, with the entire audience chanting classic one-liners: 'Fasten your seatbelts – it's going to be a bumpy night!'
> *City Lights* (1931) Filmed in San Francisco by star/director Charlie Chaplin, this poetic silent masterpiece has SF's landmark bookstore (p47) named in its honor.
> *The Conversation* (1974) Mall-like Union Square never seemed so sinister as when Gene Hackman spies on an unwitting couple, only to get stalked by Harrison Ford and Robert Duvall himself.
> *Harold and Maude* (1971) The ultimate May–December romance features metaphorically apt SF locations: the eternal spring of the Conservatory of Flowers and the fabulous ruin of the Sutro Baths.
> *Vertigo* (1958) The Golden Gate Bridge sets the stage for dizzying drama when acrophobic Jimmy Stewart watches Kim Novak leap into the bay at Fort Point.

You don't need to slip into a phone booth to explore new identities in the Castro – just saunter into Femina Potens. By day the gallery showcases the talents of women and transgender artists with queer travel photography shows and an Accessible Art Store of items under $100 – but by night the scene is transformed by the Queer Philosophy Salon, Sizzle literary erotica reading series and Open Eyes film screenings, bringing balance and perspective to the XY-centric Castro scene.

### ◉ SAN FRANCISCO LESBIAN GAY BISEXUAL TRANSGENDER COMMUNITY CENTER

☎ 865-5555; www.sfcenter.org; 1800 Market St; ☼ noon-10pm Mon-Fri, 9am-10pm Sat; 🚌 F, J, K, L, M, 6, 7, 71; ♿ 👶

'The Other City Hall' is home to indispensable nonprofits and host to same-sex wedding celebrations, job fairs, drag showcases, political rallies and other pursuits of happiness – it even provides free childcare services to parents during events. The glorious historic aqua Victorian has been opened up in the middle and outfitted with a sheer glass front, like a closet propped permanently open to let in the light.

# 🛍 SHOP

### ▢ A DIFFERENT LIGHT BOOKSTORE Books

☎ 431-0891; www.adlbooks.com; 489 Castro St; ☼ 10am-11pm; 🚌 F, K, L, M, 24, 33

SF's premier queer literary venue, hosting revelatory reading series, open mics, bear calendar release parties, gay relationship advice book launches, magazine soirees and coming out stories since 1979. One-stop-shopping for racy Victor Decimus vampire novels, Armistad Maupin's latest *Tales of the City* sequel, children's books for kids of GLBT parents, queer theory anthologies and a how-to book with a suggestive subtitle that says it all: *A Work of Non-Friction*.

### ▢ CLIFF'S VARIETY
*DIY Supplies*

☎ 431-5365; www.cliffsvariety.com; 479 Castro St; ☼ 8:30am-8pm Mon-Fri, 9:30am-8pm Sat, 11am-6pm Sun; 🚌 F, K, L, M, 24, 33; ♿ 👶

When your theme party or costume requires serious construction, Cliff's has the essentials: lumber, silver glitter paint, jars of rubber nuns, beeswax candles and more cocktail toothpicks than anyone can safely use in a lifetime. A neighborhood landmark since 1936 with window displays as chic as Barneys New York, only with hardware.

## 🏠 HUMAN RIGHTS CAMPAIGN ACTION CENTER & STORE *Gifts*
☎ 431-2200; www.hrc.org; 600 Castro St; ⏰ 9am-5pm Mon-Fri; 🚊 F, K, L, M, 24, 33; ♿

Make more than just a fierce fashion statement in a signature HRC tee designed by *Project Runway*'s Christian Siriano, Marc Jacobs, Heatherette and other fashion-forward-thinkers, with proceeds supporting GLBT civil rights initiatives. While you're here, you can write a postcard to a politician, sign up for equal rights email action alerts or just show some love for the volunteers for getting out the vote.

## 🏠 KENNETH WINGARD
*Home Design – Local Designer*
☎ 431-6900; www.kennethwingard .com; 2319 Market St; ⏰ 10am-8pm Mon-Sat, 11am-7pm Sun; 🚊 F, K, L, M, 24, 33; ♿

Upgrade from IKEA with dashingly handsome home design courtesy of SF's own Kenneth Wingard. Bachelor pads get a boost from sunburst mirrors, chocolate leather desk sets and tiki-inspired pillows in aquatic colors – plus goldfish-silkscreened Supermaggie tees so you can blend in with your mod new decor.

It's a mod, mod, mod, mod world at Kenneth Wingard

NEIGHBORHOODS

CASTRO

### ☐ SUI GENERIS
*Vintage Men's Clothing*
☎ 436-9661; 218 Church St; ☽ noon-7pm Tue-Thu, noon-8pm Fri & Sat, noon-4pm Sun; 🚇 F, J, K, L, M, N, 22, 37
Even guys who thought they'd never go back in the closet crowd into this walk-in closet of a boutique, packed with rakish fedoras, fly windbreakers, retro-butch Pendleton wool shirts and other choice vintage. The selection is best for men who can squeeze into small to medium sizes – today's buff Castro boys have access to more protein powders and personal trainers than they did back in the '50s.

### ☐ UNDER ONE ROOF
*Gifts & Home Design*
☎ 503-2300; www.underoneroof.org; 518A Castro St; ☽ 10am-8pm Mon-Sat, Sun 11am-7pm; 🚇 F, K, L, M, 24, 33; ♿ ⚥
All the fabulous gift ideas under this roof are donated by local designers and businesses, so AIDS service organizations get 100% of the proceeds from your indispensable elephant tape dispenser and adorable Jonathan Adler vase. Those sweet sales clerks are volunteers, so you can thank them for raising – get this – $11 million to date.

## 🍴 EAT

### 🍴 BURGERMEISTER *Burgers* $
☎ 437-2874; 138 Church St; www.burgermeistersf.com; ☽ 11am-midnight Mon-Sat; 🚇 F, J, K, L, M, N, 22, 37; ♿ Ⓥ ⚥
Just when *Supersize Me* turned you off Mickey D's forever, Burger-Meister reels you back in with juicy

---

#### REAL BEEFCAKE
**BurgerMeister** (above) Half a pound of Niman Ranch beef from coastal cows put out to pasture for a low-stress California lifestyle. Optional fixings: fries, grilled onions, blue/cheddar cheese, bacon, a range of mustards and steak sauces, half an avocado (oof, too much). Cheap, decadent and satisfying, like a good Friday-night date.
**Magnolia** (p152) Grilled Prather Ranch beef. Optional fixings: fries, organic green salad, local Swiss/cheddar/blue cheese, bacon, beer made in-house. Pleasing and reliable midrange burger as long as you don't mind Magnolia's brewery smell, which might remind you of that time you shacked up with a sports fan...
**Zuni Café** (p96) Mesquite-grilled, sustainably farmed prime beef gone upscale on rosemary focaccia. Optional fixings: Portobello mushrooms, housemade pickled onions, gorgonzola/Gruyère cheese, greens, aioli. Shoestring fries sold separately; burger isn't always available between 6pm and 10pm. High-end, high-maintenance and as demanding as dating a personal trainer, but worth it.

NEIGHBORHOODS

CASTRO

grilled patties of pasture-raised, hormone-free Niman Ranch beef. Skeptical Nebraskans and erstwhile vegetarians are among the regulars ordering the slippery house special with grilled onions, blue cheese and mesclun greens, best eaten two-handed.

### 🍴 CATCH Seafood $$
☎ 437-2874; www.catchsf.com; 2362 Market St; 🕑 11:30am-3pm & 5:30-9:30pm Mon-Thu, 11:30am-3pm & 5.30-11pm Fri, 11:30am-3:30pm & 5:30-11pm Sat, 11:30am-3:30pm & 5:30-9:30pm Sun; 🚇 F, K, L, M, 24, 33

As in, 'of the day' – monkfish, Dungeness crab, oysters – not necessarily a reference to that silver fox by the fireplace. The crowd consists almost entirely of men in turtlenecks and leather jackets accessorized with same, but like the menu, the conversation can get unexpectedly saucy. Try the vat-sized cioppino, and maneuver away from the piano to hear the hot dish being served by fellow diners. Book ahead.

### 🍴 DESTINO Nuevo Latino $$
☎ 552-4451; www.destinosf.com; 1815 Market St; 🕑 5-10pm Mon-Thu, 5-11pm Fri & Sat, 11am-2pm & 5-10pm Sun; 🚇 F, J, K, L, M, N, 6, 7, 71; ♿ 👶

Generous Peru-Cal small plates full of big ideas: ahi ceviche with organic mango, avocado and achiote oil; quinoa salad laced with Meyer

lemon; and purple potatoes with zesty Huancaina (Peruvian cheese) sauce. The white sangria with chardonnay, grapefruit and pineapple, and freshly baked Peruvian butter cookies with *dulce de leche* (milk-caramel) filling will make you want to worship at the altars on the wall here on a regular basis.

### 🍴 FRISEE Californian $$
☎ 558-1616; www.friseerestaurant .com; 2367 Market St; 🕑 11am-9pm; 🚇 F, K/T, L, M, N, S, 24, 33, 35, 37; Ⓥ

Fresh main-size salads featuring very little of the namesake garnish in favor of more substantial mesclun greens, grilled fish or artisan cheese, plus slow-roasted grass-fed meats or nut-rich vegan menu options for the $35 three-course weekday prix fixe. Tasty stuff, though the 'sustainable light fare' approach could use further thought: everything on the menu is organic or responsibly harvested, yet many ingredients and wines are flown in. But they're new yet, and working out the local sourcing details – give them an encouraging nudge.

### 🍴 HOME New American $$
☎ 503-0333; www.home-sf.com; 2100 Market St; 🕑 5-10pm Mon-Thu, 5-11pm Fri, 10am-2pm & 5-11pm Sat, 10am-2pm & 5-10pm Sun; 🚇 F, J, K, L, M, 22, 37, 33; ♿ Ⓥ 👶

There's no place like it, especially if you enjoy your comfort food

There's no place like Home

fireside with a $3 happy-hour margarita and a gaggle of gym-fresh men. Midwestern favorites get an upgrade here: mac 'n' cheese with sneaky cayenne zing, roasted chicken spiked with rosemary, butter lettuce salads with Point Reyes blue cheese dressing. The savvy set arrives before 6pm midweek for the Chef's Early Bird Special: starter, main and a glass of wine for $13. Book ahead.

### 🍽 SPARKY'S *Diner* $
☎ 626-8666; 242 Church St; ☽ 24hr;
🚊 F, J, K, L, M, N, 22, 37
By day it's a family-friendly burger joint, but around midnight Sparky's becomes the unofficial drunk tank of the Mission and Castro, with regulars stumbling in their leather chaps (that single step at the door gets everyone), divas trailing boas demanding home fries and omelets, plenty of Tabasco and grease, and the occasional impromptu sing-along.

### 🍽 SUSHI TIME *Sushi* $$
☎ 552-2280; 2275 Market St; ☽ 5:30-10:30pm Mon-Sat, 5-9pm Sun; 🚊 F, J, K, L, M, N, 22, 24, 37; Ⓥ
Devour sashimi in the tiny glassed-in patio like a shark in an aquarium or nosh on Barbie, GI Joe and Hello Kitty rolls at this tiny, surreal sushi spot hidden below a bookstore and gym, Tokyo-style. Several vegan, raw-food menu options make this six-table eatery a good place to cozy up to a Hollywood starlet. Happy-hour specials run from 5pm to 6:30pm.

### 🍽 WOODHOUSE FISH CO
*Seafood* $$
☎ 437-2722; www.woodhousefish.com; 2073 Market St; ☽ 11:30am-9:30pm Mon-Thu, 11:30am-10pm Fri & Sat, 11:30am-9:30pm Sun; 🚊 F, K/T, L, M, N, S, 24, 33, 35, 37
Bicoastal seafood at the Castro/Mission border, with a classic tiled New England diner look, service with West Coast sass, and East Coast/West Coast menu

loyalties divided between the fried Ipswich clams and the Pescadero artichoke overflowing with local Dungeness crab (in season) and bay shrimp – but since this is SF, you can always go both ways. The restaurant is still working on local sourcing for East Coast recipes, so sustainability-minded diners should ask the servers for best menu recommendations.

# ☥ DRINK

## ☥ 440 CASTRO *Gay Bar*
☎ 621-8732; www.the440.com; 440 Castro St; ☽ noon-2am; ☒ F, K, L, M, 24, 33
When you need a drink, some understanding, and a guy willing to strip, come to the 440. This is your average friendly neighborhood bar, if your neighborhood consists mostly of bears (burly gay men) wearing nothing but boxer briefs and boots on Mondays and taking advantage of $2 to $2.50 beer specials most nights.

## ☥ CAFÉ FLORE *Café & Bar*
☎ 621-8579; www.cafeflore.com; 2298 Market St; ☽ 7am-11pm Mon-Fri, 7am-midnight Sat & Sun; ☒ F, K, L, M, 24, 33; ☥
The see-and-be-seen, indoor-outdoor corner café at the center of the gay universe. Eavesdrop on blind dates and post-gym dish sessions with a bracing cappuccino or knee-weakening absinthe. Wi-fi is on the house and free entertainment is provided by your fellow patrons, who'll interject opinions on everything from string theory to your ex-boyfriend.

## ☥ LIME *Cocktail Lounge*
☎ 621-5256; www.lime-sf.com; 2247 Market St; ☽ 5pm-midnight Mon-Thu, 5pm-1am Fri, 11am-3pm & 5pm-1am Sat, 10:30am-3pm & 5pm-midnight Sun; ☒ F, J, K, L, M, N, 22, 24, 37, 33; ☥
Meet George Jetson, his ex Judy, and his new partner Joe, all getting chummy over the signature citrus cocktails. Perch atop the outer-space fungi that passes for seating and slurp a key lime martini or two amid cute Castro boys and their strictly platonic girlfriends. At brunch, order the bottomless $6 mimosa at your own risk.

## ☥ LOOKOUT *Gay Bar*
☎ 431-0306; www.lookoutsf.com; 3600 16th St; ☽ 3pm-2am Mon-Fri, 1pm-2am Sat & Sun; ☒ F, K, L, M, 24, 33, 35, 37
When locals call this corner balcony bar a magnet for twinks (fresh-faced boy-toys), they're not kidding: one corn-fed, Chuck Taylor-sporting cutie arrived carrying the latest Harry Potter.

Passable pizza and weekend DJ sets are served piping hot, so you could conceivably spend all day Sunday among the shirtless boys at Jock.

### MOBY DICK *Gay Bar*
☎ 626-9320; www.mobydicksf.com; 4049 18th St; ⏰ 2pm-2am Mon-Fri, noon-2am Sat & Sun; 🚌 F, K, L, M, 24, 33; ♿

Put the naughty back in nautical at this dive bar complete with sharks circling the pool table, the occasional sailor at the bar, and two-for-one frozen margaritas that'll shiver your timbers. On the off chance you missed the double entendre here, check out the aquarium: tropical fish flit blithely past something that looks like a great white whale, but, um, isn't.

### ORBIT ROOM
*Cocktail Lounge*
☎ 252-9525; 1900 Market St; ⏰ 7am-midnight Mon-Thu, 7am-2am Fri & Sat, 8am-midnight Sun; 🚌 F, J, K, L, M, N, 22, 24, 33, 37

The cocktail bar of choice for SF's gourmet set, with standing-room-only crowds gloating over seasonal custom cocktails. Bartenders keep busy inventing their next concoction with house-infused spirits and fresh-squeezed juices, so don't go expecting bar banter or speedy service – just a tasty drink so original it doesn't even have a name yet.

### SAMOVAR TEA LOUNGE
*Tea Lounge*
☎ 626-4700; www.samovartea.com; 498 Sanchez St; ⏰ 10am-11pm; 🚌 F, K, L, M, 24, 33; ♿

Anytime is high time for iron pots of tea with scintillating side dishes, especially pumpkin dumplings, honeycomb with blue cheese, and chocolate brownies with green-tea mousse. This is the hangout of choice for Castro's clean and sober crowd, and what a coincidence, the tea costs about the same as a cocktail.

## ⭐ PLAY
 **THE BAR** *Gay Club*
☎ 626-7220; www.thebarsf.com; 456 Castro St; ⏰ 4pm-2am Mon-Fri, 2pm-2am Sat & Sun; 🚌 F, K, L, M, 24, 33; ♿

You haven't been to the Castro until you've passed The Bar. Red lights, frozen cosmos and $4 drink specials set the scene, and when the DJ serves the house with a side of funk, it's every man for himself on the dance floor. Despite the shirts-on policy, overheated hotties have taken to stripping down to their socks right outside the door, like a porn-star airport security check.

## HEY LADIES...

All dressed up and no place to go with your lady-lovin' lady friends? SF will fix that. San Francisco's premier lesbian bar is the **Lexington Club** (p127), also known as the Lex or the Hex, because the chances of running into an ex by the pool table here are that high. At **Wild Side West** (p128) the women are out among the palms, birdbaths and strumming guitarists in the backyard – though straight girlfriends and little brothers or other estrogen-challenged company are perfectly acceptable accessories here. You'll hear laments about women's bars turning into trendy gay/hipster hotspots with a token lesbian night in SF, just like you do anywhere else, but the **Rickshaw Stop** (p99), **The Café** (below) and **El Rio** (p129) manage to maintain lesbian street creds while branching out in gay/bi/trans/straight/whatever directions. And when SF's historic gay clubs throw a dance party for the ladies, look out: Fridays at **The Stud** (p113) and Saturdays at **The EndUp** (p113), they sure know how to show a girl a good time. For events ranging from political rallies to DIY erotica nights, check the bulletin boards at the **Women's Building** (p119) and the schedule at **Femina Potens** (p134). For good clean family fun, join the stroller parade on 24th St in Noe Valley with umpteen other proud moms.

### ⭐ THE CAFÉ GLBT Club

☎ 861-3846; www.cafesf.com; 2369 Market St; ⏰ 4pm-2am Mon-Fri, 3pm-2am Sat, 2pm-2am Sun; 🚊 F, J, K, L, M, 24, 33; ♿

The pool tables were recently replaced because go-go dancers tore them to shreds – uh-huh, it's that kind of place, has been for decades. The eclectic mix sometimes lapses into interminable house numbers; grab a gimlet and pace yourself until the samba whistles kick in. Anyone in hot pants is welcome on the dance floor, though Fridays favor fellas and every third Saturday shows lesbians the love. Cover can be up to $8, but two-for-one drinks from 5pm to 9pm compensates.

### ⭐ CAFÉ DU NORD/SWEDISH AMERICAN HALL

*Live Music, Comedy & Spoken Word*

☎ 861-5016; www.cafedunord.com; 2170 Market St; bar admission free, shows $10-20; ⏰ 7pm or 8pm-2am except when closed for private events; 🚊 F, J, K, L, M, N, 22, 37; ♿

Push past the curtains to the downstairs 1930s speakeasy for front-row dinner seating (by reservation), and enjoy a burger and beer practically sitting in the laps of the rockers, chanteuses, comedians and raconteurs that perform here nightly. Go early for snappy banter with budding novelists at the bar, and stay late for pulled-on-stage performances by the regular crowd of off-duty musicians. The Hall upstairs features bigger acts, balcony seating and Scandinavian woodworking, but no booze – hard to argue with these acoustics though.

⭐ **MINT** *Karaoke*
☎ **626-4726; www.themint.net; 1942 Market St;** 🕐 **4pm-2am;** 🚌 **F, J, K, L, M, N, 22, 37;** ♿

More heart-rending ballads and off-pitch cringes than a first-round *American Idol* audition, plus strong drinks and an audience that will cheer you on as long as you put your back into that Gwen Stefani number. The most powerful individual in SF is surely the Mint's karaoke maestro, who with flattery, flirting and tips might let you onstage to apply your signature vocal stylings to 'Baby Got Back.' This crowd is serious about show tunes, though, so prepare to have your best Barbara Streisand upstaged by a banker with a boa and a mean falsetto.

# >HAIGHT

Guy walks down Haight St dressed as a sunflower, holding a sunflower, wearing a paper-plate mask covered with sunflower seeds. Passersby grin, but since this is the Haight, no one assumes he's some kind of corporate mascot or headed to a costume party. He's just another guy doing his thing, bringing some flower power to a foggy Monday at the corner of Haight and Ashbury.

This legendary intersection was the place to be in the psychedelic '60s, and certain flower-child habits have stuck since the Summer of Love. This is where a mysterious continental drift brings rebels and misfits, and the clock overhead always reads 4:20 – better known in herbal circles as International Bong-Hit Time. But the hedonist Haight has also built a serious rep for green politics, drug rehabs, community nonprofits and potent coffee. Skaters and hipsters cruise downhill past flamboyant Victorians to the Lower Haight between Divis(adero) and Webster, for local-designer hoodies, dive bars and cheap eats. But if you'd rather be a sunflower, dude, the Haight is the place to do it.

## HAIGHT

### 🔵 SEE
| | | |
|---|---|---|
| Alamo Square | 1 | F2 |
| Grateful Dead House | 2 | C4 |
| Haight Ashbury Food Program | 3 | B4 |

### 📷 SHOP
| | | |
|---|---|---|
| Ambiance | 4 | C4 |
| Amoeba Records | 5 | A4 |
| Aqua Surf Shop | 6 | B4 |
| Bound Together Anarchist Book Collective | 7 | D4 |
| Braindrops | 8 | D4 |
| Coco-Luxe | 9 | B4 |
| Doe | 10 | G3 |

| | | |
|---|---|---|
| Piedmont | 11 | C4 |
| SFO Snowboarding & FTC Skateboarding | 12 | B4 |
| Upper Playground | 13 | G3 |
| Wasteland | 14 | B4 |

### 🍴 EAT
| | | |
|---|---|---|
| Axum | 15 | F3 |
| Cole Valley Cafe | 16 | B4 |
| Escape from New York Pizza | 17 | B4 |
| Little Star Pizza | 18 | E1 |
| Magnolia | 19 | C4 |
| Rosamunde Sausage Grill | 20 | G3 |
| Uva Enoteca | 21 | G3 |

### 🍸 DRINK
| | | |
|---|---|---|
| Aub Zam Zam | 22 | B4 |
| Coffee to the People | 23 | C4 |
| Mad Dog in the Fog | 24 | G3 |
| Madrone | 25 | E2 |
| Noc Noc | 26 | G3 |
| Toronado | 27 | G3 |

### ⭐ PLAY
| | | |
|---|---|---|
| Booksmith | 28 | B4 |
| Club Deluxe | 29 | C4 |
| Red Vic Movie House | 30 | B4 |

Please see over for map

# ◎ SEE

## ◎ ALAMO SQUARE

**Cnr Hayes & Scott Sts;** 🚊 **21, 22, 24**
SF's finest restaurants can't provide views as spectacular as the picnic tables atop Alamo Square park overlooking downtown and facing Postcard Row, a lineup of pastel Victorian 'Painted Lady' houses on Steiner St with gingerbread detailing and frosting flourishes that'll leave you craving dessert. Stroll around the square between Steiner and Scott, and you'll spot Painted Ladies with more outrageous drag-diva color palettes. Make it to the crest of the hill, and you'll find old shoes creatively reused as planters among the windswept pines.

## ◎ GRATEFUL DEAD HOUSE

**710 Ashbury St;** 🚊 **6, 7, 33, 37, 71**
Hippies may dimly recognize this candy-colored Victorian from the

## MAKING QUEEN VICTORIA BLUSH

The city's signature architectural style is usually called 'Victorian,' but demure Queen Victoria would surely be shocked by the eccentric architecture perpetrated in her name in San Francisco. True Victorians tend to be drab, stately, earth-toned structures – nothing like San Franciscan 'Painted Ladies' with candy-jar color palettes, lavish gingerbread woodworking dripping off steeply peaked roofs, and gilded stucco garlands swagging huge, look-at-me bay windows. Only a fraction of the older buildings you'll see in SF were built during Victoria's 1837–1901 reign, and the rest are cheerfully inauthentic San Franciscan takes on a vaguely Anglo-Continental style.

Of the 19th-century buildings that survived the 1906 fire and earthquake, many belong to other architectural categories.

> Italianate (1860s–80s): Around Jackson Square, you can still see original Italianate brick buildings with elevated false facades capped with jutting cornices, a straight roofline and graceful arches over tall windows.

> Stick (1880s): In the Lower Haight and Pacific Heights, you'll notice some squared-off Victorians built to fit side-by-side in narrow lots, usually with flat fronts and long, narrow windows.

> Queen Anne (1880s–1910): Alamo Square has several exuberant examples built in wood with fish-scale shingle decoration, rounded corner towers and decorative bands to lift the eye skyward.

> Edwardian (1901–14): Most of the 'Victorians' you'll see in San Francisco are actually from the post-fire Edwardian era, and art-nouveau, Asian-inspired, and Arts and Crafts details are the giveaway. You'll notice the stained-glass windows and false gables in homes in the inner Richmond and Castro.

See also p23.

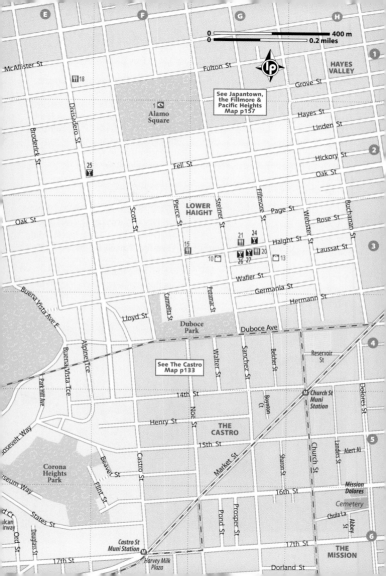

0               400 m
0             0.2 miles

**E**      **F**      **G**      **H**

McAllister St

Fulton St      **HAYES VALLEY**

Grove St

18

See Japantown, the Fillmore & Pacific Heights Map p157

Hayes St

Broderick St

Divisadero St

1

**Alamo Square**

Linden St

Hickory St

25

Fell St

Oak St

Oak St

Scott St

Pierce St

**LOWER HAIGHT**

Steiner St

Fillmore St

Page St

Webster St

Rose St

Buchanan St

15

21 24

Haight St

Laussat St

10

26 27

20

13

Walter St

Germania St

Potomar St

Hermann St

Buena Vista Ave E

Lloyd St

Camelita St

**Duboce Park**

Duboce Ave

Alpine Tce

Buena Vista Tce

See The Castro Map p133

Walter St

Sanchez St

Belcher St

Reservoir St

Park Hill Ave

14th St

Noe St

Boynton Ct

Church St Muni Station

Dolores St

Roosevelt Way

Henry St

**THE CASTRO**

Corona Heights Park

15th St

Market St

Sharon St

Church St

Landers St

Alert Al

useum Way

Beaver St

Castro St

16th St

**Mission Dolores**

Flint St

States St

Cemetery

Chula La

Abbey St

d Ct
irway

Douglass St

Prospect St

Pond St

17th St

**THE MISSION**

17th St

Castro St Muni Station

Harvey Milk Plaza

Dorland St

1960s, when it was the famous flophouse where the Grateful Dead blew minds, amps and brain cells until the cops raided the place. The new owners would be most Grateful you paid Jerry your respects with the silence of the Dead – though no one minds commemorative dancing bears in chalk on the sidewalk.

### HAIGHT ASHBURY FOOD PROGRAM

☎ 566-0366; www.thefoodprogram .org; 1525 Waller St; 🚊 N, 6, 7, 33, 37, 43, 71; ♿

Prove the Summer of Love isn't over yet by serving a meal or donating to job-training programs at this historic nonprofit, where hippie idealism meets 21st-century street smarts. It serves 61,000 hot, healthy meals a day, aided by some of the 50 training program graduates who have gone onto rewarding culinary careers and return as volunteers.

## 🛍 SHOP

### AMBIANCE Women's Clothing

☎ 552-5095; www.ambiancesf.com; 1458 Haight St; 🕙 10am-7pm Mon-Sat, 11am-7pm Sun; 🚊 6, 7, 33, 37, 43, 71

Chairs in the dressing rooms and a bench by the mezzanine sale section come in handy – even die-hard fashionistas need a breather

Enjoy the atmosphere at Ambiance

between all these swingy Betsy Johnson dresses, Free People peasant blouses and Trina Turk graphic print skirts. SF social butterflies plan their schedules around hot numbers found here: a silk smock covered with mod wine glasses suggests a wine-tasting, while a jacket with a snappy double-helix pattern demands a lecture on genome mapping.

## AMOEBA RECORDS
*Music & DVDs*

☎ 831-1200; www.amoeba.com; 1855 Haight St; ☽ 10:30am-10pm Mon-Sat, 11am-9pm Sun; 🚌 6, 7, 33, 37, 43, 71; ♿

Enticements aren't necessary to lure the masses to the West Coast's most eclectic collection of new and used music and video, but Amoeba offers listening stations, a free music zine with uncannily accurate reviews, a free concert series recently featuring the Breeders, Badly Drawn Boy and Sierra Leone's Refugee All-Stars, and a foundation that's saved more than 950 acres of rainforest.

## AQUA SURF SHOP *Surf Gear*
☎ 876-2782; www.aquasurfshop.com; 1742 Haight St; ☽ 10am-7pm Wed-Sat, 10am-5:30pm Sun-Tue; 🚌 6, 7, 33, 37, 43, 71

No locals-only attitude here: this laid-back, tiki-themed surf shop has sex wax for your board and toasty signature hoodies to brave foggy Ocean Beach, and turns even kooks (newbies) into mavericks with board and wetsuit rentals ($25 and $15 per day) and lesson referrals.

## BOUND TOGETHER ANARCHIST BOOK COLLECTIVE
*Books & Zines*

☎ 431-8355; www.boundtogetherbooks .com; 1369 Haight St; ☽ 11:30am-7:30pm; 🚌 6, 7, 33, 37, 43, 71

Given the state of the world lately, an anarchist bookstore seems like the go-to place for answers. You don't have to be a lifetime subscriber to *Eat the State* to be awed by this vast selection of free speech, from academic arguments against marriage to conspiracy-theory comics. Since 1976, this volunteer-run nonprofit bookstore has kept regular hours, coordinated the Anarchist Book Fair and expanded its 'Anarchists of the Americas' storefront mural – making us tools of the state look like slackers.

## BRAINDROPS
*Tattoos & Body Jewelry*

☎ 621-4162; www.braindrops.net; 1324 Haight St; ☽ noon-8pm Mon-Sat, noon-7pm Sun; 🚌 6, 7, 33, 37, 43, 71

New Yorkers and Berliners fly in for custom designs by top tattoo artists here – bring design ideas to your consultation or trust them to make suggestions. Piercings are done gently without a gun, with body jewelry ranging from pop-star opal belly-button studs to modern tribal septum bones, dainty gold nose rings to mondo jade ear spools.

### COCO-LUXE
*Chocolates – Local Maker*
☎ 367-4012; www.coco-luxe.com; 1673 Haight St; ⏰ noon-8pm; 🚌 6, 7, 33, 37, 43, 71

The gold rush may be over, but the sugar rush is definitely on at this SF chocolatier reinventing American dessert classics like devil's food cake, malted milkshakes and banana splits as truffles. Cinnamon-candied almonds dunked in chocolate and dusted with cocoa make Block Party Almonds the kind of treat you might not be inclined to share with neighbors.

### DOE
*Clothing & Gifts – Local Designer*
☎ 558-8588; www.doe-sf.com; 629A Haight St; ⏰ noon-7pm Mon-Sat, noon-6pm Sun; 🚌 N, 6, 7, 22, 71

One-stop-shopping for that California casual look and alternative SF souvenirs, all in a tiny converted Victorian garage. Make yourself comfortable in California-sewn Joe's jeans with Doe's own belt featuring the fogged-in Sutro Tower on the buckle, local designer She-Bible cotton tunic dresses or a necklace with a gold California-shaped pendant with a gem inset (where else?) for San Francisco.

### PIEDMONT
*Clothing & Accessories – Local Designer*
☎ 864-8075; www.piedmontsf.com; 1452 Haight St; ⏰ 11am-7pm; 🚌 6, 7, 33, 37, 43, 71

Glam up or get out at this supplier of drag fabulousness: faux-fur hot pants, airplane earrings and a wall of feather boas. These getups aren't cheap, honey, because they're custom-designed in-house, built to last and in demand by cabaret singers, cross-dressers, Burning Man devotees, strippers and people who take Halloween very seriously – in other words, everyone in SF.

### SFO SNOWBOARDING & FTC SKATEBOARDING
*Snowboarding & Skateboarding Gear – Local Designer*
☎ 626-1141; www.sfosnow.com; 1630 Haight St; ⏰ 11am-7pm Mon-Sat, 11am-6pm Sun; 🚌 6, 7, 33, 37, 43, 71

Big air and big style are the tip at this snowboard and skateboard outfitter, featuring designs by local artists. Show some local style as you grab air on a Western Edition deck tricked out with drawings of Fillmore jazz greats and ramshackle Victorian houses, or hit the slopes with Tahoe-tested gear. Check the website for upcoming SF street games and current Tahoe snow conditions.

### ⬛ UPPER PLAYGROUND
*Clothing – Local Designer*
☎ 861-1960; www.upperplayground .com; 220 Fillmore St; ⏲ noon-7pm; 🚌 N, 6, 7, 22, 71
Score instant street cred and the best SF non-souvenirs at this local designer of SF skater chic: Grotesk Golden State hoodies, a knit Muni cap and 'I'm in a San Francisco State of Mind' tees. Girly-shaped tees are next door down, and if Fifty24SF Gallery next door isn't open, get the slacker at the register to let you in to see slick art made with street finds.

### ⬛ WASTELAND
*Vintage Clothing*
☎ 863-3150; www.thewasteland.com; 1660 Haight St; ⏲ 11am-8pm Mon-Sat, noon-7pm Sun; 🚌 6, 7, 33, 37, 43, 71
Flashbacks come with the territory at Wasteland, with trippy '60s psychedelic print maxi dresses, '70s Frye boots, cocoonlike '80s wrap shirts by Yohji Yamamoto, and ironic '90s failed dot-com T-shirts. Hip occasionally verges on hideous with patchwork suede

vests and lace-up pirate shirts, but at these prices, you can afford to take fashion risks.

## 🍴 EAT

### 🍴 AXUM *Ethiopian*                    $
☎ 252-7912; www.axumcafe.com; 698 Haight St; ⏲ 5-10:30pm; 🚌 6, 7, 22, 71; ♿ Ⓥ
When you've got a hot date with a vegan, an activist's salary or the munchies of the Haight's many medical marijuana prescription-holders, Axum's vegetarian platter for two is your saving grace: generous dollops of lip-tingling red lentils, fiery mushrooms and mellow yellow chickpeas, scooped up with spongy *injera* bread.

### 🍴 COLE VALLEY CAFE
*Sandwiches & Snacks*                    $
☎ 668-5282; www.colevalleycafe.com; 701 Cole St; ⏲ 6:30am-8:30pm Mon-Fri, 7am-8pm Sat & Sun; 🚌 N, 6, 7, 33, 37, 43, 71; Ⓥ ♨
Powerful coffee, free wi-fi and hot gourmet sandwiches that are a bargain at any price – let alone $6 for lip-smacking thyme-marinated chicken with lemony avocado spread, or the smoky roasted eggplant with goat cheese and sundried tomatoes. Friendly owner Jawad knows the entire Haight by name and lunch order, and will remember you and yours when you come back for more.

### 🍴 ESCAPE FROM NEW YORK PIZZA *Pizza* $

☎ 668-5577; www.escapefromnewyork pizza.com; 1737 Haight St; ⏱ 11:30am-midnight Sun-Thu, 11:30am-2am Fri & Sat; 🚍 N, 6, 7, 33, 37, 43, 71; ♿ Ⓥ ♨

The Haight's obligatory mid-bender stop for a hot slice. Pesto with roasted garlic and potato will send you blissfully off to carbo-loaded sleep, but the sundried to-mato with goat cheese, artichoke hearts and spinach will recharge you to go another round.

### 🍴 LITTLE STAR PIZZA *Pizza* $$

☎ 441-1118; www.littlestarpizza.com; 846 Divisadero St; ⏱ 5-10pm Tue-Thu & Sun, 5-11pm Fri & Sat; 🚍 5, 21, 24; Ⓥ ♨

Midwest weather patterns reveal Chicago's thunder has been stolen by Little Star's deep-dish pie, with California additions of cornmeal crust, fresh local veggies and just the right amount of cheese. The all-meat pizza is a Chicago stock-yard's worth of meat, and not for the faint of heart.

### 🍴 MAGNOLIA
*Sustainable Gastropub & Microbrewery* $$

☎ 864-7468; www.magnoliapub.com; 1398 Haight St; ⏱ noon-midnight Mon-Thu, noon-1am Fri, 10am-1am Sat, 10am-midnight Sun; 🚍 6, 7, 33, 37, 43, 71; Ⓥ

Organic pub grub and homebrews with laid-back, Deadhead service in the hippie heart of the Haight. Join the communal table, work your way through the beer sam-pler and consult your neighbors on the all-local menu – bet they'll recommend the organic Prather Ranch burger. Magnolia smells vaguely like a brewery because it is one, which can be a problem at brunch but is definitely an asset otherwise, with seasonal micro-brewed ales and wheat beers you won't find elsewhere.

### 🍴 ROSAMUNDE SAUSAGE GRILL *Sausages* $

☎ 437-6851; 545 Haight St; ⏱ 11:30am-10pm; 🚍 6, 7, 22, 71

Baseball games in heaven surely serve Rosamunde's divine duck, spicy lamb or wild boar sausages, fully loaded with a devilish choice of roasted red peppers, grilled on-ions, mango chutney and wasabi mustard. Get yours to go and head next door to Toronado (p154) where you can devour it with a legendary selection of seasonal microbrews.

### 🍴 UVA ENOTECA *Californian* $$

☎ 829-2024; www.uvaenoteca.com; 568 Haight St; ⏱ 5pm-midnight Mon-Fri, 10am-midnight Sat & Sun; 🚍 6, 7, 22, 71

'Wine for hipsters' is the motto here. Boys with shags and girls with bangs discover the joys of Bardolino and Barbera by the tasting glass, served with inventive small plates of local veggies, cheese and charcuterie boards by a sassy staff of tattooed Lower Haight hotties.

#  DRINK

## ▼ AUB ZAM ZAM
*Cocktail Lounge*

☎ 861-2545; 1633 Haight St; ⏱ 3pm-2am Mon-Fri, 1pm-2am Sat & Sun; 🚍 6, 7, 33, 37, 43, 71

Arabesque arches, jazz on the jukebox and enough paisley to make Prince feel right at home pay homage to dearly departed Persian cocktail purist Bruno, who'd throw you out for ordering a vodka martini. Now Zam Zam is more gently run by Bruno's former customers, who carry on the venerable tradition of top-shelf cocktails at low-shelf prices for an eclectic Haight St crowd of writers, vintage shoppers and characters straight out of an R Crumb comic.

## ▼ COFFEE TO THE PEOPLE
*Café*

☎ 626-2435; www.coffeetothepeople .squarespace.com; 1206 Masonic Ave; ⏱ 6am-8pm Mon-Fri, 7am-9pm Sat & Sun; 🚍 6, 7, 33, 37, 43, 71

The people, united, will never be decaffeinated at this utopian coffee shop with free wi-fi, 5% of sales pledged to coffee-growers' nonprofits, leftist bumper stickers covering the tables, a social-change reading library and enough fair-trade coffee to revive the Sandinista movement.

## ▼ MAD DOG IN THE FOG
*Sports Bar*

☎ 626-7279; 530 Haight St; ⏱ 5pm-2am; 🚍 6, 7, 22, 71

Footie fans watch matches live on GMT, and know-it-alls arrive by 8:30pm Tuesdays and Thursdays to compete for free beer and bragging rights in SF's most eclectic pop culture trivia nights. There's no hard liquor or credit-card machine, but cash will get you beer, darts and occasionally live rockabilly.

## ▼ MADRONE *Cocktail Lounge*

☎ 241-0202; www.madronelounge.com; 500 Divisadero St; ⏱ 6pm-midnight Sun & Mon, 6pm-2am Tue-Sat; 🚍 5, 21, 24

Upbeat hip-hop and giggling cuties come as a surprise in a Victorian bar that's gone a little *Psycho*, decorated with animal skulls, front-parlor sofas, creepy murals of uprooted madrone trees and art suggesting untimely demises. The drink menu lets you play Jekyll-and-Hyde with your choice of infused vodkas and mixers – but consult the professionals behind the bar before you find out the expensive way that apricot vodka with pomegranate juice tastes evil.

### NOC NOC *Dive Bar*

☎ 861-5811; www.nocnocs.com; 557 Haight St; ☺ 5pm-2am; 🚌 6, 7, 22, 71

Who's there? Dreadlocked graffiti artists, electronica DJs and Mad Max–inspired fashion designers, that's who. This place looks like a postapocalyptic cartoon cave dwelling designed by Tim Burton, and serves a sake cocktail that'll keep you buzzed until the next Burning Man. Beer and sake drinks only; bring cash.

### TORONADO *Beer Bar*

☎ 863-2276; www.toronado.com; 547 Haight St; ☺ 11:30am-2am; 🚌 6, 7, 22, 71

Glory hallelujah, beer-lovers: your prayers have been heard, and this bar is proof (about 15 proof, but close enough). Bow before the chalkboard altar listing 46 specialty beers on tap and hundreds more bottled, including spectacular seasonal microbrews. Bring cash, come early, and drink up with a sausage from Rosamunde Sausage Grill (p152) next door. For believers in the almighty hop, Toronado's Barley Wine Festival in mid-February is a sacred event.

## ⭐ PLAY

### ⭐ BOOKSMITH *Literary Events*

☎ 863-8688; www.booksmith.com; 1644 Haight St; ☺ 10am-10pm Mon-Sat, 10am-8pm Sun; 🚌 7, 33, 37, 43, 71

There's (liquid) gold in them thar hills at Toronado

Since SF remains one of the country's top three book markets, your favorite author is bound to come through town – and probably to the Booksmith's Author Series. Prizewinners come through before and after they've hit the big time, including Kazuo Ishiguro, Art Spiegelman, Robert Hass and Maya Angelou. Every famous '60s personality from Timothy Leary to Neil Young has appeared here since 1976, but sci-fi is another major draw, with readings by Ursula Le Guin, Ray Bradbury and original *Star Trek* cast members.

### ⭐ CLUB DELUXE *Live Music*

☎ 552-6949; www.liveatdeluxe.com; 1511 Haight St; cover on music nights $3-5; 🕒 7pm-2am Mon, Wed & Fri, 2pm-2am Tue, Thu, Sat & Sun; 🚋 7, 33, 37, 43, 71

Adjust your fedora and straighten out the back seams on those fishnets: this is a class establishment.

The swing bands are better than the standup comedians, but those Tom Collins highballs may get a giggle out of you yet. Recuperate on Sundays with live bossa nova and a Bloody Mary containing a farmers market's worth of veggies – here's to your health.

### ⭐ RED VIC MOVIE HOUSE *Cinema*

☎ 668-3994; www.redvicmoviehouse .com; 1727 Haight St; tickets $7; 🚋 N, 7, 33, 37, 43, 71

Collectively owned and operated for decades, the Red Vic has preserved a funky '70s vibe right down to the dilapidated couch seating and popcorn served in wooden snack bowls with optional brewer's yeast. Surfer documentaries, cult classics, rockumentaries and movies by local filmmakers pack the place out, so get in line if you hope to avoid the seats with the busted springs goosing you.

# >JAPANTOWN, THE FILLMORE & PACIFIC HEIGHTS

A fitting soundtrack for an uphill bus ride through these eclectic neighborhoods would include psychedelic rock, fusion jazz played on a Japanese *koto* (dulcimer), and spooky amplified white noise. The Fillmore thrived when African Americans arrived to support SF's WWII shipbuilding boom, fostering a blues-rock scene that launched Jimi Hendrix, Janis Joplin and psychedelia. When a 1960s redevelopment plan demolished entire blocks of Victorian townhouses in the Fillmore, the district rallied with its Japantown neighbors. Together these communities preserved local low-income housing, and turned Fillmore St below Geary into SF's Jazz District.

Japantown had survived hard times itself since 1860, when local laws began limiting employment for Japanese immigrants. In 1942, Japantown residents were ordered to government internment camps, bringing only what they could carry. After the war, residents were resettled in makeshift apartments, often not far from the Victorian homes they'd once owned. But 'Little Osaka' rallied for civil rights, and began rebuilding.

Today Japantown remains the master of reinvention, with hip boutiques, anime-themed hotels and an all-green independent cinema.

## JAPANTOWN, THE FILLMORE & PACIFIC HEIGHTS

**A**
**B**
**C**
**D**

Green St

Vallejo St

Broadway

Pacific Ave

Bromley Pl

Jackson St

Washington St

Clay St

Lafayette Park

University of the Pacific

Clay St

Sacramento St

Buchanan St

Laguna St

Octavia St

Gough St

Franklin St

Polk St

Van Ness Ave

**NOB HILL**

See North Beach & the Hills Map pp42-3

California St Cable Car Turnaround

Swedenborgian Church (0.5 miles)

Spruce (0.6 miles)

5

14

PACIFIC HEIGHTS & JAPANTOWN

Pine St

California St

Austin St

15

Fern St

Tataki (0.2 miles)

Orben Pl

Webster St

Wilmot St

Bush St

Octavia St

Sutter St

Post St

Peter Yorke Way

Geary St

Cedar St

11

2

Kintetsu Mall

12

4

9

10

Sutter St

Starr King Way

Myrtle St

Avery St

18

17

8

13

3

Peace Plaza

Japan Center

Geary Blvd

Laguna St

Cleary Ct

Cathedral of St Mary the Assumption

See Hayes Valley, Civic Center & the Tenderloin Map p85

16

6

O'Farrell St

Byington St

Fillmore St

Steiner St

Hollis St

Ellis St

Willow St

**THE TENDERLOIN**

Raymond Kimball Playground

Ellis St

19

Eddy St

Eddy St

Webster St

Gough St

Turk Blvd

Jefferson Square

Hayward Playground

Golden Gate Ave

Elm St

Franklin St

Van Ness Ave

**Opera Plaza**

**State Building**

McAllister St

0 — 200 m
0 — 0.1 miles

Compared with retro-futurist Japantown, the frilly white Victorians in uphill, upscale Pacific Heights might seem starchy. But behind those graceful doors, weekly séances and ambient-music concerts take place – never underestimate SF eccentricity.

# SEE

## AFRICAN ORTHODOX CHURCH OF ST JOHN COLTRANE

☎ 673-7144; www.coltranechurch.org; 1286 Fillmore St; ⏱ mass noon-3pm Sun; 🚌 21, 22, 24

Cymbals shudder and the bassist plucks the opening notes of 'A Love Supreme.' The Sunday liturgy has begun, and the entire congregation joins in the three-hour devotional jam session. Overseeing the celebration from mesmerizing icons on the wall is the musician known here as St John Will-I-Am Coltrane, shown with flames leaping from his saxophone.

## COTTAGE ROW

Off Bush St btwn Webster & Fillmore Sts; 🚌 2, 3, 4, 22, 38

Amid the starchy Victorians and supersized mansions of Pacific Heights is this row of laid-back, quintessentially Californian cottages. These low 19th-century houses hang back along a brick-paved promenade and let plum trees, flowering shrubs and bonsai take center stage. The homes are private but the mini-park is public, and perfect for a sushi picnic.

## PEACE PAGODA

Peace Plaza; 🚌 2, 3, 4, 22, 38

When the people of Osaka gifted Yoshiro Taniguchi's stark minimalist concrete stupa to Osaka's sister city of San Francisco in 1968, the city was stupa-fied over what to do with it, and kept trying to cluster shrubs to hide its naked base. But with some well-placed cherry trees and a low channel fountain, the pagoda is finally in its element au naturel.

## RUTH ASAWA FOUNTAINS

Buchanan Pedestrian St; 🚌 2, 3, 4, 22, 38

Grab a seat inside the fountain, splash around and stay awhile: celebrated modern sculptor and former WWII internee Ruth Asawa designed these fountains to be lived in, not viewed from a distance. The bronze origami dandelions drizzle water onto the sloping stone floor below, where kids douse themselves with glee and weary shoppers refresh aching tootsies.

## SWEDENBORGIAN CHURCH

☎ 346-6466; www.sfswedenborgian .org; 2107 Lyon St; 🚌 1, 24, 43

Eighteenth-century Swedish theologian Emanuel Swedenborg was a scientist and occasional conversationalist with angels who believed that humans are (as the Police would sing centuries later) spirits in a material world, unified by nature, love, and 'luminous intelligence' – a lovely idea embodied in an enchanting 1894 church by architect Arthur Page Brown with naturalist John Muir and California Arts and Crafts leader Bernard Maybeck. A modest brick archway leads through a garden sheltered by trees from around the world, and into a rustic sanctuary with roughhewn maple chairs, Madrone trees supporting the roof, and California landscapes that took muralist William Keith 40 years to complete.

# 🛍 SHOP

## 🏠 CLARY SAGE ORGANICS
*Body & Bath Products, Women's Clothing – Local Maker*
☎ 673-7300; www.clarysageorganics.com; 2241 Fillmore St; ⏰ 10am-7pm; 🚌 1, 3, 12, 22, 24

To top off your spa day at Kabuki Hot Springs (p163), Clary Sage will outfit you with effortlessly flattering tunics made from organic California cotton, cozy organic knitwear, organic plant-based cleansers and lotions with light, delectable scents and homeo-

pathic flower-essence stress remedies.

## 🏠 HARPUTS MARKET
*Clothing – Local Designer*
☎ 923-9300; www.harputsmarket.com; 1525 Fillmore St; ⏰ 11am-7pm Mon-Sat, noon-6pm Sun; 🚌 1, 3, 12, 22, 24

Futuristic Tokyo style meets streetwise Fillmore cool at this old-school storefront that rocks fat-lace sneakers with Yohji Yamamoto zipper-front military sweaters, for that Sugarhill Gang–meets–James Bond look. Harputs also produces its own design linen overalls and patch-pocket A-line dresses for ladies, worn with Pleasure Principle's kimono-style hooded sweatshirt for *Blade Runner* chic.

## 🏠 ICHIBAN KAN
*Gifts & Home Design*
☎ 409-0472; www.ichibankanusa.com; No 540, 22 Peace Plaza; ⏰ 10:30am-8pm; 🚌 2, 3, 4, 22, 38

Really, it's a wonder you got this far in life without octopus stickers, anime character bento lunchboxes, chocolate-covered pretzel 'Men's Pocky,' and the ultimate in gay gag gifts, the handy 'Closet Case' – all for under $2. But the best is yet to come in the last aisle: soap dishes with feet, eraser cell-phone charms shaped like hamburgers, and pink forks in the shape of scowling giraffes.

NEIGHBORHOODS

JAPANTOWN, THE FILLMORE & PACIFIC HEIGHTS

## KINOKUNIYA
*Books & Stationery*
☎ 567-7625; www.kinokuniya.com;
1581 Webster St; ⏰ 10:30am-8pm;
🚌 2, 3, 4, 22, 38

Like warriors in a shogun show-down, the bookstore and station-ery divisions compete fiercely for the attention of shoppers. Side with stunning contemporary photography books, manga comics and Harajuku fashion mags, or choose cherry-blossom-printed *washi* paper, Sakura gel pens and notebooks that declare they're 'For-ever Optimistic with a Theme and a Purpose' – either way, you win.

## SOKO HARDWARE
*DIY Supplies, Kitchenware & Home Design*
☎ 931-5510; 1698 Post St; ⏰ 9am-5:30pm Mon-Sat; 🚌 2, 3, 4, 22, 38

Iron Chef dreams come true with a killer selection of Japanese chef's knives, sushi-rolling mats and me-dievally cool cast-iron utensils and teapots. Tough guys lurk upstairs among the knives, hardware and gardening tools for a respectably manly interval before heading downstairs to ogle the selection of ikebana vases, wind chimes, chopstick rests and bonsai pots.

## SUPER 7
*Clothing & Toys – Local Designer*
☎ 409-4701; www.super7store.com;
1628 Post St; ⏰ noon-7pm Mon-Thu,

Hangin' out at Soko Hardware

noon-8:30pm Fri, 11am-8:30pm Sat, 11am-7pm Sun; 🚌 2, 3, 4, 38

After tiresome T-shirt trends of self-promotion ('Porn Star') and retro-irony ('Virginia is for Lovers'), it's a shock to find piles of limited-edition T-shirts this original. 'Superterrific Animal Friendlies' announces one Super7 T-shirt with an unlikely superhero team of cuddly owls, bats and monkeys; 'Martial Art Garfunkel' proclaims another, with the *Mrs Robinson* crooner striking a karate pose. Godzilla fans cannot miss the se-lection of rare action figures here, though Japanese toy collectors enter at their own risk.

## 🖼 ZINC DETAILS
*Home Design & Gifts*
☎ 776-2100; www.zincdetails.com;
1905 Fillmore St; ⏰ 11am-7pm Mon-Sat,
noon-6pm Sun; 🚌 2, 3, 4, 22, 38
Pacific Heights chic meets
Japantown mod at Zinc Details,
with vintage '60s orange and red
lacquerware, Alessi soy dispensers
shaped like songbirds, recharge-
able nightlights shaped (rather
counterproductively) like ghosts,
and Noguchi table lamps that look
like an alien starship landed on
your end table.

# 🍴 EAT
## 🍴 BENKYODO
*Sandwiches & Mochi* $
☎ 922-1244; www.benkyodocompany
.com; 1747 Buchanan St; ⏰ 8am-5pm
Mon-Sat; 🚌 2, 3, 4, 22, 38
Everything you really need in life
is within reach of your stool at
Benkyodo. The perfect retro lunch
counter cheerfully serves an old-
school egg-salad sandwich for a
paltry $2.25 or pastrami for $2.50 –
unless you spring the whopping
25 cents extra for cheese. Across
the aisle are glass cases featuring teriyaki-flavored pretzels and
*mochi* (chewy Japanese cakes
with savory/sweet fillings) made
in-house – come early for popular
green tea and chocolate-filled
strawberry varieties.

## 🍴 NIJIYA SUPERMARKET
*Sushi & Snacks* $
☎ 563-1901; www.nijiya.com; 1737 Post
St; ⏰ 10am-8pm; 🚌 2, 3, 4, 22, 38
Picnic under the Peace Pagoda with
sushi or teriyaki bento boxes fresh
from the deli counter, and a swig of
Berkley-brewed Takara Sierra Cold
sake from the drinks aisle – and
save enough change from $20 for
mango-ice-cream-filled *mochi* or
chocolate-filled panda cookies.

## 🍴 SPRUCE *Californian* $$
☎ 931-5100; www.sprucesf.com;
3640 Sacramento St; ⏰ restaurant
11:30am-2:30pm Mon-Fri, 5-10pm daily,
bar & lounge 11:30am-10pm Mon-Fri;
🚌 1, 2, 4, 33
VIP all the way, with studded
ostrich-leather chairs, mahogany
walls and your choice of 1000
wines. Expense-accounters forget
business and feast on pork tenderloin with crispy pork belly, and
ladies who lunch dispense with
polite conversation and devour
lavish salads of warm duck confit,
plums and greens grown on the
restaurant's own organic farm.

## 🍴 TATAKI *Sustainable Sushi* $$
☎ 931-1182; www.tatakisushibar.com;
2815 California St; ⏰ 11:30am-2pm &
5:30-10:30pm Mon-Thu, 11:30am-2pm
& 5:30-11:30pm Fri, 5:30-11:30pm Sat;
🚌 1, 2, 4, 24
Sustainable sushi chefs Kin Lui
and Raymond Ho are here to save

the day for eco-conscious seafood fans, cleverly substituting buttery kampachi for hamachi and delicate arctic char for wild salmon, and serving local crabmeat salad with a scintillating sake gelee. Compliment your chefs on their sumptuous creations, and they'll demurely compliment you back on your eco-smart good tastes.

 # DRINK
##  BITTERSWEET CAFÉ
*Chocolate Café*

☎ 346-8715; www.bittersweetcafe.com; 2123 Fillmore St; ☼ 10am-8pm Sun-Thu, 10am-10pm Fri & Sat; 🚌 1, 2, 3, 4, 22

Hot chocolate so thick it's actually chewy is the specialty here, but why stop there? The occasional chocolate tastings are so extravagant you'll expect Oompa Loompas to leap out and chide you in song – but back off, Wonka flunkies, because there's redeeming educational value in learning about single-origin beans, fair-trade cocoa and chocolate-wine pairings.

# ⭐ PLAY
## ⭐ AUDIUM
*Musical Performances*

☎ 771-1616; www.audium.org; 1616 Bush St; tickets $15; 🚌 1, 2, 3, 4, 22

If these walls could talk, they would sing – and in fact, they do. Built in 1962 by a wealthy eccentric, the

Audium was specifically sculpted to produce bizarre acoustic effects and eerie soundscapes. Sit in total darkness as musician Stan Shaff plays his hour-plus room compositions, which sometimes degenerate into digestive rumbles and B-movie sci-fi sound effects before resolving into oddly endearing Moog machine wheezes.

## ⭐ THE FILLMORE
*Live Music & Comedy*

☎ 346-3000; www.thefillmore.com; 1805 Geary Blvd; tickets $20-40; ☼ box office 10am-4pm Sun, 7:30-10pm show nights; 🚌 2, 3, 4, 22, 38

There's no way to say, 'Yeah, I saw that at the Fillmore' without

Keep on rockin' at the Fillmore

sounding like you're bragging. The legendary birthplace of 1960s psychedelic rock reels in major acts (Stereolab, Lucinda Williams, Ozomatli, Chris Rock) to play a relatively small 1250-capacity setting, where you can grab a table if you're early or squeeze in next to the stage if you're polite about it. Upstairs, see '60s history unfold in all its Day-Glo glory in the Fillmore's poster art gallery, from the Grateful Dead through Janis Joplin and Jefferson Airplane.

### ☆ KABUKI HOT SPRINGS Spa

☎ 922-6000; www.kabukisprings.com; 1750 Geary Blvd; Mon-Fri $20, Sat & Sun $25; ⏲ 10am-9:45pm; 🚌 2, 3, 4, 22, 38
Soak away your Telegraph Hill Tendonitis, Haight Patchouli Overload and Pacific Heights Sticker Shock at this urban tub retreat. All ages, shapes and sizes come here, so don't be self-conscious about your funky pinky toe – let it all hang out, unwind, and you'll see why San Franciscans seem so blithely well adjusted. The baths are open for women only on Sundays, Wednesdays and Fridays, and men only on Mondays, Thursdays and Saturdays. Tuesdays are co-ed (bathing suits required).

### ☆ KABUKI SUNDANCE CINEMA Cinema

☎ 929-4650; www.sundancecinemas .com/kabuki.html; 1881 Post St; adult/ child $9.50/6.50 plus amenities fee; 🚌 2, 3, 4, 22, 38
Robert Redford's Sundance Institute reinvented SF's beloved Kabuki Cinema – home of the revered Asian American Film Festival (p26) and San Francisco International Film Festival (p26) – as a trendsetting green multiplex. Enjoy GMO-free popcorn and local artisanal chocolates at the snack bar, extra-comfy reserved seats made of recycled materials, and the frankly brilliant Balcony Bar, where you can slurp a seasonal cocktail during your movie. Tickets cost up to $1.50 extra here for 'amenities fees,' but get this: they don't show any ads.

### ☆ YOSHI'S Jazz

☎ 655-5600; www.yoshis.com; 1330 Fillmore St; ⏲ shows 8pm & 10pm Mon-Sat, 7pm & 9pm Sun; 🚌 2, 3, 4, 22, 38
The legendary East Bay jazz venue has opened a fabulous new restaurant/club in the heart of the historic African and Japanese American Fillmore jazz district, bringing the biggest names in jazz to an intimate venue with seasonal Japanese cuisine that threatens to steal the show. Swing with legends like New Orleans' Preservation Hall Jazz Band, or get down and funky with SF's own Broun Fellinis.

# >MARINA & THE PRESIDIO

Today this stretch of waterfront is the place to go to windsurf, browse boutiques, park your yacht and enjoy vegetarian cuisine in a former army depot – but in the 19th century, the Marina reeked with dirty laundry and drunken cows. San Francisco's dirties were washed in a lagoon south of Lombard until the 1880s, when the cesspool became so pungent that it had to be filled in by chain gangs. Today's swanky Union St was then a gulch called Cow Hollow, where dairy farmers fed flatulent cattle leftovers from SF's whiskey stills. No wonder soldiers in the local *presidio* (fort) frequently abandoned their posts for greener pastures.

The spiffy Mex-Deco Marina as you see it today was mostly built in the 1930s, after sand and debris from the 1906 quake were brought in to bury the pollution. Residents blithely ignored the area's shaky foundations until 1989, when the Loma-Prieta earthquake left millions of dollars in damages. While the Marina cleaned up, the Presidio finally retired from military duty, and returned to its bucolic origins as a national park in 1996.

# MARINA & THE PRESIDIO

## ◉ SEE
| | | |
|---|---|---|
| Baker Beach | 1 | A5 |
| Crissy Field | 2 | E3 |
| Exploratorium | 3 | E3 |
| Palace of Fine Arts | 4 | E3 |

## ⬛ SHOP
| | | |
|---|---|---|
| ATYS | 5 | G4 |
| Mingle | 6 | H4 |
| My Roommate's Closet | 7 | G4 |
| Past Perfect | 8 | G4 |

| | | |
|---|---|---|
| PlumpJack Wines | 9 | G4 |
| Sports Basement | 10 | D3 |
| Sumbody | 11 | G4 |

## 🍴 EAT
| | | |
|---|---|---|
| A16 | 12 | F4 |
| Greens Restaurant & Greens to Go | 13 | H2 |
| La Boulange | 14 | H4 |
| Warming Hut | 15 | C2 |

## ▼ DRINK
| | | |
|---|---|---|
| California Wine Merchant | 16 | G3 |
| MatrixFillmore | 17 | G4 |

## ★ PLAY
| | | |
|---|---|---|
| BATS Improv | 18 | H2 |
| Fort Mason | 19 | H2 |
| Magic Theatre | 20 | H2 |

Please see over for map

NEIGHBORHOODS

MARINA & THE PRESIDIO

# ◎ SEE
## ◎ BAKER BEACH

**Presidio; ☼ sunrise-sunset; 🚌 28, 29**
A scenic mile-long stretch of
sandy beach with windswept
pines uphill, cliffs with craggy
good looks and a whole lot of
exposed goose bumps on the
breezy, clothing-optional north
end of the beach. Yes, you're still
in the city, with spectacular views
of Golden Gate Bridge and the
Lincoln Golf Course to prove it. On
sunny weekends, crowds descend
in a motley parade.

## ◎ CRISSY FIELD

**Btwn Mason St & Golden Gate Prom-
enade; ☼ sunrise-sunset; 🚌 28, 29,
30, 76**
War is definitely for the birds in
this nature preserve that was once
a military airstrip. Birdwatchers
huddle in reclaimed tidal-marsh
rushes where once there was
oil-stained asphalt, and the airstrip
is now a favorite spot of kite-flyers and lolling puppies. Veer off
the coastal path to explore the
100-acre urban wildlife preserve
stretching from the Marina docks
toward the Golden Gate Bridge.
On sunny days you might head to
Fort Point under the bridge – but
on blustery ones, pause at the
Warming Hut (p171) for fair-trade
coffee and watch the fog billow
past.

## ◎ EXPLORATORIUM

**☎ 397-5673, 563-7337; www.explora
torium.edu; 3601 Lyon St; adult/senior/
child $12/9.50/8, 1st Wed of month free;
☼ 10am-5pm Tue-Sun; 🚌 28, 30, 43,
76; ♿**
Finally, answers to all the questions you always wanted to ask
in science class: do robots have
feelings too, does gravity apply
to skateboarding and do toilets
really flush counter-clockwise in
Australia? Try out a new hairdo at
the static electricity conductor,
grope your way through the pitch-
black maze of the Tactile Dome
(separate admission $17; reserva-
tion only), and try your hand at
the phonoharp, a cross between

Little Einsteins love the Exploratorium

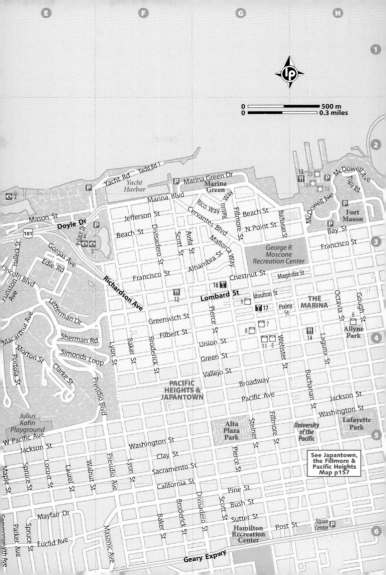

a DJ turntable and a stringed instrument invented by Exploratorium sound artist (and 2008 MacArthur Genius Grant winner) Walter Kitundu. Afterwards, follow Yacht Rd to the tip of the Marina jetty to the Exploratorium's Wave Organ, where changing tides make sounds like drum rolls, nervous humming, a gurgling baby or prank-call heavy breathing.

### PALACE OF FINE ARTS
☎ 567-6642; www.palaceoffinearts.org; 3301 Lyon St; 🚌 28, 30, 43, 76
This fake Greco-Roman ruin was originally built in wood, burlap and plaster by Bernard Maybeck as a picturesque backdrop for the 1915 Panama-Pacific Expo – but since this city has always been a sucker for a glorious folly, San Francisco decided to make it permanent in concrete and steel. The relief on the rotunda shows Art under attack by Materialists, with Idealists leaping to her rescue.

# SHOP

### ATYS *Home Design & Gifts*
☎ 441-9220; www.atysdesign.com; 2149B Union St; 🕑 11am-6:30pm Mon-Sat, noon-5pm Sun; 🚌 22, 41, 45
Designer version 2.0 of essential household goods: elephant-shaped 'Hannibal' tape dispensers, streamlined Alessi espresso makers, locally designed 'Wooly

Hoodwinks' stuffed animals made of reclaimed tweeds, and large acrylic dewdrops that add instant atmosphere if you want to take your own San Franciscan fog home.

### MINGLE
*Clothing – Local Designer*
☎ 674-8811; www.mingleshop.com; 1815 Union St; 🕑 11am-6:30pm Mon, Wed-Fri, noon-6pm Tue, 10am-7pm Sat, 11am-6pm Sun; 🚌 41, 45, 47, 49, 76
When you're tired of seeing the same clothes in your closet and the world over, it's time to get out there and Mingle. This place features dozens of one-offs by local designers, including limited-edition AYA tees with original designs created at the San Francisco Art Institute (p44), Donna Lou's surfer-chick sundresses, Nepacena's vintage-print oilcloth bowling bags, and artist-designed monster iPod covers by TinyMeat.

### MY ROOMMATE'S CLOSET
*Women's Clothing*
☎ 447-7703; www.myroommatescloset .com; 3044 Fillmore St; 🕑 11am-6:30pm Mon-Fri, 11am-6pm Sat, noon-5pm Sun; 🚌 22, 28, 41, 43, 45
The same designer numbers you'll find at the chichi Union St boutiques, brand new, only at least 50% off the high-end retail price. Clothing is organized by color, and

lately the black rack offered strictly minimal 3.1 Phillip Lim charcoal jackets, orange included African-inspired Tory Burch tunics, pale peach yielded Nanette Lepore camis, and green was all about slinky Diane von Furstenberg silk wrap dresses. Check out the shoes for bronze Sigerson Morrison kitten heels and Costume National flats your roommate will try to beg, borrow and steal from you.

### PAST PERFECT *Antiques*
☎ 929-7651; 2230 Union St; ⏱ 11:30am-7pm; 🚌 22, 41, 45

If you wonder how Pacific Heights eccentrics fill up those mansions, here's your answer: funky Big

Sur '70s ceramic candelabras, 19th-century Chinese snuff bottles shaped like lucky goldfish and wall-to-wall mid-century Danish teak credenzas. The store is a collective, so prices are all over the place – some sellers seem to believe their belongings owe them back-rent, while others are happy to be rid of wedding presents from first and second marriages.

### PLUMPJACK WINES *Wine*
☎ 346-9870; www.plumpjack.com; 3201 Fillmore St; ⏱ 11am-8pm Mon-Fri, 10am-8pm Sat, 11am-6pm Sun; 🚌 22, 28, 41, 43, 45

Before SF Mayor Newsom took office, he plied the electorate

Souse yourself SF-style at PlumpJack Wines

with 900 fine Italian, French and of course Californian wines as the owner/founder of PlumpJack and the local PlumpJack winery. A man of the people, he offers many vintages for under $15 and ecofriendly screw-cap bottles that'll have you slurring 'Thanks, Gav!'

### ☐ SPORTS BASEMENT
*Sports Gear*

☎ 437-0100; www.sportsbasement .com; 610 Old Mason St; ⏱ 9am-8pm Mon-Fri, 8am-7pm Sat & Sun; 🚌 2, 3, 4, 27, 30, 38, 45, 91

The Presidio's former US Army PX (army base retail store) has been converted into 70,000 sq ft of sports and camping equipment, which is why you'll find hiking boots near the Fresh Produce sign. Guzzle free coffee and hot cider while you shop for tracksuits to take on Crissy Field's running paths, snow gear for Tahoe slopes, and yoga gear to strike warrior poses under the Golden Gate Bridge.

### ☐ SUMBODY
*Body & Bath Products – Local Maker*

☎ 775-6343; www.sumbody.com; 2167 Union St; ⏱ 11am-7pm Mon-Sat, 11am-6pm Sun; 🚌 22, 41, 45

You don't actually have to live through a chilly San Francisco summer to get that fogged-in-for-months-fresh face. This local company uses all natural ingre-

dients to polish the skin, and the rich coconut and cream salt scrub has the bizarre effect of sealing in moisture as you're taking your shower, leaving you as emollient as a Pier 39 sea lion.

## 🍴 EAT

### 🍴 A16 *Pizza* $$

☎ 771-2216; www.a16sf.com; 2355 Chestnut St; ⏱ 11:30am-2:30pm Wed-Fri, 5-11pm Fri & Sat, 5-10pm Sun-Thu; 🚌 28, 30, 43, 91

At SF's 2008 James Beard award–winning Neapolitan pizzeria, there's always a wait to be seated and served, even with reservations. The housemade mozzarella burrata and chewy-but-not-too-thick-crust pizza (especially the kicky calamari) makes it worth your while. Skip the spotty desserts and concentrate on adventurous house-cured salumi platters, including the delectable spicy pig's ear terrina (no, really).

### 🍴 GREENS RESTAURANT & GREENS TO GO
*Californian Vegetarian* $$

☎ 771-6222; www.greensrestaurant .com; Fort Mason; ⏱ restaurant noon-2:30pm Tue-Sat, 10:30am-2pm Sun, 5:30-9pm Sun-Fri, to go 8am-8pm Mon-Thu, 8am-5pm Fri & Sat, 9am-4pm Sun; 🚌 22, 28, 30; V ☗

Military discipline has definitely slipped since this dockside army barracks became an organic vegetarian restaurant – but dawdling over smoked black bean chili with crème fraîche and pickled jalapeños can't be helped, especially with sparkling bay views and seasonal peach crumble for dessert. You don't have to be vegetarian to appreciate the vibrant flavor of ingredients grown on a Zen farm in Marin, but if you're planning a sit-down weekend dinner or Sunday brunch, you'll need reservations.

### 🍴 LA BOULANGE
*Cal-French Bakery*                               $
☎ 440-4450; www.baybread.com; 1909 Union St; ⏱ 7am-7pm Mon-Sat; 🚌 22, 41, 45, 47, 49, 76; V ♿
Even the most die-hard boutique trawlers need to refuel sometime, and La Boulange offers caffeine and house-baked carbo-loading in the middle of the Union St strip. La Combo is a $7 lunchtime deal to justify your next Union St boutique purchase: half a *tartine* (open-faced sandwich) with soup or salad, plus all the Nutella and pickled *cornichons* (gherkins) you desire from the condiment bar.

### 🍴 WARMING HUT
*Snacks & Sandwiches*                          $
☎ 561-3040; www.parksconservancy .org; 983 Marine Dr; ⏱ 9am-5pm; 🚌 29
Wet-suited windsurfers and Crissy Field (p165) kite-fliers thaw out with fair-trade coffee, organic

pastry and organic hot dogs at the Warming Hut, while browsing an excellent selection of field guides and sampling honey made by Presidio honeybees. This eco-shack below the Golden Gate Bridge has walls ingeniously insulated with recycled denim and a heartwarming concept: all purchases fund Crissy Field's ongoing conversion from US Army airstrip to wildlife preserve.

## 🍸 DRINK

### 🍸 CALIFORNIA WINE MERCHANT *Wine Bar*
☎ 567-0646; www.californiawinemer chant.com; 2113 Chestnut St; ⏱ 10am-midnight Mon-Wed, 10am-1:30am Thu-Sat, 11am-11pm Sun; 🚌 22, 28, 30, 43, 91
Pair your pick of 35 to 50 local wines by the glass with mild flirting in this wine cave, and be surprised by the unexpected nuances of Central Coast Pinots and Marina playboys earnestly trying to improve their game. Prices range from $3.50 for a taste of California crowd-pleasers to $20 a glass for 'cult wines' like Opus One.

### 🍸 MATRIXFILLMORE
*Cocktail Lounge*
☎ 563-4180; www.matrixfillmore.com; 3138 Fillmore St; ⏱ 8pm-2am Mon-Thu, 6pm-2am Fri-Sun; 🚌 22, 28, 30, 41, 43, 45, 91
The one bar in town where the presumption is that you're

straight and interested. The smoky glass and fireplace give off a sexy '70s key-party vibe, though the stockbroker/sales rep crowd doesn't do macramé or sideburns. The overall effect is modern and sleek, if not especially subtle – and the same can be said of the crowd.

## ⭐ PLAY

### ⭐ BATS IMPROV

*Comedy & Theater Classes*

☎ 474-6776; www.improv.org; 3rd fl, Bldg B, Fort Mason Center; shows $5-20, workshops vary; 🕑 shows 7pm or 8pm weekends, workshops weekday nights & weekend afternoons; 🚌 22, 28, 30

Crash an office party, sabotage a fast-food drive-thru, meet your long-lost twin in jail: Bay Area Theatersports throws ordinary people into awkward scenarios and lets hilarity ensue. Watch what happens next at completely improvised week-end shows, or take center stage yourself at an improv comedy workshop. Think fast: classes fill quickly.

### ⭐ FORT MASON *Fairs & Classes*

☎ 474-8935; www.fortmason.org; Bldg A, Fort Mason Center; 🕑 shows 7pm or 8pm weekends, workshops weekday nights & weekend afternoons; 🚌 22, 28, 30; ♿

Right this way for fun at Fort Mason

Herbst Pavilion tends to steal the spotlight as the landmark host of photo fairs, wine tastings, designer sales and gala fundraisers, but Fort Mason's other converted military buildings are known for hands-on events galore. Parents can sign up high-energy kids for sailing classes, kung fu workshops and Children's Arts Center programs, and book screenwriting, theater and tai chi workshops for themselves. Check the online calendar for details.

⭐ **MAGIC THEATRE** *Theater*
☎ 441-8822; www.magictheatre.org; 3rd fl, Bldg D, Fort Mason Center; tickets $25-75; 🚌 22, 28, 30
Now that the upstart theater company is over 40, will it settle down? Not a chance. The Magic is known for risk-taking, provocative plays by Terrence McNally, Edna O'Brien, David Mamet and long-time playwright in residence Sam Shepard, performed by talents like Ed Harris, Sean Penn and Woody Harrelson. Watch the next generation break through in professionally staged works written by teenagers.

# >GOLDEN GATE PARK & THE AVENUES

When other Americans want an extreme experience, they head to San Francisco – but when San Franciscans go to extremes, this is where they can be found. Surfers brave walls of water on blustery Ocean Beach, runners try to keep pace with the stampeding bison in Golden Gate Park and dim sum gluttons attempt just one more round of dumplings in the Richmond or Sunset.

Whenever something is clearly impossible, San Franciscans seem determined to do it, and Golden Gate Park is living proof. In 1866, San Franciscans petitioned City Hall with an impossible demand: to transform 1017 acres of sand dunes into parkland. The task daunted even Frederick Law Olmstead, who built New York's Central Park. But at age 24, San Franciscan engineer William Hammond Hall took on the 20-year project, battling casino developers and amusement-park lobbyists to unveil Golden Gate Park in 1886.

## GOLDEN GATE PARK & THE AVENUES

### ◉ SEE
| | | |
|---|---|---|
| California Academy of Sciences | 1 | F4 |
| Conservatory of Flowers | 2 | G3 |
| Japanese Tea Garden | 3 | F4 |
| Legion of Honor | 4 | B1 |
| MH de Young Museum | 5 | F3 |
| Ocean Beach | 6 | A4 |

### ⌂ SHOP
| | | |
|---|---|---|
| Green Apple | 7 | G2 |
| Mollusk | 8 | B5 |
| Park Life | 9 | G2 |
| Wishbone | 10 | G5 |

### ⑪ EAT
| | | |
|---|---|---|
| Aziza | 11 | E2 |
| Be My Guest Thai Bistro | 12 | F2 |
| Burma Superstar | 13 | G2 |
| Genki | 14 | G2 |
| Kabuto | 15 | E2 |
| Park Chow | 16 | F4 |
| PPQ Dungeness Island | 17 | D2 |
| Roadside BBQ | 18 | G2 |
| Spices | 19 | F2 |
| Taiwan | 20 | G2 |
| Ton Kiang | 21 | E2 |
| Underdog | 22 | E4 |

### ⅄ DRINK
| | | |
|---|---|---|
| Beach Chalet | 23 | A4 |
| Java Beach Café | 24 | B5 |
| Plough & the Stars | 25 | G2 |
| Rohan Lounge | 26 | G2 |
| Toy Boat | 27 | G2 |

### ★ PLAY
| | | |
|---|---|---|
| Balboa Theater | 28 | C3 |
| Four Star Theatre | 29 | D2 |
| Lawn Bowling Club | 30 | G4 |
| Lincoln Park Golf Course | 31 | C2 |

Please see over for map

Modest row houses soon sprang up nearby, and transplanted immigrant communities thrived and mingled alongside the park's botanical transplants. Famished strollers and surfers began frequenting the area's bargain restaurants, and the fog belt became San Francisco's most out-there neighborhood.

# 👁 SEE

## 🔵 CALIFORNIA ACADEMY OF SCIENCES

☎ 379-8000; www.calacademy.org; 55 Concourse Dr; adult/senior & student/child 7-11yr/child under 7yr $25/20/15/free; 🕥 9:30am-5pm Mon-Sat, 11am-5pm Sun; 🚊 N, 5, 21, 44; ♿

California's fascination with weird and wonderful wildlife is suitably showcased in Pritzker Prize–winning architect Renzo Piano's weird and wonderful 2008 landmark green building, capped with a 'living roof' of California wildflowers. The academy houses 38,000 animals in custom habitats: a white alligator stalks the swamp, butterflies flutter through the four-story rainforest dome and balding Pierre the Penguin paddles his massive new tank in a custom-made wetsuit (shhh, don't mention the molting; he's sensitive).

## 🔵 CONSERVATORY OF FLOWERS

☎ 666-7001; www.conservatoryofflowers.org; Conservatory Dr W; adult/senior & youth/child 5-11yr $5/3/1.50; 🕥 9am-4:30pm Tue-Sun; 🚊 5, 7, 21, 33, 71; ♿

Flower power is alive and well inside this grand Victorian greenhouse, where orchids sprawl out like bohemian divas, lilies float contemplatively and carnivorous plants give off odors that smell exactly like insect belches. The original 1878 structure is newly restored, and the plants are thriving.

## 🔵 JAPANESE TEA GARDEN

☎ 752-1171; 7 Hagiwara Tea Garden Dr; adult/senior & child $3.50/1.25; 🕥 8:30am-6pm Mar-Oct, 8:30am-5pm Nov-Feb; 🚊 N, 5, 21, 44; ♿

Mellow out in the Zen Garden, sip toasted-rice green tea overlooking a waterfall, and admire doll-sized

### COASTING THE COAST

Hit your stride on the 9-mile **Coastal Trail** (A2; 🕥 sunrise-sunset; 🚊 N, 28), starting at Fort Funston and wrapping around the Presidio paralleling Lincoln Blvd to end at Fort Mason. The 4 miles of sandy Ocean Beach will definitely work those calves and numb your toes – yep, the water's about that cold year-round. Casual strollers will prefer to pick up the trail near Sutro Baths, head around Lands End for a peek at Golden Gate Bridge and then duck into the Legion of Honor (p178) at Lincoln Park.

China Beach
Sea Cliff Ave
Lincoln Blvd

**A** **B** **C** **D**

**1**

El Camino del Mar

Lincoln Park

Lands End

Coastal Trail

34th Ave

⭐ 31

Fort Miley

**2**

Seal Rock Dr

Point Lobos Ave

Clement St

Geary Blvd

31st Ave
30th Ave
29th Ave
28th Ave
27th Ave
26th Ave
25th Ave
24th Ave

🍴 17
⭐ 29

Sutro Heights Park

48th Ave
47th Ave
46th Ave
45th Ave
44th Ave
43rd Ave
42nd Ave
41st Ave
40th Ave
39th Ave
38th Ave
37th Ave
36th Ave
35th Ave
34th Ave
33rd Ave
32nd Ave

Anza St

⭐ 28

**3**

Balboa St

Cabrillo St

Fulton St

Spreckels Lake Dr
Spreckels Lake
John F Kennedy Dr

North Lake

36th Ave

Golden Gate Park

🍴 23

John F Kennedy Dr

Golden Gate Municipal Golf Course

Golden Gate Park Equestrian Center & Stadium

Middle Dr W

Metson Lake

Mallard Lake

**4**

Ocean Beach

📷 6

Upper Great Hwy

Middle Lake

Martin Luther King Dr

South Lake

*PACIFIC OCEAN*

La Playa St

🛏 8

45th Ave
44th Ave
43rd Ave
42nd Ave
41st Ave

Irving St

31st Ave
30th Ave
29th Ave
28th Ave
27th Ave
26th Ave
25th Ave

**5**

🍴 24

Judah St

48th Ave
47th Ave
46th Ave
40th Ave
39th Ave
38th Ave
37th Ave
36th Ave
35th Ave
34th Ave
33rd Ave
32nd Ave

Kirkham St

Lawton St

Sunset Recreation Center

Upper Great Hwy

Great Hwy

Moraga St

**THE SUNSET**

**6**

Noriega St

Sunset Blvd

0 ———— 500 m
0 ———— 0.3 miles

Fort Funston
(4.2 miles)

Sunset Reservoir

trees that are pushing 100. These bonsai are a credit to the dedicated gardeners of the Hagiwara family, who returned from WWII Japanese American internment camps to discover their bonsai had been sold. The Hagiwaras spent the next two decades tracking down the trees, and returned the bonsai grove to its rightful home.

### ◉ LEGION OF HONOR

☎ 750-3600; www.famsf.org; 100 34th Ave; adult/senior/student/child under 12yr $10/$7/6/free, $2 discount with Muni transfer, 1st Tue of month free; 🕑 9:30am-5:15pm Tue-Sun; 🚌 1, 2, 18, 38; ♿ 👶

Alma de Bretteville Spreckels was a nude sculptor's model who married well and never lost her love of art or San Francisco. She donated the Legion to the city as a tribute to Californians killed in France in WWI, and today it houses a world-class collection spanning medieval to 20th-century European art, with highlights including the Achenbach Foundation for Graphic Arts, Impressionist paintings, and in honor of 'Big Alma's' early career, a sizable collection of sculpture by Auguste Rodin and Henry Moore.

### ◉ MH DE YOUNG MUSEUM

☎ 750-3600; www.famsf.org; 50 Hagiwara Tea Garden Dr; adult/senior/student/child under 12yr $10/7/6/free, $2 discount with Muni transfer, 1st Tue of

month free; 🕑 9:30am-5:15pm Tue-Sun, until 8:45pm Fri; 🚌 N, 5, 21, 44; ♿ 👶

You'd think the art would be upstaged by Swiss architects Herzog & de Meuron (of Tate Modern fame) and their sleek building, with its perforated copper cladding drawn from aerial photography of the park and oxidizing green to become part of the scenery. But the landmark collection of arts and fine crafts from around the world puts California's own artistic pursuits into global perspective and hides a surprise around every corner – don't miss 19th-century Oceanic ceremonial masks and stunning Central Asian rugs from the textile collection's 11,000-plus works.

Groove is in the art: the MH de Young Museum

**Daniel Handler,**
*aka Lemony Snicket, San Francisco author of* **A Series of Unfortunate Events** *and* **Adverbs,** *plus sometime accordion player for the Magnetic Fields*

**Best unintentional humor in San Francisco** Tourists, shivering in shorts in July, waiting for the streetcar. **Most magic-realist San Francisco location** City Lights (p47) bookstore. They carry more magic realism than anyone. **Goths risk losing their anomie at…** Anyplace that serves those tapioca-ball drinks on Clement. The decorations are always Pee-Wee-Herman Acide Nightmare. **Favorite SF place to thrill even jaded kids hooked on Grand Theft Auto** Ocean Beach. The Pacific has a majesty nobody can touch. **San Francisco at its bizarre best** The bison in the park, with their constant reminder that this nation was at least partially founded on a sport that's much like sneaking up on a leather sofa.

Blockbuster temporary shows range from Hiroshi Sugimoto's haunting time-lapse photographs of drive-in movies to Dale Chihuly's bombastic glass sculpture. Access to the tower viewing room is free, and worth the wait for the elevator.

### 🎦 OCEAN BEACH
🕑 sunrise-sunset; 🚌 N, 5, 18, 31, 48

Aspiring Renzo Pianos build sand castles and beachcombers strike it rich in sand dollars by day, while at night Burning Man devotees huddle against the fog around ritual bonfires in new artist-designed tiled fire pits. Be sure to follow park rules about fire maintenance and alcohol (not allowed) or you could get fined. On rare sunny days the waters may beckon, but only serious, sober swimmers and sea lions should brave these riptides.

## 🛍 SHOP

### 📕 GREEN APPLE Books
☎ 387-2272; www.greenapplebooks .com; 506 Clement St; 🕑 10am-10:30pm Sun-Thu, 10am-11:30pm Fri & Sat; 🚌 1, 2, 33, 38, 44; ♿

The opium den of SF's literary set, where readers lose track of the hours spent poring over shelves of excellent staff picks, piles of bargain-priced remainders and displays of tantalizing new releases. Just when you tear yourself away, you realize there's another

floor of poetry and nonfiction, and yikes, an entire annex of used fiction and CDs two doors down.

### 📕 MOLLUSK Surf & Skate Gear
☎ 564-6300; www.mollusksurfshop .com; 4500 Irving St; 🕑 10am-6:30pm; 🚌 N, 18; Ⓟ

Back home no one can bite your SF style, with boards by celebrity shapers and local-artist-designed Mollusk hoodies to warm up in style after a gnarly session. Surf books, local-artist-designed skate decks, sculpture installations by the Society of Driftwood Enthusiasts, and Matt Volla's ink diagrams of wave physics provide SF surf-subculture thrills without the damp wetsuit.

### 📕 PARK LIFE Gifts, Books & Art
☎ 386-7275; www.parklifestore.com; 220 Clement St; 🕑 11am-8pm; 🚌 1, 2, 33, 38, 44; ♿

The Swiss Army knife of hip SF stores: design store, indie publisher and art gallery all in one. Standout souvenirs and gift options include smiling cupcake tees, Park Life's catalog of SF jazz portraitist Ian Johnson, and librarian-chic laser-cut necklaces that command READ. The back gallery of emerging local artists is strong on whimsical, streetwise folk imagery, like Zachary Rossman's drawings of people turning into mushrooms and molten lava.

### WISHBONE *Gifts & Toys*
☎ 242-5540; www.wishbonesf.com;
601 Irving St; ⏱ 11:30am-7pm Mon-Sat,
11:30am-6pm Sun; 🚌 N, 44, 71; ♿
Certain gifts never fail to please:
bobblehead picture frames, prize
ribbons reading 'computer whiz,'
build-it-yourself charm bracelets
and local designer Gama-Go's
big-eyed birdie tote. Wishbone
has kids' gifts in the bag, from Pee
Pee Teepees that prevent sudden
spraying mid-diaper-change to a
fuzzy, plaid stuffed animal called
'Yes, a Cat Named Marty Cohen.'

#  EAT
### AZIZA *Cal-Moroccan*                    $$
☎ 752-2222; www.aziza-sf.com;
5800 Geary Blvd; ⏱ 5:30-10:30pm Wed-
Mon; 🚌 2, 29, 38; Ⓥ
The inspiration is Moroccan, the
produce Californian, and the
flavors out of this world: crostini
slathered with fava bean, ricotta
and tender almonds, quail with
huckleberry and cumin-orange
glaze, and prawn tagine with
Meyer lemons that's pure pizzazz
in a pot. Glitz and belly dancing are
kept to a minimum so as not to distract you from chef Mourad Lahl-
ou's seasonal, sustainably sourced
and often organic creations.

### BE MY GUEST THAI BISTRO
*Cal-Thai*                                  $$
☎ 386-1942; www.bemyguestthai
bistro.com; 951 Clement St; ⏱ 11am-
10:30pm Sun-Thu, 11am-11pm Fri & Sat;
🚌 1, 2, 28, 38, 44; Ⓥ ♿
This is one invitation you won't
want to refuse, with enticing, mod
orange-and-white decor, a full
cocktail bar and clever variations
on Thai themes. The marinated
Volcano Chicken is served flaming
and melts in your mouth, while
the mango tango prawns and
sea bass edamame bring surf to
California turf with tangy, earthy
flavors.

### BURMA SUPERSTAR
*Burmese*                                   $$
☎ 387-2147; www.burmasuperstar
.com; 309 Clement St; ⏱ 11am-3:30pm
& 5-9:30pm Sun-Thu, 11am-3:30pm &
5-10pm Fri & Sat; 🚌 1, 2, 4, 33, 38, 44
Rain or shine, there's always a line
for aromatic catfish curries and
green-tea-leaf salad tarted up with
lime and dried shrimp. Reservations aren't accepted, so ask the
host to call you at the café across
the street and enjoy a glass of
wine while you wait.

### GENKI *Japanese Desserts*              $
☎ 379-6414; www.genkicrepes.com;
330 Clement St; ⏱ 2-10:30pm Mon,
10:30am-10:30pm Tue-Thu & Sun,
10:30am-11:30pm Fri & Sat; 🚌 1, 2, 33,
38, 44; Ⓥ ♿
A teen scene until late at night,
with much squealing over French
crepes served Tokyo-style with
green-tea ice cream and Nutella,

and vigorous slurping of tropical-fruit tapioca bubble tea. While you wait, check out the attached Japanese convenience store, where the snack/beauty supply aisle satisfies sudden Pocky/purple-hair-dye whims.

### 🍴 KABUTO *Californian Sushi*  $$
☎ 752-5652; www.kabutosushi.com; 5121 Geary Blvd; ⏱ 5:30-10:30pm Tue-Sun; 🚍 2, 28, 38, 91

Anyone who believes sushi is just raw fish is about to undergo a conversion experience. Every night there's a line out the door to witness sushi chef Eric administer the sacrament of unagi with foie gras and chocolate sauce, ono with grapefruit and crème fraîche, and the most religious experience of all: the 49er oyster with sea urchin, caviar, a quail's egg and gold leaf, chased with rare sake.

### 🍴 PARK CHOW *Californian*  $$
☎ 665-9912; 1238 9th Ave; ⏱ 8am-10pm Sun-Thu, 8am-11pm Fri & Sat; 🚍 N, 29, 44, 71; Ⓥ 🔥

Cozy up by the fireplace downstairs or the patio heat lamps upstairs, and shake that fog-belt chill with reliable, comforting California dishes like mild curry Smiling Noodles, stalwart spaghetti with meatballs, and caramel gingerbread with pumpkin ice cream. This is one of the most kid-friendly and pet-positive restaurants in San Francisco, with booster seats available and water bowls by the door.

### 🍴 PPQ DUNGENESS ISLAND
*Vietnamese Seafood*  $$
☎ 386-8266; 2332 Clement St; ⏱ 11am-10pm Wed-Mon; 🚍 1, 2, 29, 38; 🔥

Dungeness crab season lasts most of the year in San Francisco, which means now is probably the right time to enjoy one whole atop garlic noodles or dredged in peppercorn-laced flour and lightly fried for a typical market price of about $20 per person (depending on weight and season). Ignore everything else on the menu, and put that bib to good use.

### 🍴 ROADSIDE BBQ *BBQ*  $
☎ 221-7427; www.roadside-bbq.com; 3751 Geary Blvd; ⏱ 11:30am-10pm Sun-Thu, 11:30am-11pm Fri & Sat; 🚍 2, 33, 38

Don't call it fast food: the generous $8 pulled-pork sandwiches and $10 racks of ribs are slow-cooked in a smoker, and the baked beans, sweet-potato fries and coleslaw 'roadsides' are made fresh from scratch – diets are definitely roadkill here.

### 🍴 SPICES *Szechuan*  $
☎ 752-8884; www.eatspices.com; 294 8th Ave; ⏱ 11am-9:45pm; 🚍 1, 2, 28, 38, 44; Ⓥ

The menu reads like an oddly dubbed Hong Kong action flick, with dishes labeled 'explosive!!' and 'stinky!' But the chefs can call zesty pickled Napa cabbage with chili oil, silky ma-po tofu and brain-curdling spicy chicken whatever they want – it's definitely worthy of exclamation. Cash only.

### 🍴 TAIWAN *Taiwanese* $
☎ 387-1789; 445 Clement St; 🕙 11am-10pm Sun-Thu, 11am-midnight Fri, 10am-midnight Sat; 🚌 1, 2, 33, 38, 44; Ⓥ ♿
When you're the one treating to dinner, this is the place to go for the most lavish banquet for four you'll ever get for $28: smoky dry braised green beans, feisty black-bean

Use your noodle at Taiwan

squid, grassy vegetable dumplings made by hand in the front window and scrumptious, housemade Shanghai sesame hot-sauce noodles with pickled vegetables.

### 🍴 TON KIANG *Dim Sum* $$
☎ 752-4440; www.tonkiang.net; 5821 Geary Blvd; 🕙 11am-9pm Mon-Thu, 11am-9:30pm Fri, 9:30am-9:30pm Sat, 9am-9pm Sun; 🚌 2, 29, 38; ♿ ♿
Don't bother asking what's in those bamboo steamers: choose some on aroma alone and ask for the legendary *gao choy gat* (shrimp and chive dumplings), *dao miu gao* (pea tendril and shrimp dumplings) and *jin doy* (sesame balls) by name. A running tally is kept at your table, so you could conceivably quit while you're ahead of the $20 mark – but wait, here comes another cart…

### 🍴 UNDERDOG
*Organic Hot Dogs* $
☎ 665-8881; www.underdogssf.com; 1634 Irving St; 🕙 4pm-2am Mon-Fri, 9am-2am Sat & Sun; 🚌 N, 28, 29, 44, 71, 91; ♿ Ⓥ
For $4 to $5 organic meals on the run in a bun, Underdog is the clear winner. The roasted garlic and Italian pork sausages are USDA certified organic, and the smoky veggie chipotle hot dog could make dedicated carnivores into fans of fake meat.

GOLDEN GATE PARK & THE AVENUES

# ▼ DRINK

## ▼ BEACH CHALET
*Microbrewery*

☎ 386-8439; www.beachchalet.com;
1000 Great Hwy; 🕑 9am-10pm Sun-Thu,
9am-11pm Fri & Sat, brunch 8am-2pm Sat
& Sun; 🚍 N, 5, 18, 31, 38; Ⓟ ♿

Brews with views: sunsets over the Pacific go down even smoother with small-batch beer brewed on the premises. Wander downstairs to admire Lucien Labaudt's recently restored 1930s Works Project Administration frescoes showing a condensed history of San Francisco and Golden Gate Park. The grassy lawn out back is a boon to parents, who can keep an eye on the kiddies through the bottom of a pint glass.

## ▼ JAVA BEACH CAFÉ *Café*

☎ 665-5282; www.javabeachcafe.com;
1396 La Playa St; 🕑 5:30am-11pm Mon-
Fri, 6am-11pm Sat & Sun; 🚍 N, 18

Compare session notes with the wetsuit crowd at SF's surf hangout, where the fearless go to fuel up on coffee and carbs before riding the walls of water just over the dunes. This is the last stop on the N Judah and the first before you hit Ocean Beach, with plenty of outdoor seating in a small park to strike up conversations about sex wax. To understand why that's not as raunchy as it sounds, check out the surfer-slang decoder at www.riptionary.com.

## ▼ THE PLOUGH & THE STARS
*Pub*

☎ 751-1122; www.theploughandstars
.com; 116 Clement St; 🕑 3pm-2am Mon-
Thu, 2pm-2am Fri-Sun; 🚍 1, 2, 33, 38

The Emerald Isle by the Golden Gate. Jigs are to be expected after the first couple of rounds and rousing Irish fiddle tunes are played most nights by top Celtic talent, but put down your pint first on the long lunchroom tables so as not to splash your new best mates.

## ▼ ROHAN LOUNGE
*Soju Cocktail Lounge*

☎ 221-5095; www.rohanlounge.com;
3809 Geary Blvd; 🕑 6pm-midnight Mon-
Thu, 6pm-2am Fri & Sat, 6-11pm Sun;
🚍 1, 2, 33, 38

*Soju* sophistication: Korea's answer to vodka gets mixed with cool cucumber into a Bond-worthy sojutini, or serves the funk with lemon-lime, OJ and blue curaçao in the mighty Superfly. Wednesdays are binges waiting to happen with half-price all night on cocktails and inspired bar bites from garlic edamame to the kimchee sampler. Easy there, lightweight: soju goes down smoother than vodka and stays with you awhile, like the chill-out DJ beats on Saturdays.

## ▼ TOY BOAT *Café & Toy Store*

☎ 751-7505; www.toyboatcafe.com;
401 Clement St; 🕑 7:30am-11pm Mon-

Thu, 8:30am-midnight Fri & Sat, 8:30am-11pm Sun; 🚌 1, 2, 33, 38, 44; ♿
The triple threat of Double Rainbow ice cream, toys and mechanical pony rides ensures that anyone with kids winds up here eventually. Coffee and tea, free *San Francisco Bay Guardian*s and displays of vintage toys keep adults occupied while the kids bond.

#  PLAY

### ⭐ BALBOA THEATER *Cinema*
☎ 221-8184; www.balboamovies.com; 3630 Balboa St; double features adult/senior & child $9/6.50, matinees $6.50; 🚌 31, 38
Double features perfect for foggy weather – including film fest contenders hand-picked by the director of the Telluride Film Festival – in a renovated 1926 art-deco cinema. If you need something more than popcorn with your choice of butter or hot sauce between shows, the cinema is surrounded on all sides by cheap, tasty Vietnamese and Chinese restaurants.

### ⭐ FOUR STAR THEATRE *Cinema*
☎ 666-3488; www.hkinsf.com/4star; 2200 Clement St; double features evening/matinee $8.50/6.50; 🚌 1, 2, 29, 38
International art-house double features take you around the world in a day. Long before John Woo,

Ang Lee and Wong Kar Wai hit multiplex marquees, they brought down the house in the Four Star's postage-stamp-sized screening rooms. This diminutive cinema is still the audience testing ground for emerging international cinema, and directors have even shown up to do Q&A for a full house of 25.

### ⭐ LAWN BOWLING CLUB
*Lawn Bowling*
☎ 487-8787, 753-9298; Bowling Green Dr; 🚌 N, 44, 71
Pins seem ungainly and bowling shirts unthinkable once you've stepped onto Golden Gate Park's spongy lawn bowling green in your classic sweater-and-slacks combo. Free lessons are available Wednesday at noon, Wednesday evenings in summer or by appointment.

### ⭐ LINCOLN PARK GOLF COURSE *Golf*
☎ 221-9911; www.lincolnparkgc.com; 300 34th Ave; adult/junior Mon-Thu $32/10, Fri-Sun $36/19; 🚌 1, 2, 18, 38; 🅿 ♿
Whack that ball but don't slice it, or you'll end up taking a penalty for shooting into the Pacific. Greens fees are surprisingly low to spend a day on the Lands End links amid the windswept grandeur of Monterey pines, but you'll need to make reservations at least seven days in advance.

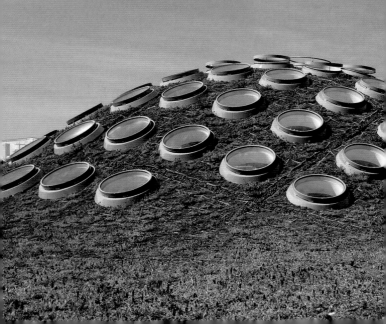

Wake up to Victorian splendor, brunch organically, sunbathe naked with a good book, hit the galleries, stores and clubs, and get eco-savvy over movies and cocktails: no matter how eclectic your tastes, San Francisco has you covered.

How green was my roof: the California Academy of Sciences (p175)

# ACCOMMODATIONS

Every possible interest can be accommodated in San Francisco at an average room rate of about $160, though you can find decent places for around $100 or even less in the elusive low season between December and March, dodging holidays and major conventions. Competitive rates are January to February, and the highest from July to November.

Where you'll want to stay in town depends on what you want to do here – we assume you'd rather not spend all day on buses and trolleys. Why stay in a faceless Fisherman's Wharf hotel alongside roving packs of restless conventioneers far from downtown restaurants when you can enjoy waterfront views and gourmet dining at **Hotel Vitale** (www.hotelvitale .com) on the Embarcadero, or find boho bliss at **Hotel Bohème** (www.hotelbohe me.com) amid North Beach cafés? You'll be spoiled for choice with nearby taquerias and views from the rooftop bar at the hipster **Elements Hostel** (www.elementssf.com), while **Laurel Inn** (www.thelaurelinn.com) offers the life of a local foodie with your own kitchen near the restaurants and groceries of Clement St. Most chains have airport hotels (15 minutes from downtown) good for catching early flights, but inconvenient for longer stays.

Some may prefer the formal hotels atop Nob Hill, such as the **Ritz** (www.ritz carlton.com/hotels/san_francisco), **Fairmont** (www.fairmont.com) or **Mark Hopkins** (www.mark hopkins.net) – missing the point of casual, quirky San Francisco. Downtown designer digs are accessible to all budgets, from minimalist **Mosser Hotel** (www .themosser.com), slick **Hotel Diva** (www.hoteldiva.com) and arty-chic **Hotel des Arts** (www.sf hotelsdesarts.com) to the cool, contemporary **Hotel Adagio** (www.thehoteladagio.com), girls-night glam of the San Francisco **W** (www.whotels.com) and the bedside PDA

Need a place to stay? Find and book it at lonelyplanet.com. Over 60 properties are featured for San Francisco — each personally visited, thoroughly reviewed and happily recommended by a Lonely Planet author. From hostels to high-end hotels, we've hunted out the places that will bring you unique and special experiences. Read independent reviews by authors and other travelers, and get practical information including amenities, maps and photos. Then reserve your room simply and securely via Hotels & Hostels — our online booking service. It's all at lonelyplanet.com/hotels.

tech of the tricked-out **St Regis Hotel** (www.stregis.com/sanfrancisco). If it's Victorian charm you're after, head for the gabled rooftops of Haight and Castro B&Bs.

In this easygoing, individualist town, there's a place for everyone. Kids will appreciate the pool and splashy colors of the **Hotel del Sol** (www.thehotel desol.com), pugs prefer the pet-friendly policies of **Hotel Monaco** (www.monaco -sf.com) and trees everywhere appreciate the certified-green **Orchard Garden Hotel** (www.theorchardgardenhotel.com). For those who don't mind being extras in the backstreet dramas of the sketchy Theater District (aka the Tenderloin), the friendly, well-kept **King George Hotel** (www.kinggeorge.com), the rocker-chic **Hotel Phoenix** (www.jdvhospitality.com) and the up-to-date **Adelaide Hostel** (www.adelaidehostel.com) will save you plenty for front-row tickets.

## WEB RESOURCES
For accommodation deals, check out www.lonelypanet.com, and also:
**www.bbsf.com** Independent B&Bs in neighborhoods away from the downtown hustle.
**www.jdvhospitality.com** Package deals and rates from a San Francisco boutique hotel chain.
**www.onlyinsanfrancisco.com** The Visitors Information Center website shows a wide range of options from hostels and B&Bs to luxury hotels, and helps with reservations.
**www.sanfrancisco.com** Big-name hotel deals, mostly downtown and Fisherman's Wharf chains.

### BEST ON A BUDGET
> Mosser Hotel (wwww.themosser.com)
> Hotel Diva (www.hoteldiva.com)
> Hotel Tomo (www.jdvhospitality.com)
> Elements Hostel (www.elementssf.com)
> Hayes Valley Inn (www.hayesvalley inn.com)

### BEST ON AN EXPENSE ACCOUNT
> Hotel Vitale (www.hotelvitale.com)
> Hotel Adagio (www.thehoteladagio .com)
> Orchard Garden Hotel (www.theor chardgardenhotel.com)
> Palace Hotel (www.sfpalace.com)
> Hotel Palomar (www.hotelpalomar .com)

### BEST VICTORIAN B&BS
> Belvedere House (www.belvedere house.com)
> Chateau Tivoli (www.chateautivoli.com)
> Inn San Francisco (www.innsf.com)
> Parker Guest House (www.parker guesthouse.com)
> Inn 1890 (www.inn1890.com)

### BEST FOR SAN FRANCISCO CHARACTER
> Hotel Bohème (www.hotelboheme .com)
> Red Victorian B&B (www.redvic.com)
> Hotel des Arts (www.sfhoteldesarts .com)
> Inn on Castro (www.innoncastro.com)
> Hotel Rex (www.jdvhospitality.com)

# FOODIES

Tell a San Franciscan you're coming to town, and the next thing you'll hear is: 'Dude, there's this place you *have* to go for dinner…' Locals do tend to proselytize about their restaurant scene – but really, where else are your options this fresh, varied and divine? San Franciscans are culinary polytheists who worship the chef's $100 tasting menu and the lowly $2.50 sandwich equally, and believe in dishes from around the Pacific Rim and across the Mediterranean, all made with farm-fresh California produce.

Deciding where to eat is tougher than choosing a religion here. Getting foodies to agree on a place for dinner can require some delicate negotiating that makes the UN Charter look like a cinch: two people might object that they just had Thai for lunch; one might make a motion for sustainable seafood, or propose Mexican; another is opposed in principle to burritos outside the Mission. But according to local rules of hospitality, as the visitor you hold the veto power. Wield it wisely with some help from the lists below, and additional input from www.eatersf.com, www.burritoeater.com and www.chowhound.com. For the broadest range of options without reservations, try San Francisco's best eat streets: Clement (Richmond), Mission (Mission), Irving (Sunset) and Geary (Richmond). To assemble sublime picnics, head to the Ferry Plaza Farmers Market (p59), Heart of the City Farmers Market (p94) and Molinari (p50).

When (not if) you fall for a signature SF dish, you can recreate it at home. Refine your palate and hone your skills with classes at Sur La Table (p61), the Cheese School (p54), Cav Wine Bar (p97) and Bittersweet Café chocolate tasting events (p162). Kitchen equipment is available from Sur La Table, and if you don't feel like lugging that Dutch oven in your carry-on, it also sells online. Find SF recipes and inspiration in the cooking section at Green Apple (p180) and online at www.slowfood.com and www.cookhereandnow.com, and savor juicy foodie gossip at www.tablehopper.com and www.eatersf.com. Bon appétit, dude.

## BEST CHEAP EATS
> La Taqueria (p124)
> Udupi Palace (p126)
> Greens to Go (p170)
> Tu Lan (p95)
> Heart of the City Farmers Market (p94)

## BEST SUSTAINABLE CUISINE
> Jardinière (p94)
> Tataki (p161)
> Millennium (p95)
> Magnolia (p152)
> Mission Pie (p125)

## BEST TO IMPRESS A DATE
> Gary Danko (p62)
> 1550 Hyde (p49)
> Michael Mina (p73)
> Hog Island Oyster Company (p62)
> Bar Crudo (p72)

## BEST FOR ADVENTUROUS EATERS
> Jai Yun (p82)
> Kabuto (p182)
> Aziza (p181)
> Spices (p182)
> Lahore Karahi (p94)

**Left** Drink your way around the world at Cav Wine Bar (p97)

SNAPSHOTS

# GAY/LES/BI/TRANS

Singling out the best places to be queer in San Francisco is almost redundant. The Castro is awash in rainbow flags, SoMa loves the leather, and the Mission is a lesbian and transgender magnet, but the entire city is indisputably the center of the known GLBT world – hence the number of out elected representatives in City Hall at any given time and a Pride celebration that takes the entire month of June, starting with the Gay and Lesbian Film Festival (p27) and ending with the grand finale Pride Parade (p27).

Back in the pre-1960s bad old days of police raids, bars would euphemistically designate Sunday afternoons as 'tea dances,' appealing to gay crowds to make money at an otherwise slow time. The tradition makes Sundays one of the busiest times for SF's gay bars, though now you can also find your choice of gay bars open any other day of the week – and most will accommodate well-behaved straight friends (hint: tip well and don't stare). Drag shows are popular with San Franciscans of all persuasions, though this is not a town where you need a professional reason to cross-dress. If you're here, and queer, welcome home.

## BEST QUEER DANCE CLUBS
> The EndUp (p113)
> El Rio (p129)
> The Stud (p113)
> The Café (p142)
> The Bar (p141)

## BEST PLACES TO HAVE A DEEP CONVERSATION (COULD THIS BE LOVE?)
> Gay and Lesbian Film Festival (p27)
> San Francisco Lesbian Gay Bisexual Transgender Community Center (p135)
> Femina Potens (p134)
> Samovar Tea Lounge (p141)
> Café Flore (p140)

## BEST GAY PLACES TO BRING STRAIGHT FRIENDS
> Human Rights Campaign Action Center & Store (p136)
> Castro Theatre (p134)
> Under One Roof (p137)
> Pride Parade (p27)
> Lime (p140)

## BEST PLACES TO HAVE A SHALLOW CONVERSATION (COULD THIS BE SEX?)
> Folsom Street Fair (p28)
> Eagle Tavern (p111)
> Lexington Club (p127)
> The Lookout (p140)
> Moby Dick (p141)

# BOOKISH

Defying all pronouncements of the imminent demise of books in the internet age, books remain wildly popular here in the capital of new technology. San Francisco has more writers per capita than any other US city, buys more books per capita than any other North American burg, and hoards three times the national average of library books – and San Franciscans will gladly argue about any book, whether or not they've actually read it (ahem).

But San Francisco's literary tradition doesn't just hang out on book shelves. Allen Ginsberg's ecstatic readings of *Howl* continue to inspire slam poets at LitQuake (p29) and spoken-word nights at Edinburgh Castle Pub (p99), and Beat authors like Kerouac freed up generations of monologists at the Marsh (p130) and Progressive Reading Series at the Make-Out Room (p129) from the tyranny of tales with morals and punctuation. R Crumb paved the way for future generations of graphic novelists at Alternative Press Expo (p29), but also the street art on view in Clarion Alley (p115).

The local zine scene has supplied notes from the underground since the '70s brought punk and V Vale's *RE/Search* to San Francisco, and you can read the latest word at San Francisco Public Library Main Branch (p88), Needles & Pens (p122) and the Bound Together Anarchist Book Collective (p149). The most successful local zine of all, *McSweeney's*, is the doing of Dave Eggers, who used the proceeds from his memoir *A Heartbreaking Work of Staggering Genius* to start 826 Valencia (p115), a nonprofit writing program for teens. *McSweeney's* also publishes an excellent map of literary San Francisco, so you can get out there and walk the talk.

## BEST BOOKSTORES
> City Lights (p47)
> Green Apple (p180)
> Booksmith (p154)
> Adobe Books & Backroom Gallery (p119)
> Babylon Falling (p46)

## BEST SOURCES FOR LITERARY INSPIRATION
> San Francisco Public Library Main Branch (p88)
> Sterling Park (p46)
> Caffe Trieste (p52)
> 826 Valencia (p115)
> Jack Kerouac Alley (p45)

# BOOZEHOUNDS

First came the gold rush, then came the rush on the bar…or was it the other way around? San Francisco's hooch purveyors seem to have come out ahead of every boom and bust, and even fire couldn't prevent AP Hotaling's whiskey warehouse (p68) from shilling the rye. Wines from nearby Napa and Sonoma appear on every self-respecting San Francisco bar and restaurant menu, but SF's own microbrewed beer is not to be overlooked, and the Bay Area makes its own standout spirits, including Hangar One vodka, 209 gin and Takara sake, and pours a mean cocktail – martinis were invented in SF.

Neighborhoods where you'll never want for drink are North Beach, the Mission, SoMa, Union Square and the Tenderloin, with watering holes ranging from trendy to seedy and some unusual locations for happy hour: a log cabin dominated by Bigfoot (p51), a speakeasy entered through a secret library passageway (p97) and a grass hut where tropical rainstorms erupt every 20 minutes (p53). Smoking is officially banned inside all bars, clubs, coffeehouses and restaurants, though some bars have smoking patios.

## BEST HOLE-IN-THE-WALLS
> Hemlock Tavern (p97)
> Aub Zam Zam (p153)
> Aunt Charlie's (p98)
> Specs Museum Café (p53)
> Noc Noc (p154)

## BEST LIQUID EDUCATION
> Cav Wine Bar (p97)
> Anchor Brewing (p111)
> Ferry Plaza Wine Merchant (p61)
> California Wine Merchant (p171)
> Elixir (p127)

## BEST BEER
> Toronado (p154)
> City Beer Store & Tasting Room (p111)
> Bar Crudo (p72)
> Zeitgeist (p128)
> Magnolia (p152)

## BEST BARS FOR HOT DATES
> Top of the Mark (p53)
> Tsar Nicolai Caviar Café (p63)
> Bar Bambino (p123)
> Rohan Lounge (p184)
> Absinthe (p96)

# ART SCENE

The lines to get into some gallery openings are long enough to warrant a red-velvet rope, but that's not the kind of art scene San Francisco has going. There's no real barrier between the street and the gallery here, so the art you'll see on SF gallery walls is often like the murals you'll find in SF back alleys: rabble-rousing, surprisingly meticulous, and more concerned with big ideas than big bucks. Graduates from SF's distinguished art schools as well as street artists converge on the walls of risk-taking Luggage Store Gallery (p88), Yerba Buena Center for the Arts (p108), Gallery Paule Anglim (p69) and Jack Hanley Gallery (p115).

San Francisco is a photogenic city with the distinguished photography tradition to prove it, from technical innovators like Pirkle Jones and Ansel Adams to high-concept photographers like Larry Sultan and Todd Hido – all part of the collection at San Francisco Museum of Modern Art (p107). But video and digital art have also taken SF by storm, especially at New Langton Arts (p107), Catharine Clark Gallery (p103) and Hosfelt Gallery (p106).

Many world-class San Francisco art collections begin with surprisingly affordable works from local nonprofits, including San Francisco Arts Commission Gallery (p88), Intersection for the Arts (p129) and Southern Exposure (p119). See something you like at a commercial gallery? Repeat these magic words: 'installment plan.'

## BEST GALLERIES FOR LOCAL ART
> Catharine Clark Gallery (p103)
> Gallery Paule Anglim (p69)
> Marx & Zavattero at 77 Geary (p68)
> Gregory Lind Gallery at 49 Geary (p68)
> Stephen Wirtz Gallery at 49 Geary (p68)

## BEST MURALS
> San Francisco Art Institute's Diego Rivera Gallery (p44)
> *History of San Francisco* mural at Rincon Annex Post Office (p61)
> Clarion Alley (p115)
> Women's Building (p119)
> Galería de la Raza's Digital Mural Project (p115)

# RETAIL THERAPY

Though it's been weaned off most of the harder drugs since the '60s, San Francisco still has one adrenaline-elevating weakness: shopping. Local designers provide a steady supply of distinctive souvenirs, from bejeweled collars at Velvet Da Vinci (p48) to ultramod Iranian beaten-felt rugs at Peace Industry (p92) and tiny prints by local artists at Electric Works (p106). In this town, you'll never have to settle for Alcatraz beach towels from China Bazaar (p80) or snow globes from Far East Flea Market (p81) if what you really want to remember San Francisco by is a surfboard from Mollusk (p180), poetry from City Lights (p47) or a new tattoo (p120). Fashionistas get their SF style on at Residents Apparel Gallery (p92), Mingle (p168), Doe (p150), Dema (p120), Delilah Crown (p47) and Sunhee Moon (p123), while guys work local looks ranging from Sui Generis vintage (p137) and MAC chic (p91) to Upper Playground streetwear (p151), Madame S & Mr S leather (p109), and Piedmont drag (p150). Foodies are spoiled for choice: local chocolates from Recchiuti (p61), local vintages from PlumpJack Wines (p169) and local taste treats from Ferry Plaza Farmers Market (p59) and Bi-Rite Market (p123). When the retail high goes to your head, just keep telling yourself: you can quit anytime you like.

## BEST PLACES TO SHOP WELL & DO GOOD
> Under One Roof (p137)
> Human Rights Campaign Action Center & Store (p136)
> Community Thrift (p120)
> 826 Valencia (p115)
> Eco Citizen (p48)

## BEST NONSOUVENIR SOUVENIRS
> Golden Gate belt buckles at Doe (p150)
> Limited-edition local artwork from Electric Works (p106)
> Ferry Plaza Farmers Market treats (p59)
> Golden State hoodie at Upper Playground (p151)
> CDs of local bands from Aquarius Records (p119)

# ARCHITECTURE

Superman wouldn't be so impressive in San Francisco, where most buildings are low enough for even a middling superhero to leap in a single bound. The Transamerica Pyramid (p70) is a helpful compass needle to orient newcomers, skinny Market St flatirons help you track your progress down SF's main drag, and Coit Tower (p41) adds an exclamation point to the city skyline.

But San Francisco's low-profile buildings are its highlights: the historic Italianate brick buildings in the former Barbary Coast, now Jackson Square in the Financial District; Renzo Piano's landmark green building California Academy of Sciences (p175), with its 'living roof' of native wildflowers; Julia Morgan's tastefully restrained East-meets-West Zen Center (p88) and pagoda-topped brick Chinatown YWCA (now the home of the Chinese Historical Society, p78); and architects Herzog & de Meuron's low-slung, copper-clad MH de Young Museum (p178), rapidly oxidizing green to match the park (and other architects' envy). Still, your favorite landmarks may be the ones you discover as you wander the streets of the Haight, Mission and Castro: Victorians in outlandish designs that do justice to their residents. Some attractive oversize Victorians are now B&Bs, so you too can live large in the swanky San Francisco digs of yore; see p188.

## BEST HISTORIC BUILDINGS
> Victorian Painted Ladies of Alamo Square park (p145)
> Mission Dolores (p118)
> Columbus Tower (p44)
> City Hall (p86)
> Swedenborgian Church (p158)

## BEST MODERN ARCHITECTURE
> California Academy of Sciences (p175)
> MH de Young Museum (p178)
> Federal Building (p87)
> SFMOMA (p107)
> Yerba Buena Gardens at Yerba Buena Center for the Arts (p108)

# OUTDOORS

Claustrophobes, rejoice: that city-shut-in sensation you get surrounded by NY skyscrapers or LA freeways isn't a problem here. San Francisco wasn't exactly planned, with sailors abandoning their ships in the harbor as they swarmed ashore to get in on the gold rush. But naturalist John Muir and Golden Gate Park (p174) champion William Hammond Hall were among the early arrivals who saw beauty and not just gold in these hills.

Today virtually every hilltop in San Francisco has a precious green toupee it wouldn't be seen without, including scenic Telegraph Hill (p19) and Sterling Park (p46). Some architects have worked with the local landscape to create organic landmarks: Nagao Sakurai's 1951 Zen Garden at the Japanese Tea Garden (p175), the 1996 AIDS Memorial Grove at Golden Gate Park and Renzo Piano's flower-capped 2008 California Academy of Sciences (p175).

As real-estate prices rise to nosebleed heights, there's always a fear that San Francisco's outdoor living-room spaces will be swallowed up by private development. But San Francisco's motley coalition of neighborhood councils, dog walkers, environmentalists, parents, kite-flyers and Green Party members keeps a keen eye on urban green spaces, and helped lobby for the US military to hand over the Presidio military base including Baker Beach (p165) and Crissy Field (p165) for use as public parks.

## BEST URBAN HIKES
> Golden Gate Park (p174)
> Filbert Steps (p41)
> Lands End path (p175)
> Ocean Beach (p180)
> Crissy Field to Golden Gate Bridge (p165)

## BEST OUTDOOR ACTIVITIES
> Parades! (p25)
> Free opera, bluegrass, Shakespeare and love in Golden Gate Park (p174)
> Exploring alleyway murals in the Mission with Precita Eyes (p118)
> Street fairs (p25)
> Sunning naked at Baker Beach (p165)

# KIDS

No, it's not just a trick of the eye: there aren't a lot of kids in San Francisco. Residents here have fewer children per capita than anywhere else in the US – and while that means your kids will have fewer playmates while they're here, they're going to get a whole lot more attention. Except for a few swanky restaurants that toddlers probably wouldn't appreciate anyway, the admiration is mutual between San Francisco and kids.

There's a certain storybook quality to this city, which kids can relate to: wild parrots squawking indignantly at passersby on Telegraph Hill (p19), murals in hidden alleys awaiting discovery, slumbering sea lions nudging one other off the docks and into the water at Pier 39 (p60) with a comical *sploosh!* Educational opportunities abound for kids with a scientific or artistic bent, and the Asian Art Museum (p86), Legion of Honor (p178), MH de Young Museum (p178) and Museum of the African Diaspora (p106) are free to kids under 12. When spirits and feet begin to drag, there's plenty of ice cream and kid-friendly meals to pick them back up, plus toy stores to bribe them up that last hill – look for the 🧒 symbol throughout this book.

**BEST FAMILY FUN**
> California Academy of Sciences (p175)
> Musée Mécanique (p59)
> Chinatown Alleyways Tour (p205)
> Sea lions at Pier 39 (p60)
> Aquarium of the Bay (p59)

**BEST HANDS-ON LEARNING EXPERIENCES**
> Exploratorium (p165)
> Zeum (p108)
> 826 Valencia workshops (p115)
> Fort Mason's Children's Arts Center (p172)
> Ferry Plaza Farmers Market (p59)

# GREEN

In a place surrounded by this much natural beauty, environmentalism comes easily: to make the great outdoors stay that way, it's what happens indoors that counts. This is one town where you can eat, sleep and cavort sustainably – just look for 'sustainable' in the indexes of this book. There are many places in SF where you can see green ideas coming in from the cold: the **Orchard Garden Hotel** (www.theorchardgardenhotel.com) is the city's first green-certified hotel; the energy-conserving green Federal Building (p87) puts taxpayers' dollars to good use for a change; and California Academy of Sciences (p175) is a natural wonder, from its sustainable café to its wildflower-capped roof.

But green is more than window-dressing in SF. The US may be a lumbering two-party system, but in San Francisco, the Green Party is a power player, and Green city supervisors and emissions-reducing measures date back over a decade. San Franciscans actually use the public transport system, and some use green-minded car-sharing programs in lieu of owning a vehicle (see p215). Citizens have effectively defended parks and green spaces against developers' schemes for more than a century and even reclaimed acres of military bases and industrial sites as green space. San Francisco has one of California's most successful curbside recycling and composting programs, and its claim to fame as the US capital of creative reuse dates from '50s Beat artists' scavenged collages and assemblages. Best of all, SF's green ideas are highly portable, and make fine souvenirs to take home with you.

## BEST SUSTAINABLE ENTERTAINMENT

> Organic cocktails at Elixir (p127)
> Communing with nature indoors at the green California Academy of Sciences (p175)
> Kabuki Sundance Cinema (p163)
> Kite-flying at Crissy Field (p165)
> Walking, biking or skating Golden Gate Park (p174)

## BEST ECO-SAVVY SHOPPING

> Ferry Plaza Farmers Market (p59)
> Wasteland (p151)
> Rainbow Grocery (p123)
> Eco Citizen (p48)
> Sui Generis (p137)

# MUSIC

If San Francisco history had a soundtrack, it would start with opera and bluegrass, then segue into West Coast jazz – the cool-cat kind, Dave Brubeck with Paul Desmond on saxophone or Maya Angelou singing low and bluesy. Gradually it would speed up and break down into bebop, and splinter off into folk: think Bob Dylan and Joan Baez in the days of their West Coast affair. Next the amps get turned on and so does Jimi Hendrix, Janis Joplin wails herself hoarse, Jim Morrison mumbles onstage and Grace Slick hits ear-splitting notes to clear the air. The Grateful Dead just keep playing on and on, while the Dead Kennedys wage aural anarchy and the Sex Pistols break up onstage here. The echo of '70s funk from Oakland meets Mission salsa and disco in the Castro, until synthesizers take over and '80s anthems ensue. Grunge trickles down from Seattle in the '90s and stomps out the power pop. Then the soundtrack loops back to the beginning, with jazz-inflected hip-hop from Oakland and Tupac's tough-love West Coast style. What's up next? All of the above remixed nightly on the dance floor, and something else entirely at SF street fairs and music festivals.

## BEST FOR MUSIC & DANCING YOUR STYLE
> Pogo: Hemlock Tavern (p97)
> Bollywoodish: Rickshaw Stop (p99)
> Vaguely merengue: El Rio (p129)
> Hot, sweaty and shirtless: The Stud (p113)
> That flopping thing Deadheads do: Hippie Hill in Golden Gate Park (p11)

## BEST FOR LIVE MUSIC
> Davies Symphony Hall (p98)
> Great American Music Hall (p99)
> The Fillmore (p162)
> Yoshi's (p163)
> War Memorial Opera House (p100)

# SHOWTIME

There's a San Francisco syndrome known as the Monday Night Cringe, when you're browsing online, talking on the phone with a friend or rifling through last week's *Bay Guardian* only to discover you missed out on an incredible show last weekend. Ouch, that hurts. Still, it's unavoidable: there's always too much going on in this city for any one person to know about and score tickets to, no matter how tapped into the film and performing-arts scenes you are. Your only defense is to have a ticket to some promising performance next weekend already in your wallet – or failing that, to get on Craigslist quick and see who's selling their tickets to the opera or San Francisco International Film Festival on the cheap.

You'll never know what you've been missing until you check out some of SF's independent cinemas and theaters, where films by unknown directors become cult classics and acts you've never heard of are polished into sleeper hits. But if you can't score a seat, there's always the street theater of San Francisco's street fairs, protests and parades. Call us Monday and tell us what we missed.

## BEST CINEMAS
> Castro Theatre (p134)
> Kabuki Sundance Cinema (p163)
> Roxie Cinema (p131)
> Balboa Theater (p185)
> Four Star Theatre (p185)

## BEST STREET THEATER
> Pride Parade (p27)
> Bay to Breakers (p26)
> Folsom Street Fair (p28)
> Lunar New Year Parade (p26)
> Weekends on Haight St (p144)

## BEST WAY-OFF BROADWAY THEATER
> American Conservatory Theater (p98)
> Exit Theater (p99)
> Magic Theatre (p173)
> Marsh (p130)
> Theatre Rhinoceros (p131)

## BEST DANCE
> ODC (p130)
> Yerba Buena Center for the Arts (p108)
> San Francisco Ballet (p100)
> Theater Artaud (p131)
> Mission Cultural Center (p130)

Step out of vine at the California Academy of Sciences' indoor rainforest (p175)

# BACKGROUND
## HISTORY
### MISSION IMPOSSIBLE

Before gold changed everything, San Francisco was a hapless Spanish mission. Without immunity to European diseases, many native Californians conscripted to build the 1776 mission didn't survive to see the end result – some 5000 Ohlone and Miwok are buried under Mission Dolores, 'Our Lady of Sorrows' (p118). The mission settlement never really prospered: the sandy fields were difficult to farm, the 20 soldiers manning San Francisco's Presidio (army encampment) made more trouble than they prevented, and fleas were a constant irritation. Spain had stopped sending supplies long before the unmanageable colony was lost to Mexico, who surrendered the troublesome backwater to the US without much of a fight.

### GOLD FEVER

Mexico couldn't have had worse timing: within days of signing away California in the Treaty of Guadalupe Hidalgo, gold was discovered in the Sacramento River. From 1847 to 1849, San Francisco's population ballooned from 800 to 100,000 prospectors from South America, China, Europe and Mexico, and California was fast-tracked for statehood in 1850. But nominal rule of law didn't change SF's saloons, where a buck would procure whiskey, opium, opera tickets or one of the women frolicking on swings rigged from saloon ceilings (publicly revealing they weren't wearing bloomers 150 years before Britney Spears). The lawless harbor known as the 'Barbary Coast' soon filled with ships abandoned by crews with gold fever.

Early arrivals panned for gold side by side and returned to San Francisco with fortunes to splurge on Chinese takeout, French food and Australian-imported wines. In 1848, each prospector earned an annual average of about $300,000 in today's terms; by 1865 that mining income had dipped to $35,000. Surface gold became harder to find, and the real money was made by San Francisco's robber-barons, who hoarded the machinery for deep-mining operations.

When gold was discovered in Australia, panic ensued, and irrational resentment turned on Australians and Chinese dockworkers. In 1870, ordinances restricted housing and employment for anyone born in China, and the 1882 US Chinese Exclusion Act barred Chinese from immigration and citizenship until 1943. Anti-Asian sentiment was a windfall for San Francisco's robber-barons, who recruited Chinese San Franciscans on the cheap to do the dangerous, dirty work of dynamiting through the Sierras and building railways to mining claims.

## UP FROM THE ASHES

Anxious to distract attention from waterfront fleshpots and attract legitimate business interests, San Francisco decided to build a beaux-arts Civic Center (p84). These grand plans were destroyed in under a minute on April 18, 1906, when a quake estimated at a terrifying 7.8 to 8.3 on today's Richter scale struck. For 47 seconds, the city emitted unholy groans as streets buckled, windows popped and brick buildings keeled over. Fire-fighters couldn't pass through rubble-choked streets to put out blazes, and fires raged for three days. When the smoke lifted, the devastation was clear: as many as 3000 people were dead or missing, and 100,000 were left homeless.

Some survivors fled San Francisco, but those who stayed rebuilt the city at an astounding rate of 15 buildings per day. Although all but one of San Francisco's 20 theaters were destroyed, theater tents were set up while the city still smoldered, and opera divas performed for free to boost

---

**TOP FIVE WALKS THROUGH SAN FRANCISCO HISTORY**

**Chinatown Alleyways Tours** ( ☎ 984-1478; www.chinatownalleywaytours.org/tourinfo; adult/youth 10-17yr/child 6-9yr/child under 6yr $18/12/5/free; ☒ 11am-1pm Sat; ♿ ) Get the inside scoop on Chinatown from resident old pros who happen to be teenagers. Nonprofit-run tours leave from Portsmouth Square (p79) and must be reserved five days in advance.

**City Guides' Victorian architecture walking tours** ( ☎ 557-4266; www.sfcityguides .org) Learn to tell your Queen Annes from your Sticks with prime examples in Pacific Heights and Alamo Square. Free tours are led by local volunteers and last about 2½ hours; donations are appreciated.

**Haight-Ashbury Flower Power Walking Tour** ( ☎ 863-1621; www.haightashburytour .com; adult/child under 9yr $20/free; ☒ 9:30am Tue & Sat, 2pm Thu, 11am Fri) Take a long strange trip through 12 blocks of hippie history in 1½ to two hours, starting at the corner of Stanyan and Waller Sts.

**Cruisin' the Castro** ( ☎ 255-1821; www.webcastro.com/castrotour; cnr Castro & Market Sts; adult/child incl lunch $35/25; ☒ 10am-2pm Tue-Sat) Find out what it was like to be gay back in the day on this Castro circuit, followed by lunch at a popular restaurant. Tours meet at Harvey Milk Plaza; reservations required.

**Precita Eyes** ( ☎ 285-2287; www.precitaeyes.org; 2981 24th St; adult/senior & student/ child under 12yr from $10/5/2; ☒ 10am-5pm Mon-Fri, 10am-4pm Sat, noon-4pm Sun) Muralist-led weekend mural tours of the Mission on foot and by bike; see also p118.

morale. A city plan was concocted to relocate Chinatown to less desirable real estate in Hunter's Point, but was dropped after the Chinese consulate, Waverly Place temples and several gun-toting Chinatown merchants refused to vacate. With the mysterious, highly flammable exception of AP Hotaling's whiskey warehouse (p68), most of the Barbary Coast had burned, and the city rebuilt the ragged pirate piers into a major port.

## ROCKING THE BOAT

But longshoremen pulling long hours unloading heavy cargo for scant pay didn't see the upside of San Francisco's new port. In 1934, a coordinated strike among 35,000 workers along the coast lasted 83 days, while shipments spoiled dockside. Finally police and the National Guard intervened, killing 34 strikers and wounding 40 sympathizers. The strategy backfired: public sympathy helped force concessions from the shipping magnates, and WPA (Works Progress Administration) murals in Coit Tower (p41) capture the 1930s pro-worker sentiment that swept the city.

WWII brought a shipbuilding boom, fueled largely by African Americans and women working the assembly lines. But not everyone benefited from wartime expansion. Two months after the attack on Pearl Harbor, President Franklin Delano Roosevelt signed Executive Order 9066, ordering 120,000 Japanese Americans to internment camps. The San Francisco–based Japanese American Citizens League challenged the measure, and after a historic 40-year effort, won reparations and a formal letter of apology signed by President George HW Bush in 1988 – and along the way, set key precedents for the civil rights movement.

WWII sailors discharged in San Francisco for insubordination and homosexuality soon found themselves at home among the bohemian coffeehouses and anarchic alleyways of North Beach. When the rest of the country took a sharp right turn with McCarthyism in the 1950s, rebels and romantics headed for the Left Coast, where jazz broke down barriers in desegregated clubs and José Sarria led gay bar patrons in nightly choruses of 'God Save Us Nelly Queens.' San Francisco became America's home of free speech and free spirits, and soon everyone who was anyone was getting arrested: Beat poet Lawrence Ferlinghetti for publishing Allen Ginsberg's epic poem *Howl*, African American–Jewish anarchist Bob Kaufman for taunting police in rhyme, comedian Lenny Bruce for uttering the F-word onstage and burlesque dancer Carol Doda for going topless.

## FLOWER POWER

But it wasn't ribald jokes, striptease, gay bars or even uncompromising poetry that would pop the last button of conventional morality in San

Francisco – no, this would be a job for the CIA. The federal spy agency inadvertently kicked off the psychedelic era when an operation tested psychoactive drugs intended to create the ultimate soldier on writer Ken Kesey, who promptly introduced LSD to the masses at the legendary 1966 San Francisco Acid Tests. At the January 14, 1967, Human Be-In in Golden Gate Park, tripmaster Timothy Leary urged a crowd of 20,000 hippies to dream a new American dream, and 'turn on, tune in, drop out.'

For weeks, months, even a year or two, depending whom you talk to and how stoned they were at the time, San Francisco was the place where it seemed possible to make love, not war. There were draft-card–burning protests in Golden Gate Park and free food, love and music in the Haight until 1969, when the assassinations of Bobby Kennedy and Martin Luther King Jr brought a sudden chill to the Summer of Love.

## PRIDE

As the fog settled in over the Haight, San Francisco gays ditched hetero hippie communes for sunny Victorians in the Castro, and proceeded to make history to a funky disco beat. The Castro was triumphant when local entrepreneur Harvey Milk became the nation's first openly gay elected official in 1977, but the news sent washed-up politician Dan White on a Twinkie binge and down to City Hall, where he shot Milk and then-mayor George Moscone. The charge was reduced to manslaughter due to the infamous 'Twinkie Defense' faulting the high-sugar snacks; White committed suicide a year after his 1984 release.

By then the city was preoccupied with a strange illness appearing in local hospitals. The gay community was hit hard by the virus initially referred to as GRID (Gay-Related Immune Deficiency). A social stigma became attached to the virus, compounding a grim prognosis with patient isolation. But San Francisco healthcare providers and gay activists rallied to establish standards for care and prevention of the pandemic now known as HIV/AIDS, and vital early interventions made possible through local fundraisers saved untold lives around the world.

Another item on the community's political agenda is same-sex marriage, first authorized by SF Mayor Newsom in time for Valentine's Day, 2004. California courts voided those contracts, but in 2008 ruled that same-sex marriage falls within California's constitutionally protected civil rights. Six months later, a statewide voter referendum banning same-sex marriage passed, calling into question the 9000 same-sex marriages already legalized; at press time, the ACLU and other activist groups were preparing legal challenges to continue the fight for marriage equality.

## GEEKING OUT

Industry dwindled steadily in San Francisco after WWII, but the brains of military-industrial operations found work in Silicon Valley. At San Francisco's first West Coast Computer Faire in 1977, 21-year-old Steve Jobs and Steve Wozniak introduced the Apple II, the first mass-produced PC, with a then staggering 4kB of RAM, 1MHz microprocessor and networking capabilities, and a retail price of US$1298 (about $4300 today). Skeptics were stumped: what would consumers do with a computer network?

By the mid-'90s, a modest computer network had grown into a World Wide Web selling vegan dog food, art by the yard and extra socks – until venture capital funding dried up in 2000 and multimillion-dollar dot-coms shrank into oblivion. Yet San Francisco managed to retain its talent pool, and still has more entrepreneurs with advanced degrees than any other US city. It's a self-selecting community that's OK with the risk of earthquakes and a volatile economy based on technology and tourism, but more people keep opting in each year. New booms in the works include biotech in Mission Bay and Web 2.0 in former downtown dot-com headquarters.

# LIFE AS A SAN FRANCISCAN

Conversation is easy to strike up in San Francisco: just ask locals to recommend a restaurant or political candidate. But ask them to describe a day in the life of a typical San Franciscan and they'll claim they can't help you, because no San Franciscan likes to be considered typical. Praise them as brilliant creatives or deride them as total slackers, and they'll gleefully contradict you. San Franciscans are highly educated and hold more patents per capita than anywhere else in the US, yet somehow all these innovators also find time to frequent the most medical marijuana clubs per capita in the US. Here in the capital of the Left Coast, Republicans are viewed with scorn, curiosity and even pity, like declawed circus tigers. But San Franciscans bristle at being referred to as hippies; they prefer to think of themselves as forward-thinking idealists, and to that end support some 2000 local nonprofits.

So how do you recognize a San Franciscan when you encounter one? True to California surfer stereotypes, you'll probably overhear 'right on,' 'hella' and even 'gnarly' uttered with no trace of irony. Other than dudespeak, there is no dominant language in San Francisco, where half the population speaks a language other than English at home and one in three claim Asian heritage. Look around, and you'll notice the city is blessed with an uncanny metabolism: despite an obsession with food and thousands of restaurants, San Francisco has the lowest body-mass index of any US city.

Still, gym-ripped abs raise suspicion as being 'too LA.' Really, who has time to spend all day doing crunches when there are protests to be organized, concerts and art openings to be blogged about, and online avatars that need designing? And honey, please: those parade costumes aren't going to make themselves.

All this earnest endeavor is endearing, if almost always just a bit over the top. After a couple of days in San Francisco, you may begin to doubt how many of the latest Web 2.0 technologies are all that revolutionary, how tattoos and drag can still be transgressive when they're so ubiquitous, if graffiti artists who sell their work for five figures in galleries still qualify as 'street', and whether the umpteenth documentary film about San Francisco subcultures can still be described as 'shattering stereotypes.' San Franciscans will take any opportunity to prove reality wrong, and that contrarian streak could itself become predictable if not for some truly astonishing breakthroughs: Beat poetry, free speech, gay liberation, sustainable cuisine, new media art, green public architecture and Folsom Street Fair getups that may permanently impair your ability to blush. Never mind, you won't be needing those inhibitions anyway – you're in San Francisco now.

# FURTHER READING

## NONFICTION

**The Electric Kool-Aid Acid Test** (1967) Tom Wolfe follows Ken Kesey, the Merry Pranksters, the Grateful Dead and Hell's Angels as they turn on, tune in and drop out.

**Hell's Angels: A Strange and Terrible Saga** (1966) Hunter S Thompson's gonzo account of the outlaw Bay Area motorcycle club disturbed the deluded peace of middle America.

**On the Road** (1957) The book Jack Kerouac banged out on one long scroll of paper in a San Francisco attic over a couple sleepless months of 1951 woke up America.

**Slouching Towards Bethlehem** (1968) Joan Didion's essays burn right through the hippie haze to reveal glassy-eyed teenage revolutionaries adrift in the Summer of Love.

## POETRY

**A Coney Island of the Mind** (1958) An indispensable doorstop for the imagination by SF's poet laureate Lawrence Ferlinghetti.

**Howl and Other Poems** (1956) Allen Ginsberg's ecstatic improvised mantra chronicling the waking dreams of a generation that rejected postwar suburban complacency.

**The Other Side of the Postcard** (2005) Ordinary San Franciscans hold forth in free verse about their city, creating a portrait of a city lost and found in the details. Edited by Devorah Major.

**Time and Materials** (2007) In the latest collection by Robert Hass, the Berkeley-based poet and winner of the 2008 Pulitzer Prize for Literature, every word is as essential as a rivet in the Golden Gate Bridge.

## FICTION

**The Man in the High Castle** (1962) Bestselling Berkeley sci-fi writer Philip K Dick imagines San Francisco c 1962 if Japan and Nazi Germany had won WWII.

**Martin Eden** (1909) Semi-autobiographical account of Jack London, San Francisco's first literary star, who got by on his wits in the illicit oyster trade.

# SAN FRANCISCO AT THE MOVIES

## CLASSICS

**Escape from Alcatraz** (1979) Clint Eastwood stars in this story based on Frank Morris' famous escape attempt using only a spoon and his wits.

**Harold and Maude** (1971) The ultimate May-December romance features metaphorically apt SF locations: the eternal spring of the Conservatory of Flowers and the fabulous ruin of the Sutro Baths.

**Maltese Falcon** (1941) Dashiell Hammett's classic noir tale features Humphrey Bogart as tough-talking private dick Sam Spade.

**Vertigo** (1958) The Golden Gate Bridge sets the stage for dizzying drama when acrophobic Jimmy Stewart watches Kim Novak leap into the bay at Fort Point.

## INDIES

**Chan Is Missing** (1982) When Chan disappears with their $4000, two cabbies search Chinatown for him, only to realize they don't really know Chan, Chinatown or themselves.

**Dogfight** (1991) Dashing sailor River Phoenix asks out homely Lili Taylor on a cruel bet, with consequences that neither expects.

**Tales of the City** (1993) PBS' most popular miniseries stars Laura Linney unraveling a mystery involving a pot-growing landlady, closeted Nob Hill socialites and the swinging '70s disco scene.

## DOCUMENTARIES & BIOPICS

**And the Band Played On** (1993) Randy Shilts' account of activism and inertia in the early AIDS epidemic, with Mathew Modine, Alan Alda and cameos galore.

**Milk** (2008) Sean Penn stars as Harvey Milk, following his trajectory from camera-store owner to the first openly gay elected official, and his eerie prediction of his own assassination.

**Patty Hearst** (1988) Natasha Richardson starred as the kidnapped heiress in this account by writer/director Paul Schrader (screenwriter for *Raging Bull*).

## ACTION FLICKS

**Bullit** (1968) The plot has something to do with underworld kingpins, but it's all about Steve McQueen's GTO flying over Nob Hill and landing in SoMa – hence that editing Oscar.

**Dirty Harry** (1971) Think you can mess with flinty SF detective Clint Eastwood and not get burned? Go ahead – make his day.

**Dragon: The Bruce Lee Story** (1993) Follows martial arts megastar from his birth in Chinatown's Chinese Hospital through his street-fighting years and onto international stardom.

# DIRECTORY
## TRANSPORTATION
### ARRIVAL & DEPARTURE
#### AIR
**San Francisco International Airport** (SFO; ☎ 650-821-8211; www.flysfo.com) is 14 miles south of downtown on Hwy 101. All flights from Asia, Europe and Latin America go through the International terminal; the North and South terminals handle domestic flights.

There are **information booths** (☎ 7-0018; 8am-1:30am) that can be called from the white courtesy phones on the lower (arrivals) level of all three terminals and **Traveler's Aid information booths** ( 9am-9pm) on the upper level.

Lockers ($2 for 24 hours) are located in all boarding areas and luggage storage is available in the travel agency area on the upper-level connector between the South and International terminals.

For information on getting to/from the airport, contact the **ground transportation hotline** ( ☎ 800-736-2008; 7:30am-5pm Mon-Fri); see also the boxed text (p212). Shuttle companies include the following:
**American Airporter Shuttle** ( ☎ 202-0733; http://americanairporter.onsmartpages.com)
**Bay Shuttle** ( ☎ 564-3400; www.bayshuttle.com)
**Lorrie's** ( ☎ 334-9000; www.lorries-shuttles.com)
**Quake City** ( ☎ 255-4899; www.quakecityshuttle.com) Online coupon available for $3 to $4 off.
**SuperShuttle** ( ☎ 558-8500; www.supershuttle.com)

### GETTING AROUND
Most SF destinations can be reached on foot, but hills sometimes call for a cable car or bus, and only people with a high tolerance for grit should stroll the Tenderloin, Lower Haight, SoMa or Mission by night. Public transportation is the best way to get around town when you're not pressed for time; for

---

### CLIMATE CHANGE & TRAVEL
Travel – especially air travel – is a significant contributor to global climate change. At Lonely Planet, we believe that all who travel have a responsibility to limit their personal impact. As a result, we have teamed with Rough Guides and other concerned industry partners to support Climate Care, which allows people to offset the greenhouse gases they are responsible for with contributions to energy-saving projects and other climate-friendly initiatives in the developing world. Lonely Planet offsets all staff and author travel.

For more information, turn to the responsible travel pages on www.lonelyplanet .com. For details on offsetting your carbon emissions and a carbon calculator, go to www .climatecare.org.

fastest routes and the most exact departure times, consult http://transit.511.org.

The city's principal public transportation system is **Muni** ( ☎ 673-6864, 701-2323; www.sfmuni.com), which operates nearly 100 bus lines, the streetcar system and the city's signature cable cars. Train service throughout the metropolitan area is provided by **BART** (Bay Area Rapid Transit; ☎ 989-2278; www.bart.gov).

Buses and streetcars are referred to interchangeably as Muni and marked in this book after each listing with 🚌 , while cable cars are marked with 🚃 and BART is denoted by Ⓞ . Some areas are better connected than others, but public transportation spares you the costly hassle of driving and parking in San Francisco, and is often faster than driving during rush hour (7:30am to 9:30am and 4:30pm to 6:30pm). Nighttime and weekend service is less frequent.

## TRAVEL PASSES

Pick up a one-day Muni Passport good for buses, streetcars and cable cars for $11, a three-day Passport for $18, or a week-long Passport for $24. Passports can be purchased at the Muni kiosk at the Powell Street cable car stop on Market, from the half-price ticket kiosk on Union Square and from a number of hotels.

## TRANSPORT OPTIONS TO/FROM SFO AIRPORT

|  | Taxi | BART | Shuttle | Bus |
|---|---|---|---|---|
| **Pick-up point** | Yellow zone, lower level | SFO BART stop (near International terminal) | All terminals, near Departures (upper level) | SamTrans 292 bus stop at SFO BART station |
| **Drop-off point** | Door-to-door service | Downtown BART stations (Powell Street, Montgomery, Embarcadero) | Door-to-door service | Transbay Terminal |
| **Duration** | To downtown, 20min (up to 60min in rush hour) | 30min to downtown stations | 30-90min, depending on the number of other stops | 35min to Transbay Terminal |
| **Cost** | To downtown, $35-45 | $5.35 | $15; check online for coupons | $1.50 |
| **Other** | First-come, first-served | Leaves every 20min | Makes up to 4 stops | Leaves every 35min |
| **Contact** | See p214 | www.bart.gov | See p211 | www.samtrans.org |

## MAJOR BUS ROUTES

**5 Fulton** From the Transbay Terminal, along Market and McAllister Sts to Fulton St, along the north side of Golden Gate Park all the way to the ocean.

**7 Haight** From the Ferry Building, along Market and Haight Sts, through the Haight to the southeast corner of Golden Gate Park; daytime only.

**14 Mission** From the Transbay Terminal, along Mission St through SoMa and the Mission District.

**15 Kearny** From 3rd St in SoMa, through the Financial District on Kearny St, through North Beach on Columbus Ave, then along Powell St to the Fisherman's Wharf area.

**18 46th Ave** From the Legion of Honor to the Sutro Baths, along the western edge of Golden Gate Park on the Great Hwy, past the San Francisco Zoo and Lake Merced.

**22 Fillmore** From 18th and 17th Sts in Potrero Hill, through the Mission on 16th St, along Fillmore St past Japantown to Pacific Heights and the Marina.

**74X Culture Bus** Express shuttle runs every 20 minutes between SFMOMA to California Academy of Sciences in Golden Gate Park; all-day excursion fares with unlimited stops cost adult/senior & child $7/5.

## KEY STREETCAR DESTINATIONS

**F** Fisherman's Wharf and Embarcadero to the Castro.

**J** Downtown to the Mission/Castro.

**K, L, M** Downtown to the Castro.

**N** Caltrain and AT&T Park to the Haight and Ocean Beach.

## BUS & STREETCAR

Buses and streetcars run from 5am to midnight weekdays, with reduced schedules on weekends and holidays. Arrival times can be guesstimated by consulting schedules posted inside bus shelters; underground streetcar arrivals are noted on station digital displays. Owl Service (1am to 5am) is offered on a limited number of lines, with departures about every half-hour.

Tickets cost $1.50 for adults, 50¢ for seniors and children aged five

to 17, and are free for kids under four; they're valid until the expiration time noted on your ticket. Bus tickets are available on board, but you'll need exact change. For underground streetcars, you can change bills using the BART ticket machines. Hang onto your ticket or transfer even if you're not planning to use it again – if you're caught without one by the transit police, you're subject to a $75 fine. You can use your ticket to transfer to another bus or streetcar, but not BART or the cable car.

DIRECTORY

## RECOMMENDED TRANSPORTATION BETWEEN KEY DESTINATIONS

| | Powell Street | North Beach | Embarcadero | The Castro | Mission & 16th Street | Haight & Masonic |
|---|---|---|---|---|---|---|
| **Powell Street** | – | Powell-Mason cable car; 20min | BART; 5min | F line; 15min | BART; 5min | Bus 6, 7, 71; 30min |
| **North Beach** | Powell-Mason cable car; 20min | – | Bus 41; 15min | Walk then F line; 45min | BART to Montgomery then walk; 35min | Bus 15 then bus 6, 7, 71; 55min |
| **Embarcadero** | BART; 5min | Bus 41; 15min | – | F line; 40min | BART; 10min | Bus 7, 21, 71; 50min |
| **The Castro** | F line; 15min | Walk then F line; 45min | F line; 40min | – | Bus 33; 10min | Bus 33; 20min |
| **Mission & 16th Street** | BART; 5min | BART to Montgomery then walk; 35min | BART; 10min | Bus 33; 10min | – | Bus 33; 35min |
| **Haight & Masonic** | Bus 6, 7, 71; 30min | Bus 15 then bus 6, 7, 71; 55min | Bus 7, 21, 71; 50min | Bus 33; 20min | Bus 33; 35min | – |

## CABLE CAR

Cable cars cost $10 all day or $5 one-way for adults, students and seniors; kids under four ride free. Tickets can be purchased on board or at the Muni kiosks at the corners of Powell and Market, and Hyde and Beach. Cable cars run from 6am to 12:30am; try hopping on further up the route to avoid the lines at the Powell and Market stop. Routes are noted on the city map provided with this book.

## BART

The fastest link between downtown and the Mission district also offers transit to SFO Airport, Oakland and Berkeley. Within the city, one-way fares start at $1.50. BART tickets are sold in machines in BART stations, and you'll need your ticket to enter and exit. BART services operate until about midnight, starting weekdays at 4am, Saturdays at 6am and Sundays at 8am. From San Francisco BART stations, a transfer is available to Muni bus and streetcar services.

## TAXIS

Fares start at $3.10 at the flag drop and cost $0.45 for every 1/5 mile thereafter. Add at least 10% to the taxi fare as a tip (starting at $1, even for fares under $6). Cabs are easiest to hail along downtown streets; elsewhere you may need to call. These taxi companies have 24-hour dispatches:

**Arrow Cab** ☎ 648-3181
**DeSoto Cab** ☎ 970-1305
**Green Cab** ☎ 626-4733
**Luxor Cab** ☎ 282-4141
**Yellow Cab** ☎ 333-3333

## FERRY
The authorized seller of tickets to Alcatraz is **Alcatraz Cruises** ( ☎ 981-7625; http://alcatrazcruises.com; Pier 33; ☽ call center 8am-7pm); for more information see p58. **Blue & Gold Fleet** ( ☎ 705-8200; www.blueandgoldfleet.com) ferries to Oakland ($7.75 one way), Sausalito ($11) or Tiburon ($11) depart from the Ferry Building.

## CAR
Car Share
With advance planning, **Zipcar** ( ☎ 866-494-7227; www.zipcar.com) lets you rent a car (including a Prius Hybrid or parkable Mini) by the hour for flat rates starting at $7.86 per hour, including gas and insurance, or by the day for $58.65. Be sure to rent the car for more time than you think you need, since penalties for late return are $50 per hour. If you anticipate running late, extend your reservation by phone. Watch your mileage: only the first 125 miles you drive are covered in the flat rate. Zipcar's Extra Value Plan requires a $25 application fee and $50 prepaid usage in advance (no annual or membership fees). Anyone without a US driver's license will need to obtain a copy of their driving record in English (instructions at www.zipcar.com/apply/foreign-drivers) and fax that to Zipcar at ☎ 495-1161.

Rental Cars
Renting a car is not especially recommended for transportation

### ALTERNATIVE TRANSPORT: TO/FROM SF BY TRAIN
Trains provide a low-emissions, leisurely way to travel to San Francisco. **Amtrak** ( ☎ 800-872-7245; www.amtrak.com) operates two services: the *Coast Starlight* has a spectacular 35-hour run from Los Angeles to Seattle and stops across the bay in Oakland, and the *California Zephyr* takes its sweet time (51 hours) travelling from Chicago through the ruggedly handsome Rockies and Sierra Nevada en route to Emeryville (near Oakland). Both have sleeping cars and dining-lounge cars with panoramic windows, and you can stop along the route, resuming your journey as you please. At $125 and $284 one-way respectively, these train journeys are cheaper than air travel and reduce emissions – Lonely Planet travelers have dubbed the *Zephyr* 'the trip of a lifetime.'

within San Francisco. Street parking is elusive, parking garages expensive, and parking officials ruthless about ticketing. Gas prices are rising steadily, and driving on these hills means shifting gears and applying brakes often – and contending with drivers who think they're Steve McQueen in *Bullitt*. But if you're planning a break in wine country or the redwoods, here are your best rental options:

**Alamo Rent-a-Car** ( ☎ 650-616-2400 ext: LOCAL; www.alamo.com; 780 McDonnell Rd; ☽ 24hr; 🚐 airport shuttle)

**Avis** ( ☎ 650-877-6780; www.avis.com; 780 McDonnell Rd; ☽ 24hr; 🚐 airport shuttle)

**Budget** ( ☎ 650-877-0998; www.budget.com; 780 McDonnell Rd; ☽ 24hr; 🚐 airport shuttle)

**Dollar** ( ☎ 866-434-2226; www.dollarcar.com; Lot C, San Francisco International Airport; ☽ 24hr; 🚐 airport shuttle)

**Hertz** ( ☎ 650-624-6600; www.hertz.com; 780 McDonnell Rd; ☽ 24hr; 🚐 airport shuttle)

**Thrifty** ( ☎ 877-283-0898; www.thrifty.com; 780 McDonnell Rd; ☽ 24hr; 🚐 airport shuttle)

# PRACTICALITIES
## BUSINESS HOURS
**Banks** 9am-6pm Mon-Fri, 9am-1pm Sat
**Bars & pubs** 5pm-2am
**Cafés** 8am-7pm
**Restaurants** noon-3pm lunch, 5:30-10pm dinner
**Shops** 10am or 11am-6pm or 7pm Mon-Sat, noon-6pm Sun

## EMERGENCIES
**Drug treatment** ( ☎ 362-3400)
**Police, fire & ambulance** ( ☎ 911)
**Rape crisis line** ( ☎ 647-7273)
**Suicide crisis line** ( ☎ 781-0500)

## HOLIDAYS
**New Year's Day** January 1
**Martin Luther King Jr Day** 3rd Monday in January
**Presidents' Day** 3rd Monday in February
**Easter** March or April
**Memorial Day** Last Monday in May
**Independence Day** July 4
**Labor Day** 1st Monday in September
**Columbus Day** 2nd Monday in October
**Veterans Day** November 11
**Thanksgiving** 4th Thursday in November
**Christmas Day** December 25

## INTERNET
This close to Silicon Valley, there's wireless access at almost any hotel or street-corner café and a plethora of websites that list intriguing events:

**http://laughingsquid.com/squidlist/events** Alternative culture calendar – performances, protests, art projects and DJ events.

**http://sfbay.craigslist.org** Find activities partners, short-term apartment rentals, freebies and more.

**http://sf.eater.com** Blog on SF food, nightlife and bars.

**www.dailycandy.com** Blog covering trendy shops, new restaurants and clubs.

**www.flavorpill.com** Weekly events: live music, lectures, art openings, movie premieres and more.

**www.mundanejourneys.com** Maps for offbeat walking tours of SF via non-touristy sights.

**www.sfbg.com** *San Francisco Bay Guardian* website offers theater, art, music and movie listings.

**www.sfgate.com** *San Francisco Chronicle* website, with news and comprehensive event listings.

**www.sfist.com** Blog with irreverent take on San Francisco news and politics.

**www.stretcher.org** Covers the Bay Area art scene.

**www.somalit.com/newsletter.html** Online newsletter covering SF literary scene.

**www.thrillist.com** Blog on the new and the now in SF: bars, bands, shops, restaurants and events.

## MONEY

Count on expenses starting at about $100 per day, including budget overnight accommodations, three bargain meals, public transit and recommendations from the Free Day itinerary (p34). Exchange rates are listed on the inside front cover.

## TELEPHONE

The US country code is ☎ 1, and San Francisco's area code is ☎ 415. To make an international call from the Bay Area, call ☎ 011 + country code + area code + number. US cell phones operate on either CDMA or GSM, but on different frequency bands, so be sure to check compatibility with your phone manufacturer and/or service provider. For useful operator services, see the inside front cover.

## TOURIST INFORMATION

The **San Francisco Visitor Information Center** (Map p67, A5; ☎ 391-2000; www.sfvisitor.org; 900 Market St; ☺ 9am-5pm Mon-Fri, 9am-3pm Sat & Sun) is a handy resource that provides practical travel info and runs an events hotline.

## TRAVELERS WITH DISABILITIES

All the Bay Area transit companies offer travel discounts for the disabled, and wheelchair-accessible service. For further information about wheelchair accessibility, contact the **Independent Living Resource Center of San Francisco** ( ☎ 543-6222; www.ilrcsf.org; ☺ 9am-5pm Mon-Fri).

# >INDEX

*See also separate subindexes for See (p226), Shop (p227), Eat (p229), Drink (p231) and Play (p231).*

000 map pages

## SEE

**000** map pages

INDEX

**000** map pages